CRN EUROPE AND THE PACIFIC,
FOUGHT MOMENTOUS BATTLES WHICH
DECIDED THE WAR AND THE FUTURE OF THE WORLD ITSELF

0

JUNE
1944

H. P. WILLMOTT

First published in hardback in the UK by Blandford Press

This paperback edition first published 1999
Copyright © Grub Street 1999

British Library Cataloguing in Publication Data
Willmott, H. P. (Hedley Paul), 1945-
June 1944
1. World War, 1939-1945 – Campaigns – Europe
2. World War, 1939-1945 – Campaigns – Pacific Ocean
I. Title
940.5'42

ISBN 1 902304 22 5

Printed in the UK by Biddles Ltd

ACKNOWLEDGEMENTS

JUNE 1944 would not have been possible without the help, advice and very hard work of a number of people, and for their various involvements in the book I would like to thank first and most importantly: John Davies, Roger Hammond and Robin Cross for their support of the project; second, the same John Davies and Martin Mulligan for turning the manuscript into text; third, Jerry Goldie, Simon Roulstone and Hussein Hussein for their map and chart work; fourth, Bobby Hunt and Mars for the provision of photographs.

As always, none of these or anyone else who assisted in the preparation of the text are answerable in any way for errors of omission and commission, which remain the exclusive responsibility of the author.

MAP SYMBOLS
Basic unit/formation symbol

☐	Allied
☐ (with inner bar)	Axis
☐ (open bottom)	Headquarters
⊠	Infantry
▣	Mechanized
Ⴔ	Airborne
·	Artillery
⬭	Armored
xxxxx	Army Group or equivalent
xxxx	Army
xxx	Corps
xx	Division
x	Brigade
II	Regiment
I	Battalion
⌐	All-arms unit/formation
+	Unit overstrength
–	Unit understrength

Note

Because of the problems associated with trying to compare formations of one nation with those of another, the designations used by national forces themselves have been used in the text and on maps. Thus, for example, Japanese and Soviet armies have been referred to as armies even though they would correspond to Anglo-American corps.

Because the extent of their motorization placed Anglo-American infantry divisions in a very different class from the infantry divisions of other nations, they have been marked as mechanized divisions in European situation maps.

Discrimination has been made between Allied and Axis formation symbols only when they appear on the same map.

CONTENTS

FOREWORD

Innumerable books and articles have been written about the weaponry, battles and campaigns of World War II, but with *JUNE 1944* the author has set down a record and interpretation of the war in both Europe and the Far East on the eve and during the course of this single month. *JUNE 1944* sets the developments of the month in context and provides both an account and an analysis of the events which took place in relation to the series of political decisions that preceded them and the repercussions that followed them.

The book has three parts. First, it examines the events in the northwest European and Mediterranean theaters of operation where Anglo-American efforts were concentrated. Second, it recounts and weighs the significance of events on the Eastern Front, an area of study frequently neglected by western histories of World War II. Third, it tells the story of the struggles on the Asian mainland and in the western Pacific where Japan con-fronted her many enemies. In the resulting analysis, *JUNE 1944* proves that the vital importance of this month lies in the fact that combined events ushered in the final phase of World War II. Moreover, in bringing together the various elements of global conflict, it was witness not just to the destruction of German and Japanese attempts to create a new world order but to the creation of a new international system based on the awesome reality of American and Soviet power.

THE MONTH IN CONTEXT

One of the most famous bombs of World War II was the one used by Colonel Count von Stauffenberg, Chief of Staff of the Reserve Army, in his attempt to assassinate Adolf Hitler at the Wolfsschanze, near Rastenburg in East Prussia, on 20 July, 1944.

Details of von Stauffenberg's failure and the fate that befell the hundreds of Germans implicated in the 20 July plot need no elaboration. Of all the plots directed against Hitler's life, this was the most determined and the one that came closest to success. It was the only attempt that resulted in injury to Hitler, and it killed several members of his entourage.

Von Stauffenberg had a high-mindedness and genuine loathing of Hitler and all his works that would have made him the agent of an assassination attempt if an earlier opportunity had presented itself, but the driving force behind the July plot was less a revulsion against the perversion and depravity of Nazism amongst the conspirators as the conviction that Hitler had to be removed because he was leading Germany to inevitable defeat and ruination. By July 1944 it was clear beyond any doubt that the war was lost, that the last hope of somehow avoiding defeat in the field had gone. For von Stauffenberg and those associated with him, Germany had to rid herself of Hitler if she was to have any chance of escaping retribution for all the miseries that she had brought mankind.

But in historical terms the July plot was more than just an attempt to do away with a satanic genius, to secure Germany a reprieve from the horrors that would befall her when vengeful enemies brought to her soil the scourge of war that she had inflicted on others over the previous five years. Von Stauffenberg's bomb was the death knell for Germany and, for the second time in a generation, of her hopes to secure the mastery of Europe. Moreover, it marked the eclipse of Europe itself.

Many factors contributed to the contraction of European power, prestige and influence throughout the world, but there was a direct link between this weakening and the shrinking borders and ultimate division of Germany. Germany's defeat in two world wars proved the dominant feature in the shattering and prostration of Europe as a whole: her defeats were not a reflection of Europe's declining fortunes but a major cause of them. This explains the significance of June 1944.

The period between July 1866 and May 1944 was the German era of European history, and even after her defeat in 1918 Germany remained potentially the most powerful single state within Europe. By securing an armistice in 1918 she evaded total defeat, and retained the basis on which to rebuild her military power. The reconstruction of German national power that took place under Hitler had run its course by June 1944, for in that month two non European powers emerged as the arbiters of Europe's fate. In doing so, they relegated the Continent to the site of their most intensive postwar confrontation. After June 1944 the outcome of the war was not in doubt, and what remained to be decided was when, how and in what way it would end, and the shape of the postwar world. After centuries of expansion and political and economic domination of the world, the smallest continent was in June 1944 on the point of becoming the object and no longer the subject of international power.

Half a world away, June 1944 saw the same questions posed with regard to Germany's main partner in the attempted revision of the alignment of power. In June 1944 Imperial Japan, like Germany, suffered a series of defeats that sealed her fate.

Until May 1944 both Germany and Japan retained hopes of avoiding defeat, but these slim hopes lessened with every passing day. By May 1944 the tide of war had turned against these two Axis powers after their early, easy victories, and the real failure of Germany and Japan had been their inability to consummate and consolidate those triumphs. Through miscalculation, wars that had been started by the Axis powers with the intention of limiting the scope of conflict had assumed their own momentum, condemning their authors to fight wars of attrition that they could not win against enemies larger, more populous and more powerful than themselves. This inability to prevent the spread of conflict and to force the issue to a successful conclusion when they held the upper hand led both Germany and Japan by mid-1944 into difficult situations. The cream of their armed forces had been worsted in the crucial battles of 1942 and 1943, and their remaining forces in the field had lost the initiative that had been their only compensation for matériel weakness. With little knowledge of their enemies' capabilities and intentions, they had simply to await the onslaught.

But in May 1944 Germany and Japan remained formidably strong. Enemy forces were nowhere near their homelands. Both remained well outside their prewar borders, and the extent of their conquests remained a comfort to their leaders and peoples. In these conquered areas, it seemed, were the resources needed to continue the war and the space needed to buy time and security. The reality, however, was rather different. Space was an asset only in mobile battle, and both Axis powers were saddled with rigid static strategies and beset by a lack of matériel that prevented their using space to full effect. Nor could they hold, administer and exploit their conquests since both Germany and Japan lacked the trained manpower, logistics and transport needed to convert the space and resources of the conquered territories into tangible military assets. However, in May 1944 the extent of Axis conquest remained as impressive as the quality of their field forces, and if nothing else their powers of destruction with regard to the millions of conquered people under their control remained enormous.

The Axis armies were counted in millions of well-trained and battle-tested troops with impressively high standards of dedication and professional expertise. Their naval and air forces, though savaged in earlier exchanges, remained powerful. All branches of the Axis armed forces could be depended upon to fight to the finish in defense of their homelands, and in May 1944 the German and Japanese armed services knew that the most crucial battles of the war to date were at hand and that they had to counter the next enemy moves. If either the long-awaited Anglo-American invasion of northwest Europe or the American drive into the western Pacific could be blunted then the outcome of the war might be better shaped to Axis advantage (if only in the sense that they might escape total defeat and occupation).

By July 1944 it was clear that the Axis powers had lost or were losing these critical encounters. The Americans and British had established themselves in an irreducible position in northwest Europe, and as the Germans had failed to prevent this landing they were trapped between two fronts and their final defeat assured. After July 1944 Germany's central position, hitherto so great an advantage because of the interior lines of communication it conferred, increasingly became a liability. Hitler could no longer easily switch forces between fronts as pressure from both east and west mounted. The Anglo-American landings therefore ensured their contributing in full to the land defeat of Germany and that the war would be ended with western Europe being liberated by forces from the western democracies. In the Pacific the failure of the Japanese to defeat the American landings on Saipan, and then the annihilation of Japanese naval aviation in the battle of the Philippine Sea, brought the Americans into a position from where their heavy bombers could strike at Tokyo and rupture Japanese lines of communication to southeast Asia. From an economic and strategic viewpoint, the battles in the Marianas doomed Japan as emphatically as the battle of the Philippine Sea.

In the diversity of June 1944 several facts suggest that this month marked the decline of Europe and its subjugation to the will of powers that were not European. First, the fact that until May 1944 the wars in both Europe and the Pacific had been peripheral or short. In the case of the war in the Pacific this point is obvious. A glance at the map confirms that between May 1942 and May 1944 the war barely touched the western Pacific and southeast Asia (the American submarine offensive excepted). The situation with regard to the European theater of operations is not so obvious on first appearances, but in Europe World War II before 1944 was really a series of conflicts linked by the fact that certain combatants were common to them. With one exception these campaigns were short, intensive, and relatively economical in terms of effort and losses. Poland lasted a month, Denmark and Luxembourg a matter of hours. Norway because of its peculiar geography was a more protracted affair, but heavy though German naval losses were, *overall* losses were modest. The Netherlands lasted five days; Belgium three weeks. France, the largest state in Europe with the exception of the Soviet Union, was forced out of the war in seven weeks. The cost to Germany of conquering western Europe was about 45,000 killed and missing: the French dead numbered about 90,000. Compared to the blood letting of Ypres, the Somme and Verdun, such losses were light. In Yugoslavia in 1941 the campaign lasted 11 days, and Greece and Crete succumbed in the course of a campaign that was apparently over before it began.

Only in the Mediterranean theater was there any element of continuity between 1940 and 1944 but before September 1943 this was no more than a corps-sized sideshow for Germany. In the final analysis, the battle of the Atlantic was similarly a sideshow for the Germans, as were British operations outside Europe and North Africa. In all the countries within Europe which saw battle there was horror and killing in plenty, but *after* the battle as the Nazi occupation machine established itself on its prostrate enemies.

War had made little impact on Europe in the physical sense. There was destruction, but there were no strips of murdered nature that had characterized trench warfare in World War I. War passed over the countryside swiftly, expanding outwards from central Europe cheaply and relatively cleanly. Even when a protracted and less fluid campaign developed in southern Italy after September 1943 and war began to leave deep and ugly scars on the countryside, the war was still peripheral. After June 1944 the flow of battle was back towards the heart of Europe as Germany's foes began to break through her outer defenses and the borders of the *Reich* itself. Even as late as December 1944 the Germans still stood on almost every front outside the borders on which they started the war, but the tide of destruction was beginning to engulf the *herrenvolk*. Three quarters of the bombs dropped on Germany in the entire war fell after June 1944 as part of the process whereby Allied forces fought their way to unconditional German surrender.

One fact stands out in all this. The campaigns of 1939-1941 had been fought by Europeans. Europeans had been the arbiters of their own fate. Even as late as 1938 the most serious of the interwar crises had been settled by Britain, France, Italy and Germany without reference to outsiders. Now, after June 1944, as the war began to sweep over Germany and central Europe from three directions, the destruction of Nazism was being led, almost without regard to Europeans, in the east by the Soviet Union and in the west, the south and in the air by the United States.

It was this dual emergence of the United States and the Soviet Union into their inheritance as great powers that makes the events of this month so significant. In the east, on the front that the Germans regarded as the all-important one, June began quietly enough, but before the month was over the Soviets had begun one of the largest offensives of the war. It was here, the Eastern Front, where in 1944 over 60 per cent of the German army was stationed, that there was the exception that distinguished this theater from the others in Europe. On the Eastern Front and in conquered Poland Nazi depravity manifested itself from the first day of the conflict, and on this front it was repaid in kind by a regime that had nothing to learn from Nazism in terms of cruelty and excess. The Eastern Front was the only one in the European theater of operations where the barbarity so much in evidence throughout German-occupied eastern Europe became part of the combat zone. Of the 4,200,000 Germans who died in the course of the war, perhaps half perished as a result of Soviet Army excesses after it reached German soil in August 1944. But such losses pale almost into insignificance besides the 20,000,000 dead that the Soviets incurred in the course of the war.

It is estimated that perhaps as many as 15,000,000 of the Soviet dead were amongst the civilian population and captured military personnel. In relative terms, Soviet losses equate to Britain losing about 5,000,000 people (in the course of the war Britain actually lost about 277,000 as a result of enemy action). But losses on the Soviet scale were the price to be paid for victory. Victory legitimized the Stalin regime in a way that the tyrant could not otherwise have achieved. Stalin exceeded even Hitler in the excesses of his regime, in the acts of wanton barbarism he perpetrated against his own submissive peoples, but he was successful, and the fearful toll of lives the war exacted from the Soviet Union was 'justified' by the avoidance of defeat and then the greatest victory in Russian history.

Victory brought hegemony over lands which had always lived in dread of Russia even when under other alien rule, gains that had eluded the Romanovs for more than 300 years. In June 1944 the Soviets undertook operations that resulted in their clearing the Karelian Isthmus, the success of which was to play its part in convincing Finland to defect from the German camp. In western Russia, the Soviet army stood poised to begin an offensive against

Army Group Center that would result in two things: the greatest single defeat thus far inflicted upon the German army, and the intrusion of the war deep into Poland. The Balkan and Baltic states were on the point of being overrun, the latter dumbly and despairingly resigned to absorption by the Soviets for the second time in less than five years. For the first time in the war, in June 1944 the Soviets were undertaking major operations into non-Soviet territory.

Yet while the Soviet Union stood on the brink of foreign conquest and great power status, she was a great power only within Europe. For all her size, the USSR in 1944 was to all intents and purposes a European power and not a superpower. She lacked the means to project power and influence outside eastern Europe. By June 1944 the United States, on the other hand, had a strength that clearly and distinctly separated her from countries such as Britain and the Soviet Union and placed her firmly in a class of her own.

In 1942 and for much of 1943, the United States was the junior partner of Britain in the European theater of operations. But in these years she played a critical and developing role that was essential to their joint success, and even if she was inferior on land and at sea to the British she was at least their equal in the air, and air supremacy over Germany and German-occupied western Europe was won mainly by the Americans.

In the course of the various Allied conferences of 1943, the Americans made it clear that the days of British predominance in the Anglo-American decision-making process were numbered and that they intended to exercise the power of decision in the future. But in June 1944 Britain still provided the larger contribution to the forces involved in the assault phase of the Normandy landings, though the appointment of an American as supreme commander of the Allied endeavor in western Europe was tacit recognition of who was to provide the backbone of the Allied effort. At the war's end, with their forces standing on the Elbe, the Allies had a total of 4,084,314 ground troops in northwest Europe of whom 2,618,023 were American. At that time the United States deployed five armies in Germany compared to Britain's one, and no fewer than 61 divisions compared to the nominal 12 of the British. For the latter to have 835,208 soldiers in northwest Europe – the equivalent of 20 divisions and 17 independent brigades within Twenty First Army Group – was no mean achievement, but even with their providing the basis of another 12 divisions in the Mediterranean there was no getting around the fact that although Britain retained a global presence she was no longer a global power. In effect, Normandy proved a British swansong, after which her ability to shape events and influence stronger allies declined.

For the Americans, the landings in Normandy came just two days after their forces overtook those of the British in the race to liberate Rome, and on the same day as their main forces bound for Saipan cleared Pearl Harbor and the fast carrier force left its anchorage in Majuro Atoll for its appointment with its Japanese counterpart. Moreover, in June 1944 the American strategic bombing of the Japanese homeland began, not from the Marianas as any casual observer might reasonably suspect but from bases in southern China that were supplied from India. No other country could have considered waging war in such a manner over such distances and with so much force, neither then nor now. The industrial and financial power that underpinned the American effort was awesome. At the war's end some 78,000 warships, assault ships and craft, and auxiliaries of all description were in service with the US Navy. In the course of hostilities American factories provided just over 100,000 tanks and almost three times that number of aircraft, and in financial terms the United States provided civil and military aid to her allies on a scale that would have been sufficient for her raising 2,000 infantry divisions. In June 1944, with her armed forces winning comprehensive victories over her enemies in both Europe and the western Pacific, the United States assumed superpower rank, though she could have little inkling of what such status was to entail over the coming years.

PART ONE

NORTH-WEST EUROPE AND THE MEDITERRANEAN

CHAPTER 1
STRATEGIC BACKGROUND

History has not dealt kindly with Italy and her performance in World War II, but in a very real sense she provides the key to any understanding of the evolution of Anglo-American policy between 1941 and 1944. It is impossible to follow the disputes and compromises that punctuated successive Allied conferences without grasping the fact that the Americans and British were divided on the crucial question of her role and the value of her military geography.

The British regarded Italy as an objective worthy of attention in her own right. Churchill referred to her as 'the goal' though for a time in mid-1944, unsupported by his chief military advisers, he saw her as the means of access into central and eastern Europe. The Americans regarded the road that ran the length of peninsular Italy from the impoverished south as one that in military terms led nowhere. They saw the mountains that line Italy's northern borders as an insurmountable barrier to any force that tried to fight its way up the length of the country towards southern Germany, and they doubted British claims that the elimination of the junior Axis partner would bring major political, psychological, positional and military gain to the Allied cause. In brutal terms, the American view was that Italy would never be anything other than a liability to whichever side occupied her.

THE BASIS OF ALLIED DISAGREEMENT
But in thus stating the nub of an argument that divided the Americans and British for more than two years of war there is a risk of oversimplification and confusion of cause and effect. Italy was not so much the source of discord as the issue on which Anglo-American differences crystallized and took practical form as the two Allies tried to hammer out a common strategic policy after December 1941. Dividing the two were very different philosophies of war. On the American side there was a concept of making war that was based on maneuver and concentration, on mass and firepower. Though the American high command was poorly organized institutionally, and on many occasions suffered from a lack of coherence, realism and leadership, its unerring view was that the defeat of Germany could only be achieved by beating the German army in the field by large-scale land operations.

At different times the vastness of American resources allowed the American leadership to think in terms of raising a military force first of 215 divisions and then a 13,000,000-strong army of 334 divisions in the expectation that such a force would shatter the German army in battle. From the very start of their involvement in the war, the Americans believed that it could only be won if it was carried across the English Channel, into France and thence into the heart of Germany. In the event, the United States was called upon to provide the main contribution on land to the defeat of Germany, but this was not a prospect from which the Americans flinched. The availability of such power enabled the American leadership to think in terms of invading northwest Europe in 1942 or 1943, and such strength, plus the certainty of where it should be used, was the basis of priorities that relegated all other matters to secondary status. The Americans saw Italy and matters Mediterranean to be a distraction and an irrelevance compared to the real need to concentrate for battle in northwest Europe.

The British held a more cautious concept of war, since they were in straightened circumstances. Britain's position, resources and recent historical experience did not allow so confident, assertive and optimistic a military philosophy as the one adopted by the Americans. In terms of industrial output Britain had long been overtaken by Germany, and in 1942 her population of about 48,000,000 contrasted sharply with that of a *Grossdeutsches* Reich that encompassed some 110,000,000 people and controlled as 'allies' or conquered subjects at least a similar number. The resources of Britain's possessions could not redress such an imbalance because the fragmented nature of the British empire produced local needs that ensured a dispersal of effort and power.

Britain and her empire did not have the means to destroy German supremacy within Europe, and this realization was at the heart of her strategic policy in the course of World War II. Britain knew that she could not win a war against Germany except in the company of allies who would have to shoulder the main burden of land fighting. Unable to mount large-scale operations after her expulsion from the European mainland in 1940 and in any event less than enamored with continental warfare after her experiences of World War I, Britain sought to maneuver and probe for weaknesses, to drag the enemy out of position and off balance. She sought to wear down and exhaust the enemy by forcing his dispersal of strength to meet the many threats that could be posed by superior sea power. Only when this had been accomplished would the British turn their attention to the possibility of major land operations. This was a difference with the Americans that was no mere disagreement over emphasis. The Americans saw the cross-Channel effort as essential to the defeat of Germany, but the British regarded it as one that should be made once the defeat of Germany was assured and her collapse was in the process of becoming a *fait accompli.*

Certain Americans contemptuously dismissed British ideas as periphery picking while in their turn many in the British camp regarded American thinking as crude, unimaginative and unrealistic. Such sentiments were the natural prerogatives of peoples destined to be the most intimate of allies, and in the course of the war Britain and the United States became the closest of confederates. Both had philosophies and strategic policies that were flawed in their different ways, and even at a distance of 40 years it is hard to strike a balance between their respective values.

The basic strength of the American case was that it addressed the problem of how Germany was to be defeated. She was not going to be beaten by maneuver and guile but by being shattered in battle by superior forces. The American concept of war grasped the nettle presented by this brutally vulgar fact. The British concept tried to sidestep this problem, and incorporated a basic weakness. Maneuver by the use of seapower could never result in the dispersal of enemy strength to the point where his power would be compromised without battle because in effect there was no periphery on which to maneuver. Air power and the superiority of overland communications to those by sea ensured that there was no theater where the British, for a minimal outlay, could tie down disproportionately large enemy forces. Nevertheless, the British concept had a certain validity, particularly before an invasion when the potential threat was always greater than available power.

To guard against Allied landings German forces had to be spread along the whole coast of Europe, from North Cape to the Pyrenees to Thrace. By 1944 the Germans had 12 divisions in the backwater of Norway, and some 50 divisions in southern France, Italy and the Balkans to check the Allies in Italy and to counter the possibility of further invasions in the Mediterranean theater. Such a drain on enemy resources represented at least a partial vindication of British strategy, and in reality there was a 'second front' in western Europe in terms of German commitment long before the invasion of northwest Europe took place.

The seeds of Anglo-American dispute over Italy and the Mediterranean sprang from 1940 when Germany overran western Europe, British forces were driven from the continental mainland, and Italy declared war on Britain and the already defeated France. Thereafter Britain's strategy was in large part decided for her. Beyond the defense of the homeland and her communications in the Atlantic, her priority had to be to hold Egypt, geographically the center of the empire and glacis of the British position throughout the Middle East, and to carry the war to Germany's junior partner because it was only in North and East Africa that British ground forces could grapple with those of an enemy. Britain's lack of allies, her inability to reestablish herself on the Continent, and the presence of substantial Italian forces in Libya, Eritrea, Ethiopia and Somaliland, ensured that Britain could not hope to achieve more than relatively modest objectives: clearing North and East Africa of the enemy; reopening the Mediterranean to through shipping; eliminating Italy from the ranks of her enemies. Two years after Italy's entry into the war most of these objectives seemed as far from being realized as they had been in June 1940.

The British were not without their successes in these two years, but their power, mobilized along external lines of communication, was never able to ensure a decisive superiority of numbers over German ground forces that deployed directly from the European land mass and which had a tactical doctrine and organization far superior to their own. Just as the British seldom had difficulty in repelling Italian forces, so small German forces, committed to North Africa after February 1941, consistently outfought more numerous British formations. Inferior British technique was obvious at Gazalla when a defensively deployed army was defeated by a German armored corps less than half its size.

Victory at Gazalla allowed the Germans to secure Tobruk (20 June, 1942) and then drive deeply into Egypt before being halted on the Alam Halfa-El Alamein position. By then certain decisions taken by the United States began to exert an increasingly baleful influence on Axis hopes and intentions. At the first Anglo-American conference held after the United States entered the war the two Allies had tentatively agreed that North Africa should be the scene of Allied endeavor in the course of 1942. Subsequently the Americans recognized that they would have to underwrite the British position in Egypt and the Middle East, but in the course of the first half of 1942 the Chief of the Army Staff, General George C Marshall, hardened in the view that the agreed Allied policy of 'Germany first' did not mean 'Italy first.'

THE BASIS OF ALLIED COMPROMISE

The 'German first' policy was the statement of the basic Allied aim, namely that resources should be directed to the defeat of Germany in the sure knowledge that the defeat of Italy and Japan would be assured once the strongest of the Axis partners was crushed. Marshall had little time for the Mediterranean option because he regarded it as a potential ulcer that would drain off the resources needed to mount a cross-Channel attack. What Marshall wanted was an immediate invasion of northern France, and in April he and President Roosevelt's special adviser, Harry Hopkins, arrived in London with a plan for a 48-division assault on northern France, the coast between Le Havre and Boulogne being attacked on a six-division front. The Americans insisted that this plan be implemented no later than April 1943.

It took the British three months to persuade the United States to drop these proposals for Operation Roundup and its alternative, Operation Sledgehammer, which involved a landing on the Cotentin peninsula by six to ten divisions. The Americans defended their plans with a tenacity that would have been admirable had it been supported by a single element of practicability. The Americans and British commanded neither the sea nor the air, lacked specialist amphibious shipping and assault equipment, and had no margin of assured superiority over the German army in western Europe. Moreover, there was never any chance of British acceptance of Roundup if only because American plans envisaged their contributing 18 divisions to the common cause.

Eighteen divisions was small change for an army that planned to raise 20 times that number, but it represented the sum of British strength both immediately and for some time to come. The British were not prepared to squander what little power they had on enterprises they believed unsound and doomed to defeat. The Americans finally came to realize that they could not challenge the Germans in France for the moment, and in return for a British commitment to a cross-Channel invasion at some time in the future they agreed to turn their attention for the remainder of 1942 to French North Africa as the only theater where offensive land operations might be undertaken that year. The North Africa bargain – sealing the ring around Germany – was struck between the United States and Britain on 25 July, 1942.

In the course of these negotiations both sides made concessions, though the more immediate and important ones were made by the Americans. Unfortunately, the latter came to feel that these concessions had been made to the British, whereas they had in fact been made to reality. The upshot was that the negotiations left an unpleasant aftertaste, for both sides. The British resented American attempts to intimidate them into accepting plans that were not properly thought through by threatening to revise the 'Germany first' principle in favor of the 'Japan first' option or by threatening to regulate the flow of aid in order to ensure their acquiescence.

The Americans, on the other hand, emerged from this episode with a revised view of their ally. They suspected that the British never had much heart for a cross-Channel assault and that they would renege on their undertaking if given the chance. They suspected long-term British policy and intentions in the Mediterranean. They feared that the British would try to broaden an initial American involvement in the area, thereby incurring for them an open-ended commitment in a secondary theater of operations.

They did not believe that any help could come from any state in the area, and they doubted the claim that the defeat of Italy would be to Allied advantage. They calculated that the Germans would be well rid of the Italians and that an Italian defection was unlikely to affect the position and morale of Germany one iota. Because the Americans regarded the Balkans and Italy as liabilities in that no advantages whatsoever could be derived from occupying them, they saw no reason to rid the Germans of this drain on their resources.

THE LEGACY OF CASABLANCA

Such were the reservations of the American high command when it accepted a commitment that resulted in forces landing in Morocco and Algeria in the following November. Such hesitations were confirmed and reinforced at the first of the five great Allied conferences of 1943, the Anglo-American summit at Casablanca during January. Perhaps the only time when the Americans and British negotiated as equals, this conference set out two matters: the intention (taken without regard to the other Allies) not to treat with any enemy except on the basis of unconditional surrender, and a basic framework for the immediate prosecution of the war. The latter envisaged an intensification of the war against Japan, primarily in the Pacific but also in the form of a British amphibious endeavor in the Indian Ocean; stepping up the strategic bombing offensive against Germany; clearing North Africa and Sicily, and thereby freeing the Mediterranean to through shipping.

Explicit in these arrangements was an American acceptance of the main strands of British strategic thinking: that there would be no cross-Channel invasion in 1943; that for the remainder of the year the Allies would fight where they were; and that the Mediterranean for the moment ranked above other theaters of operation. But the Americans refused to commit themselves beyond the clearing of Sicily.

The British were able to establish the principle of the Mediterranean option at Casablanca but they were unable to persuade their ally of either the need or the desirability of a campaign on peninsular Italy even though the Americans at this time entered into a double-edged commitment: both they and the British undertook to concentrate forces in Britain for an invasion of northwest Europe 'as soon as German resistance is weakened to the required extent'. Herein lay American endorsement of the British policy of maneuver and attrition to tie down enemy strength and leave him exposed to subsequent defeat, yet at the same time it involved a British recognition of northwest Europe as the primary theater of operations.

So at Casablanca the two Allies accepted the interrelationship between the Mediterranean and northwest European theaters, Allied success in any campaign in the latter being seen to be largely dependent on a preliminary campaign intended to tie down German forces in southern and southeast Europe, away from the scene of the main endeavor. Such an understanding was reached at a time when there was no inkling on the Allied side of the extent of the impact of Anglo-American air power on the battlefield and the manner in which it was to destroy the German capacity to counter an Allied landing in northwest Europe. Such calculations were made when the primary Allied consideration was to secure positional and numerical advantages that would enable them to bring a decisive superiority to bear in north-west Europe. At Casablanca the Americans and British hammered out a formula that envisaged the Mediterranean sapping the enemy's strength to the extent that his ability to respond anywhere in western Europe would be impaired. The aim of carrying the war to the Italian mainland could be either to draw the enemy forward and then to destroy him *in situ* or to gain ground that in its turn would provide the base for subsequent operations. In either eventuality the Allies would have the option of merely posing threats or developing one or more of them, and herein lay the basis of the question of whether or not the Mediterranean could or should be developed as a theater of operations of equal status to the one that was to be opened in northwest Europe.

As the events of 1944 showed, the Americans were unalterably opposed to such a development. By that time the United States carried the main burden of the strategic air offensive, contributed the largest single national contingent in the Mediterranean, and was to provide the vast majority of the forces that were to be committed to northwest Europe. Washington never had any intention of allowing itself to become committed to two major land campaigns in Europe, and at best saw the advantage of an Italian campaign in the threat it would pose to the German position throughout southern Europe.

The British attitude of 'creative opportunism,' on the other hand, came to reflect an increasing ambivalence towards the third member of the 'Grand Alliance'. The British leadership viewed the Soviet Union with mixed feelings, a mixture of suspicion and downright distrust. Soviet complicity with Germany before 1941 had not been forgotten, and constant Soviet demands for the second front that they had denied the British and French in 1940 cut little ice with the British. Nor could the British forget that the Soviets had been Hitler's willing accomplices in the destruction and dismemberment of Poland in 1939, a fact that could never be glossed over after April 1943 when the Katyn Wood affair broke and Moscow set about the systematic vilification of the London-based Polish government-in-exile. More serious, however, was the simple fact that the British

25

leadership had major reservations about Soviet long-term intentions. It saw the Soviet Union not just as an unlikely ally in the present conflict but a future rival and threat, and it had never been part of British intentions to see the German threat replaced by a Soviet menace in central and eastern Europe. But as these considerations increasingly infringed upon Churchill's calculations in the course of 1944, the fear of Soviet hegemony became tangled with several other considerations. The demands of proSoviet public opinion in the west and the needs of interalliance diplomacy ensured that the British had to portray as help to the Soviets the very moves they contemplated as the means of forestalling and frustrating them.

Moreover, the Americans did not share British concern on this score. They did not fear the Soviets, and gave little consideration to the postwar map of Europe. In any event the American political leadership was not prepared to jeopardize future relations with the Soviets because of possible difficulties over the minor states of eastern Europe. In this crucial respect the British, unlike the Americans, grasped the implications of the outcome of the war before it ended. They realized that the war would end the era of European preeminence and result in their own eclipse as a great power, that in future they could survive only as a subordinate ally to the United States. They realized too that the notion of the balance of power within Europe would be at an end, and that their own power to influence events to their advantage would be small, declining and dependent on the closest possible coordination of resources and power. But these matters were reserved for the future when the British travelled to Washington for the Trident conference of May 1943.

TRIDENT – THE TIDE TURNS?

Trident began auspiciously thanks to the completion of Allied plans for the invasion of Sicily and the end of Axis resistance in North Africa. However, the British and Americans failed to resolve their various differences on the question of what course of action was to be followed after the invasion and conquest of Sicily. The British sought to convince the Americans of the need to consolidate operations in the Mediterranean after the taking of Sicily since this theater was the only one where offensive operations might be undertaken and where the pressure on the enemy might be maintained. As the British saw things, any Allied move against mainland Italy was certain to force the Germans to strengthen their positions in southern France and the Balkans and at the same time force Hitler to undertake a potentially major commitment in either southern or northern Italy.

A lack of Italian assistance and the vulnerability of long and exposed coastal flanks suggested that Hitler would choose to stand in the north, on short lines of communication from the Reich and in the rugged mountains just south of the Po valley. But whichever way the Germans tackled the Italian problem, the British could envisage perhaps two dozen enemy divisions committed to a 'containing' role. Such a diversion of enemy strength in the British view could only prove useful to the Soviets in 1943 – and essential to Anglo-American success thereafter.

In mid-1943 tentative planning for the Allied invasion of northwest Europe envisaged an assault by four divisions, another six coming ashore inside a week and a further 20 divisions moving into the beachhead in the first 90 days after the landing. Though relieved that the American fixation with the thickest part of the fence had exhausted itself, the British view was that the initial Italian commitment had to be developed in such a way as to prevent a redeployment of enemy armored and mechanized divisions within the Continent more rapidly than the Allies could move formations by sea into a beachhead in northwest France. The American leadership could see the point of this argument, but it was not convinced by the overall British thesis. It feared that an Italian campaign could drain Allied rather than German resources because it felt the needs of an offensive campaign could bite more deeply into Allied strength than the demands of a defensive campaign would make inroads into German means. Washington was determined on the cross-Channel offensive, and it was not prepared to sanction anything that might deflect it from that aim or in any way lead to a downgrading of operations in any other theater. The Americans were determined to keep the Mediterranean as a secondary theater of operations, to ensure that it remained a complement and not a rival to northwest Europe, and it suspected British intentions on this matter. Washington failed to realize that the British chiefs of staff (but not Churchill) effectively discounted the possibility of developing Greece and the Balkans as active theaters since they knew that the Allies lacked the means to conduct offensives in both the central and eastern Mediterranean. In short, the Americans held a jaundiced view of the Mediterranean and suspected that their ally was prepared to accept an unlimited commitment there in pursuit of chimerical aims.

At Trident the British encountered obstruction and procrastination from the Americans, the very sins of which they stood accused by their ally on many occasions in World War II. The Americans had one intention: to force the British to accept a binding commitment to an invasion of northwest Europe (Operation Overlord) on or about 1 May, 1944. Beyond this matter the American attitude towards Europe was negative. Washington had no idea of how an Italian collapse might be exploited, and was of the view that because so many imponderables were involved in the Mediterranean, the Allies were best advised to wait on rather than try to shape events. Determined to ensure that the Mediterranean did not get in the way of preparations for Overlord, the most that the Americans were prepared to accept in the Mediterranean was the preparation of a number of contingency plans which might allow the Allies to exploit success after Sicily and which, if adopted, would be 'best calculated to eliminate Italy from the war and to contain the maximum number of German forces'.

Churchill and the two army chiefs of staff were authorized to proceed to North Africa in order to expedite this process, but any plans drawn up by the theater commander were subjected to two provisos. First, the Combined Chiefs of Staff reserved for themselves the power of decision with regard to all plans that might be drafted. Second, future policy in the Mediterranean would be subjected to the redeployment of three British and four American divisions from the Mediterranean to Britain in readiness for Overlord after November 1943. At the same time roughly 80 per cent of all amphibious shipping was to be moved out of the Mediterranean, either to the United Kingdom or to the Indian Ocean in readiness for operations in Burma.

Though the Americans tried hard to escape or limit commitment to mainland Italy at Trident, the Allies had little option but to carry the war precisely there. Inability to open a front outside the Mediterranean at this time forced Allied attention back to this theater and thence to peninsular Italy as the only place on the Continent where operations against the German army might be undertaken. The logic of the situation was accepted by the Combined Chiefs of Staff when, on 26 July, 1943 it sanctioned a three-pronged descent on central and southern Italy with landings in the Gulf of Salerno, and on the heel and toe of Italy. The first effort, the invasion across the Straits of Messina against Reggio di Calabria, took place on 3 September, while the other two landings were carried out six days later.

With both Salerno and Apulia approximately 300 miles from Calabria and 200 miles from each other, the Allied plan of campaign incorporated a potentially dangerous dispersal of strength since the various forces put ashore would be unable to provide mutual support in the event of their encountering strong enemy resistance. This risk was accepted because the Allies knew that the Italians would not oppose any landings. The invasion of Sicily (10 July) and capture of Palermo (22 July) had led to the dismissal and arrest of Mussolini and his replacement by Marshal Pietro Badoglio, and thereafter the Italian government was intent on trying to secure an armistice from the Allies and to keep the Germans out of the country even while it reaffirmed its loyalty to the Axis cause. But the real Allied problem was (as it always had been) not the Italians but the Germans, and in the present context that meant Hitler's determination to keep Italy in the war, hopefully as a partner – but if not as a battlefield.

HITLER AND THE INVASION OF ITALY

Hitler was determined to defend at least a part of Italy. He had committed and lost some 100,000 troops in Tunisia after November 1942, but that effort had brought a six-month respite before the war came to Sicily. Then he had tried to hold the island, and had committed a corps to its defense. This had failed to prevent the enemy from securing Sicily in the course of a five-week campaign, but German forces on the island had been able to escape to the mainland and were in a position to counter the Allied landings in September. Indeed, by the autumn, despite Italian obstruction and an uncharacteristic indecisiveness on the part of Hitler, the Germans had assembled an impressively large number of combat formations in Italy.

While Corsica played unwilling host to a single SS infantry brigade and Sardinia enjoyed the protection offered by a reinforced mechanized division, peninsular Italy supported Field Marshal Erwin Rommel's *Heeresgruppe B* in the north and Field Marshal Albert Kesselring's *Heeresgruppe C* in the south. Rommel had under his command three corps with a total of two armored and five infantry divisions while Kesselring deployed the *1st Parachute Division* in and around Foggia, a two-division corps in the Rome-Civitavecchia area, and Colonel-General HG von Vietinghoff genannt Scheel's *Tenth Army*. The latter consisted of two armored corps, the *LXXVIth Panzer Corps* in northern Calabria and the *XIVth Panzer Corps* on the west coast between Gaeta and Agropoli. It was this deployment of the *Tenth Army* in southern Italy, and particularly that of the *XIVth Panzer Corps* on the Gulf of Salerno, that did so much to shape the course of the Italian campaign after September 1943.

Hitler's initial inclination had been to fight for the whole of Italy, but he realized that southern Italy could not easily be held without Italian assistance and that this was not likely to be forthcoming. Hitler read the signs of Mussolini's fall correctly. He believed that Badoglio would sue for peace and even turn on Germany, but for the moment he was unwilling to preempt Italian ambiguity. It was not in his interest to turn on the Italians when the enemy was on the doorstep, or to do anything to upset the delicate balance in the Balkans where the Italians provided the largest single occupation force in what had been Yugoslavia. Hitler's policy after Mussolini's fall was to try to take over the whole of Italy and bind the Italians to him, despite their intentions and hopes. In this way he might still hold southern Italy and secure lines of communication and guard coastlines throughout the length of peninsular Italy.

Hitler's calculations were shaped by the knowledge that the Balkans were far more important to Germany than Italy and that it was in German interests to hold southern Italy and thereby prevent the Allies from securing a platform for operations both against the Adriatic coastline and air operations over the Balkans and the southern *Reich*. But Italian ambivalence and long exposed coastlines made the prospect of holding the south a hazardous one, and holding in northern Italy lessened the drain on German manpower and logistics. Holding in the north would save the German high command a minimum of four front-line divisions, an important consideration for an organization operating in four separate theaters without a strategic reserve on which to call. But balancing this advantage was the fact that in the late summer of 1943 the Germans had no prepared defenses in northern Italy on which to stand, and in any case it made little sense to make the main defensive effort on the last possible line of resistance behind which was no fallback position.

As summer gave way to autumn, Hitler faced an awkward choice as he deliberated on the problem of the policy to be pursued in Italy. Forced back on the defensive and increasingly obliged to conform to the moves of his enemies, Hitler knew that it was imperative to shape events to his own interest and to bring the situation in the Mediterranean under control for three reasons. First, he could not attempt to stabilize the disastrous situation on the Eastern Front while the whole of the German position in the south threatened to fall to pieces. Second, Hitler was realistic enough to see that Mussolini's fall and Italy's defection was an indication of who the Italians thought was destined to lose the war, and that their example was unlikely to be lost on his Bulgarian, Hungarian and Romanian allies. Third, Hitler knew that his own people looked to him for proof of his genius as the war turned against Germany. The fall of Mussolini and Sicily came as the climax to a disastrous six months. In the half year preceding the loss of Messina the German people had to absorb the shock of Stalingrad; defeat in North Africa; unpredented losses at sea; the defeat at Kursk-Orel; and then on 3 August, perhaps the most fearful of all, the shattering of Hamburg in a massive terror raid by the Royal Air Force. By September 1943 the German people and their allies looked to Hitler for some sign of reassurance, that he had the capacity to weather the storm.

Reassurance was to be provided from two sources – the German forces in southern Italy and inadvertently by the western Allies. It was not until 6 November that Hitler finally resolved to stand in the south, and this decision was shaped by the fact that a series of successful rearguard actions had slowed Allied progress in southern Italy to a crawl by the first week of October when the weather broke. In the month between the landings around Reggio and the onset of the autumn rains the Germans were forced to concede ground in Apulia and defeat before Salerno, but in both areas Allied victories were only partial.

The Allied armies proved unable to crush the German formations that opposed them, and on neither coast were they able to secure the speed and depth of penetration that alone would allow them to turn successive German positions and thence the enemy's reverses into a rout. On the east coast British amphibious assaults secured Bari on 23 September and Termoli on 3 October, but in the face of a faltering line of communication, appalling weather, difficult terrain and stiffening resistance their advance did not reach the Sangro valley, 40 miles beyond Termoli, until the second week of November. On the west coast Allied progress was equally slow. The *Tenth Army* made an all-out effort to drive the Allies back into the sea at Salerno between 12 and 14 September but though the British Eighth Army advancing from Calabria linked up with the US Fifth Army heading south from Agropoli on 17 September at Vallo di Lucania, it was not until 1 October that the Allies captured Naples. By then the Germans had bought enough time to devastate the city's port and civil facilities and to prepare the first set of defensive positions behind the line of the Volturno.

STANDING ON THE WINTER LINE

These positions straddled the Italian peninsula at its narrowest point, between the Volturno and Gaeta on the Tyrrhenian Sea and Termoli and Ortona on the Adriatic. Collectively these positions became known as the Winter Line, though in fact the German defenses consisted of six major defense lines of which two were designated as main lines of resistance. These were the Gustav and Hitler Lines, and in organizing these positions Kesselring sought to provide Hitler with time. For more than a year the Germans had been forced to conduct a series of retreats. Movement had been one way, and on the Winter Line the Germans could hope to hold the enemy for a minimal outlay. Static warfare would reduce the drain on fuel, resources and manpower. On the Winter Line Kesselring might provide Hitler with many months in which to effect his strategic policy – the completion of the mobilization of the economy (placed on a war footing only in February) and building up strength in order to wear down the unlikely alliance that he had raised against himself.

Kesselring's intention was to establish himself in positions that would ensure the security of the Aurunci Mountains and the huge Mount Cairo massif. By holding these positions the Germans would be able to dominate the line of the Garigliano and Rapido, and by holding the line of these rivers they would bar the natural and obvious route from the south to Rome that ran through the Liri valley under the brooding gaze of the Monte Cassino position. In this way the Germans established themselves in an immensely strong series of interdependent and mutually supporting positions, sited in depth across an extended front.

The result of their efforts was that the Liri valley would remain closed as long as their positions in the nearby hills and mountains were unreduced, and these could not be reduced unless the Allies secured the valley as the base for their clearing operations. The only way to break this conundrum was to turn a flank, but there was no flank to turn on the Winter Line itself. Siting in depth ensured that each position had to be assaulted deliberately, individually and in sequence, thus preventing the Allies from making a breakthrough in one single movement.

The professionalism involved in the choice of ground and siting of defenses became obvious in the course of the autumn. The outlaying positions, the Viktor Line, were reached by the Allies on 13 October and forced 12 days later. The Garigliano was reached on 2 November, but with Hitler finally backing Kesselring's insistence that the south could be held the Fifth Army attempt of 5-15 November to fight its way into the Liri valley via the upper Volturno and Mignano Gap was halted with heavy losses on both sides. In the course of its effort the Fifth Army all but broke the *3rd Panzer Grenadier Division* around Mignano. Had it done so, it might easily have secured an advantage that confounded Kesselring's optimism. But the Allied problem was that the effort at Mignano practically ruined the American and British divisions involved and no reserve was on hand to turn a potential success into a real one.

THE ALLIED DILEMMA

The lack of a reserve in Italy at this time was the result of decisions taken at Trident and Quadrant. As we have seen, at Trident the Americans and British agreed that seven divisions would be withdrawn from Italy after November in readiness for Overlord; and at Quadrant this decision, plus a British recognition of the primacy of Overlord, were reaffirmed in the course of a singularly bruising, ill-tempered and acrimonious conference. At Quadrant the Americans were determined to secure two things: an unequivocal British commitment to Overlord that by definition would relegate the Mediterranean to secondary status, and acceptance of their idea for a landing in southern France to coincide with Overlord. The latter idea had been raised before and at Trident, but between then and Quadrant it had become almost a *leitmotif* for the American high command as in effect it set out to make British ideas its own.

The British idea of justifying the Mediterranean effort in terms of 'relative strength' and 'interdependence of theaters' reasoning culminated in the concept of simultaneous landings in northern and southern France, and at Quebec the Americans insisted on a landing in southern France (Operation Anvil) as a complement to Overlord. The British made no objection. At this time they were more interested in the immediate needs of the Italian campaign, and while they hoped that the Allied armies would be able to reach the Pisa-Ancona line by late 1943 they had given little consideration to any subsequent course of action other than to note that an advance into northern Italy might allow the Allies to develop amphibious offensives either at the head of the Adriatic or in southern France. While at this juncture Churchill dallied with his eastern Mediterranean option – Greece, the Aegean and the Dodecanese – the British showed no obvious concern for the Balkans on account of the Soviet Union. Indeed, with the Soviet army still to reach the Dnieper at the time of Quadrant, there was no immediate cause for British worries on that particular score.

At Quadrant the British gave the undertakings that were required of them. They reaffirmed the Overlord priority, accepted its May 1944 schedule and underwrote the southern France option. But in the weeks that followed the Americans found that British acceptance of their demands was provisional on their being revised. In return for the British promises at Quadrant the Americans accepted that the Allies should continue to exert 'unremitting pressure on German forces in northern Italy', but this threatened to be an empty promise given the fact that the British 7th Armored, 50th and 51st Infantry and the US 1st Infantry, 2nd Armored, 9th Infantry and 82nd Airborne Divisions were to leave Italy after November. Indeed, because of their departure Allied strength in Italy fell from 19 divisions in October to 13 in December, and the Allies could not maintain 'unremitting pressure' on the enemy while divesting themselves of a third of their strength at the very time when the Germans were at their weakest and when the chance of recording a very substantial victory was a real one.

In the autumn the Allies came close to a swift and economical victory in Italy, but with failure they were caught in as sterile a situation as any that had ever confronted a commander on the Western Front during World War I. Ironically, at the very time when the Mediterranean was supposed to slip into secondary status, the number of Allied divisions in Italy almost doubled in the first six months of 1944, 25 being in position in June. This buildup came in readiness for Anvil and after Kesselring had imposed a stalemate on the Winter Line, when new arrivals could not exploit success but merely reinforce failure. In the autumn and winter the Allies in Italy found a favorable decision beyond them because of their lack of engineers, infantry and a reserve, and because the winter weather prevented their using their superiority at sea and in the air to full effect. But perversely, and despite British efforts to redeem the situation, the coming of spring was to bring little advantage to the Allies – because of Anvil.

Anvil could only be mounted with some of those divisions that had arrived in Italy in the first half of 1944, and their being earmarked for France was one reason why a major victory in Italy once more eluded the Allies. In fact, victory slithered through Allied fingers and the whole of the Mediterranean theater was reduced even further in status as the number of German divisions in Italy rose to exceed those of the Allies. This situation persisted for the remainder of the war, a belated and largely irrelevant endorsement of the British argument in favor of peripheral action. In a very real sense this was a rather apt comment on what was, by any standard, the rather unsatisfactory state of affairs that had characterized the entire Italian campaign and its direction on the part of the Allied high command.

When the Allies came ashore on Sicily they had no clear and settled idea of where they were to go after the island had been secured. They then came ashore in Calabria after a number of decisions that should have ensured Italy's being closed down as a major theater of operations. Even before the landings in southern Italy there was little chance that the forces committed to the campaign on the mainland would have the time, means and opportunity to exploit any initial success that came their way. So it was to prove in November 1943 when the Allies, after the battle around Mignano, stood some ten miles from the mouth of the Liri. With the Germans for the moment exhausted and overcommitted, here was one fleeting opportunity for a drive that would have broken clean through the German positions on the Winter Line. The chance was missed, and it was to take the Allies six long months to cover those ten short miles.

CHAPTER TWO
STRUGGLE FOR ITALY

The winter and spring months of 1943-1944 found the Allied and German high commands preparing for campaigns in western Europe that both knew had to come with the summer. At the same time both had to contend with the problem of trying to run a campaign in Italy the aim of which became increasingly unclear to attacker and defender alike, but which was certain to have profound repercussions for the intended campaign in northwest Europe.

The problem that confronted the Allied high command in these months was how to reconcile the demands of three potentially conflicting interests and commitments. First, failure on the Winter Line in the autumn of 1943 did not spell an end to the campaign in Italy. Failure presented the Allies with the problem of how the offensive in Italy was to be continued, and further failure in their next two moves only presented the same problem in more urgent form. Second, this question of the future of operations in Italy had to be settled in conjunction with arrangements for Anvil since in the spring of 1944 the Allied high command was not agreed on the crucial question of whether the main diversionary effort in support of Overlord should be made in Italy or in southern France. Third, the Allies had to determine the scale and timing of Overlord itself in order to make two things possible: the timely concentration of assault shipping in British ports in readiness for the invasion of northern France, and the implementation of an elaborate plan of deception designed to confuse the Germans on the critical questions of when and where the Allies would make their effort.

On the other side of the hill, the problem that confronted the German high command also manifested itself in three ways. First, *Oberkommando der Wehrmacht* (*OKW*) had to consolidate its initial success on the Winter Line and to ensure that control of the situation in Italy did not slip from its grasp. Second, as it did this it had to strike a balance between the claims on its pool of front-line divisions presented by Kesselring's *Heeresgruppe C* in Italy and Field Marshal Gerd von Rundstedt's *Oberbefehlshaber West* (*OB West*) covering the Netherlands, Belgium and France. Third, *OKW* in consultation with *OB West* had to determine its command organization, strategic deployment and tactical doctrine in readiness for the anticipated enemy landings in northern France.

Both sides faced formidable problems in trying to resolve their various difficulties, and the Allies ultimately enjoyed a greater measure of success than the Germans in settling policy. One simple fact indicates how in practice *OKW* failed to harmonize the conflicting claims made upon it. On 1 June it deployed no fewer than 24 front-line divisions – armored, mechanized, parachute and assault infantry – in France, and 23 such divisions in Italy. Moreover, another four divisions were then on their way to Italy in order to stabilize the situation in that country. Thus on the eve of the Normandy invasion more than half the German front-line divisions in the west that in theory could have been in France to counter an Allied invasion were sidetracked in a secondary theater of operations where they were quite unable to exert any influence on the more important events in the north. But such error on the part of the German high command was not one sided. Allied policy with regard to Anvil and Italy in the first half of 1944 was more than a little confused, and Anglo-American conduct of operations in Italy in the summer was no different.

PRELIMINARY PLANNING FOR OVERLORD

The problem confronting the Allied high command stemmed from its view that it lacked the means to conduct three concurrent offensives within the European theater of operations. With the Overlord commitment inviolable and its requirements having to be expanded, Allied difficulty arose from the conflicting claims within the Mediterranean theater at a time when the Americans refused to consider any widening of their contribution either in Italy or for Anvil. Moreover, the widening Overlord requirement could only be met by reducing (not expanding) Anvil, by cutting back the present allocations for the Pacific theater, or by postponement of the invasion of northwest France. The latter option, proposed on 21 January and accepted by the American Joint Chiefs of Staff on 31 January, could never be anything more than a partial solution to Allied problems, but the American high command at this time was unwilling to accept either or both of the other options.

Trident had provisionally fixed Overlord for May 1944, had allocated a total of 653 LCTs and 632 transport aircraft for the operation, and had appointed a 'Chief of Staff to the Supreme Allied Commander (Designate)' (COSSAC) to draw up plans and proposals that in fact had been under consideration for some time. On the basis of his instructions and these allocations COSSAC at Quadrant set out a proposal for a landing in the Bay of the Seine by three divisions on a 25-mile front. With another two divisions held as reserve, each division was to land on a single beach (Lion-Courseulles, Courseulles-Arromanches, Colleville-Vierville) while two airborne divisions were to land in the Caen area.

The COSSAC proposals did not get enthusiastic support at Quadrant. The Allied high command recognized that the Overlord frontage and the forces committed to the landings were inadequate. The result was that the frontage was to be extended by some ten miles to include the Lion-Ouistreham beach with the landing force increased at the expense of the reserve. Such a 'solution' threatened to create as many problems as it tried to settle, and COSSAC and those who came into contact with this plan were of the view that even in its amended form it remained unsatisfactory and underinvested. But beyond accepting that the landing force should be increased 'if possible' the Combined Chiefs of Staff (CCS) – the only authority with the power to sanction any increase – made no attempt to deal with this problem, and at Sextant in December 1943 they compounded it by settling the main outline of Anvil.

Intent on seeing Overlord and Anvil as arms of a gigantic pincer movement and unwilling to see one effort weakened in order to provide for the other, the CCS envisaged Anvil as an assault landing by two divisions (the local command suggested three) that would be followed up by French formations from Italy and ten divisions shipped directly from the United States. These divisions were to advance into central and eastern France and then take their place on the right flank of Overlord forces for the final drive into Germany. Given this strategic view, and its belief that its forces would have to secure the ports of southern France because those of northern and western France were unlikely to be able to sustain an advance into Germany, the American JCS were unwilling at the turn of the year to consider any reduction of Anvil even to meet the demands of Overlord. It was quite unwilling to accept any commitment that might in any way jeopardize Anvil.

Matters came to a head when the Overlord command appointments were made at Sextant. The then supreme commander in Italy, General Dwight D Eisenhower, was appointed supreme Allied commander for Overlord with a British deputy, Air Chief Marshal Sir Arthur Tedder, and an American chief of staff, Major General W Bedell Smith. The British provided Eisenhower's subordinate air, sea and land commanders-in-chief in the respective forms of Air Chief Marshal Sir Trafford Leigh-Mallory, Admiral Sir Bertram Ramsey and General Sir Bernard Montgomery. The latter was to be in command of all ground forces during and immediately after the assault phase, and his opposition to the amended COSSAC plans was the crucial factor in the decision to redraft them.

Supported by Eisenhower and Smith, Montgomery (after some initial wild plans of his own were quietly assigned to oblivion) insisted on an initial landing being made by five assault divisions coming ashore not just between the Orne and Vire but on a front extended to include the Quinnéville-Pouppeville beach at the foot of the Cotentin peninsula. In this way the Allied force would establish itself securely between two major river obstacles and also in a position hopefully to take Cherbourg quickly. The rapid capture of this port was considered to be very important to the success of Overlord, but the original and amended COSSAC plans had been unable to contemplate a landing north of the Carentan estuary. The proposal to land south of Quinnéville therefore represented a major improvement over the earlier intention to break into the Cotentin and Cherbourg across the Douve, Taute, Vire and Aure rivers from the original Colleville-Vierville beachhead, but because the eastern Cotentin coast was very marshy and the exits from the Pouppeville beach were few and poor, the Overlord plan envisaged the American seaborne assault being supported by airborne landings designed to secure the routes inland from the coast and into the peninsula from the rest of Normandy. At the other end of the intended beachhead, one British airborne division was to be landed in the Caen area.

Thus the final Overlord plan allowed for a landing on either side of Carentan and Isigny by five divisions, four to the east of the estuary and one to the north. Three airborne divisions were to spearhead the landings, while the seaborne divisions were to be supported by a second assault wave consisting of one reinforced armored division, one artillery division and an understrength infantry division. These three formations were to be landed on the same day as the main force landings, and the following day the balance of the understrength formation, plus another complete infantry division, were to come ashore. This plan was very different from the one drawn up by COSSAC, the main point of variance being that the latter had worked to what was available whereas Overlord was to be finally planned on the basis of what was needed.

In the end these needs were almost double those envisaged by COSSAC since in its expanded form Overlord called for enough transport aircraft and gliders to land three divisions and enough assault shipping to put the equivalent of ten divisions ashore on a single day. The five assault divisions, the three supporting divisions and the large number of non-divisional troops that had to go ashore on the day of the landings all had to be lifted by assault shipping, not transports. The latter could handle troops who were to go ashore on the second day, but on the day of the landings itself the Allies had to find sufficient assault shipping to lift a force that in the event totalled 174,320 men and 20,018 vehicles.

In January, when Montgomery, Eisenhower and the various staffs made these calculations, the difficulty inherent in such a plan was obvious: the Allies could find the ground forces for such an assault easily enough, but the assault shipping for so vast an enterprise could only be found at the expense of present arrangements in another theater. Montgomery's solution (seconded by Smith) was to dispense with Anvil, but Eisenhower and the JCS were opposed to this, and it was on 21 January, 1944 that the former suggested a postponement for Overlord in order to allow extra amphibious vessels to come into service. Hardly had Eisenhower made this proposal than the basis of any compromise that tried to maintain present arrangements for the Mediterranean was overtaken by events.

SHINGLE – AND FAILURE

The day after Eisenhower recommended that Overlord and Anvil be postponed to buy time for more matériel production, Allied forces came ashore on either side of Anzio, a small port 30 miles south of Rome and 80 miles beyond the Liri valley. An improvized affair put together at three weeks' notice with assault shipping otherwise destined to proceed to Britain in readiness for Overlord, Operation Shingle was the amphibious side of one last effort to break the deadlock in Italy before the summer and Anvil. The Allied plan called for the US Fifth Army to make a heavy and sustained attack on the Winter Line that would exert such pressure on the *Tenth Army* that Kesselring would be forced to commit his reserves to its support. With the enemy thus committed and unable to extricate himself, the Allies intended to put four divisions from VI US Corps ashore and thence across enemy lines of communication south from Rome. The hope was that at worst the enemy might be turned out of the Winter Line and then Rome, at best that *XIV Panzer Corps* might be encircled and destroyed and the Germans rolled back to the Pisa-Rimini line.

Both parts of the Allied intention miscarried. The Fifth Army proved unable to reduce the outlying defenses of the Bernhardt Line until 15 January, and all but exhausted itself in the process. It was then left with two or three days (actually stretching to five) to prepare an offensive over impassable, glutinous ground against an enemy position stocked and prepared over the previous three months. The result was an entirely predictable failure on the Rapido by II US Corps that was the subject of a postwar Congressional inquiry. The Fifth Army's attack forced Kesselring to commit his reserves, but in failing to pin these on the Winter Line it was unable to ensure that Kesselring could not thin his front to deal with a threat to his rear. But this threat failed to materialize because the Germans proved able to contain the landing of the VI Corps.

In reality the latter had been set a task beyond its means, and there was never any chance of its being able to realize the exaggerated and unrealistic hopes vested in it. It was expected to secure its own beachhead perimeter, develop an offensive to isolate the Winter Line position, and at the same time block any southwards advance of any German divisions coming down from northern Italy. With just two reinforced infantry divisions in the original assault and with no armored division that might have been able to register the depth of advance that was needed to produce success, VI Corps lacked the means to carry out its divergent tasks. By the time it secured its perimeter and concentrated all its divisions ashore, the moment for offensive action had passed. Within a week of the landing, elements from eight divisions surrounded the beachhead as the *Fourteenth Army* moved from northern Italy to protect the rear of the *Tenth Army*, and another six divisions moved into the country to take the place of those that had gone south.

Here were the roots of an increasingly unfavorable situation that consistently infringed upon Anglo-American deliberations in the first quarter of 1944. The failure of VI Corps to provide the key to the opening of the Winter Line created a double impasse for the Allies because it left them with a beachhead they could neither expand nor evacuate as Hitler, after a year on the defensive, sought to seize the initiative with a counterattack that would destroy VI Corps. He knew that a German victory at Anzio would blunt Allied power in Italy, have major repercussions throughout the Mediterranean to Germany's advantage, and have profound psychological effects for both sides as they prepared for the forthcoming 'main event' in France. German success would end a depressing run of defeats, put fresh heart into the *Wehrmacht* in France, and weaken Allied morale and perhaps resolve. The divisions gathered around the Anzio position were committed to two all-out drives to crush the beachhead (15-20 February and 28 February-4 March) but these efforts proved no more successful than renewed Allied attempts in the last week of January, mid-February and again in mid-March, to raise the siege of Anzio by breaking German resistance on the Winter Line.

With the failure of both sides to force a favorable decision the battle both on the Winter Line and around Anzio was allowed to die, but long before this happened its likely outcome had been foreseen by the Allies who were then left with urgent problems, given the pressing need for decisions to be made about Overlord and Anvil. Because of their supremacy at sea and in the air the Allies could be expected to ride out the storm at Anzio, but failure to force a favorable decision left them with a broadening commitment in Italy that they could not meet if Overlord and Anvil were to proceed. They could not cut the Italian commitment once VI Corps was sealed in its beachhead, but without such a cut they could not mount Anvil – and they could not carry out Overlord unless the Anvil commitment was reduced.

In trying to reconcile these conflicting claims the British sought to preserve Overlord, to concentrate in Italy and to rely on the threat of invasion rather than invasion itself to tie down enemy forces in southern France; the Americans sought to cut the Italian commitment in order to retain Anvil as complement to Overlord. To the Americans the British 'solution' might tie down the Germans in southern France but would not result in their destruction. That was exactly the British point, hence the inability of the two sides to agree to it.

EISENHOWER IN CONTROL?

The drift of Allied policy, a shortage of time and the desire to avoid yet another bruising exchange with their British opposite numbers led the JCS to decide to delegate American authority to Eisenhower in the hope that he could negotiate a compromise formula on strategic policy in Europe with the British that had so far eluded the CCS. In many ways Eisenhower was the ideal choice for the role of mediator since he enjoyed the confidence of both national commands, but for the independent supreme commander of Overlord to be appointed plenipotentiary with instructions to settle the conflicting claims of Overlord, Anvil and Italy represented an extraordinary abdication of responsibility on the part of the JCS. The situation was made stranger by two other decisions. First, in order to 'assist' Eisenhower make his decisions a team of advisers was sent to Britain for what promised to be a confused set of talks. Second, after making Eisenhower the arbiter of Allied policy the JCS rejected his findings.

Eisenhower's inclination was to try to maintain both Overlord and Anvil, but if forced to choose between them he had to opt for Overlord. His first efforts were directed to keeping both operations in being. By increasing the load capacity of assault shipping and providing Overlord with Anvil's landing craft in return for transports, the planners were able to 'adjust' the manifests until the needs of both operations could be met. Predictably, the British objected to such dubious expediency, Montgomery because of the tactical problems that might arise, the chiefs of staff on more substantial strategic grounds.

Their argument in mid-February was that if two or more months had to elapse between formations earmarked for Anvil being pulled out of the line in Italy and the start of the operation, the clock suggested that Anvil's moment had already passed. This was uncomfortably near the truth. The second British argument was that continuing with Anvil would leave the Allies with just 20 divisions for Italy and other commitments which might arise in the Mediterranean.

It is hard to think of any argument that might have secured less American sympathy than this, but on 22 February Eisenhower obtained British acceptance of a complicated, short-lived and ambiguous compromise. The Overlord priority was reaffirmed, but Eisenhower, giving away no more than what he might be called upon to concede in any event at some time in the future, recognized Italy as the Allied priority in the Mediterranean. The supreme Allied commander in the Mediterranean, General Sir Henry Maitland Wilson, was to draw up plans for operations intended to complement Overlord, with Anvil at the top of the list. All decisions were to be reviewed on 20 March, but for the moment there was to be a moratorium on shipping movements in and out of the Mediterranean. Irrespective of whatever decisions were taken in March, *some* assault shipping would leave the Mediterranean in April, but if Anvil was cancelled the Mediterranean theater would *lose all* its amphibious shipping other than the requirements for a single division. That would be left on station for deception purposes.

DIADEM'S ROLE AS SUPPORT FOR OVERLORD

The Eisenhower formula strongly suggested that Anvil might be dropped, and Eisenhower went so far as to recommend this to Marshall on 26 February after both London and Washington had endorsed his proposals. In effect, the 22 February formula placed Anvil under a suspended sentence, and seemed to place its fate in the hands of authorities biased against it. The Mediterranean command and the Allied command in Italy – General Sir Harold Alexander's Fifteenth Army Group – were given a month in which to force a favorable decision in Italy that would enable Anvil to proceed and result in the virtual demise of these two commands. The price of failure would be that the two commands would be allowed to do what they wanted. By this stage Fifteenth Army Group knew exactly what it wanted.

Thus far the campaign in Italy had been an extemporized affair The Allies had never had a strategy but an improvized plan of campaign that yielded increasingly meager and disappointing results with each landing. Sicily, Salerno and Anzio had shown declining returns and proof that optimism and opportunism were not effective substitutes for a properly planned strategy. The latter came within reach in the form of a paper, drawn up by Alexander's chief of staff, Lieutenant-General John Harding, which set out the basic objective of an Italian campaign: to force the enemy to commit the maximum number of divisions to . . . Italy at the time Overlord is launched.' Harding continued:

'It is obvious that the most effective way of making the enemy draw on other theaters for troops for . . . Italy is not merely to push back the enemy's line, but to destroy enemy formations in Italy to such an extent that they must be replaced from elsewhere to avoid a rout. Tactical plans should therefore be designed to bring about situations in which enemy formations can be destroyed or so reduced in strength as to be (rendered) non-effective, rather than for the primary purpose of gaining ground.'

The Harding thesis was that by securing the initiative and local superiority the Allies should fight a battle of matériel or, more accurately, that they should use superior matériel resources in battle against enemy manpower. By dictating the timing and course of events, the Harding tactical plan envisaged the enemy being broken on the Winter Line not by guile, maneuver or skill, but by superior firepower. The Allies had more tanks, aircraft and artillery than the enemy, and Harding's intention was to wait until spring dried and hardened the ground before using these advantages in a full-scale offensive. In the meantime virtue could be made of necessity by the reinforcement and reorganization of Fifteenth Army Group.

Over the previous months, armies and corps had lost their national cohesion to such an extent that in March 1944 not one of the nine Allied corps in Italy was nationally distinct and at a strength of three divisions. Harding suggested using the time before the start of a spring offensive to unravel American and American-sponsored divisions from their British, imperial and British-sponsored counterparts, and at the same time to extend the front of the British Eighth Army west of the Apennines. By thinning the Adriatic sector and relegating it to secondary status, Harding envisaged bringing the main strength of the Eighth Army to support the Fifth around the main Monte Cassino position. The Harding proposals envisaged such a reorganization and redeployment being completed by mid-April, and the recommendation was that offensive operations against the Winter Line should begin three weeks before Overlord in order to exert the greatest possible pressure on the enemy in the days immediately before the invasion of northwest Europe.

The Harding thesis was formidably complete, but it was open to three objections. First, though Harding specifically sought to use Allied matériel against enemy manpower, his proposals embraced a concept that had not lived down the evil reputation it had gained during World War I. Harding envisaged fighting the one type of battle the enemy could not win, a battle of attrition – with all the overtones of brutal insensitivity that that implied. Second, the Harding proposals called for a major reinforcement of Fifteenth Army Group but no significant offensive action for some months. Third, the reinforcement of Fifteenth Army Group on the scale envisaged by Harding was certain to spell an end to Anvil. Harding made this very point, that the Allies would have to decide between

Anvil and a major offensive in Italy. The Harding thesis was a credible alternative to Anvil, and was the basis of confused exchanges between Washington, London, Eisenhower, Maitland Wilson and Alexander that were brought to a head on 21 March when Eisenhower formally recommended the cancellation of Anvil.

The following day Wilson submitted proposals that incorporated Harding's original plan of campaign. He also observed that an offensive in Italy in April in support of Overlord in May would not allow Anvil to be carried out before mid-July. Given that the rationale for Anvil was that it should take place at the same time as Overlord, the JCS threw out Wilson's proposal on 24 March. It sanctioned the transfer of shipping from the Mediterranean that had been foreshadowed under the terms of the February compromise, but refused to cancel Anvil. However, it accepted Wilson's provisional timetable, and indicated that it was willing to see Anvil postponed until mid-July.

Given the earlier JCS insistence on the synchronization of Overlord and Anvil, the 24 March decision made little military sense, and led to bitter Anglo-American recriminations as spring gave way to summer. But the JCS sanctioned the Harding plan though hardly had it done so than it became clear that the reorganization of Fifteenth Army Group would take longer than expected and that its offensive against the Winter Line – Operation Diadem – could not begin until mid-May. Anvil, as a result, could not start until mid-August. This did not unsettle the JCS. It was determined to launch Anvil some time in the summer regardless. The extent to which Anvil was less an element of a war-winning strategy than the means of bending the British to the American will became clear with the unprecedented JCS offer to send assault shipping from the Pacific (ie from the sacrosanct resources devoted to the US Navy's real war) to the Mediterranean *on condition the British accepted a June Anvil*. The British refused to entertain such a notion and with the situation unresolved Anglo-American attention had to switch from internal dispute to the mastery of the Winter Line.

A FATAL GERMAN MISCALCULATION

The Diadem plan envisaged the Allies staging an elaborate deception plan with landings on the Tyrrhenian or French coasts designed to tie down German mobile divisions in the rear areas, while the *Tenth Army* was shattered by a massive frontal assault conducted by no fewer than five Allied corps in the sector between the sea and Monte Cassino. With 14 divisions committed to the attack, Diadem envisaged the use of II US Corps on the coast and the French Expeditionary Corps in the Aurunci massif in supporting roles while three of the Eighth Army's corps ruptured the enemy front. The hope and expectation was that II Polish Corps would break German resistance at Cassino while XIII British Corps opened a breach in the Liri valley which the reserve, I Canadian Corps, would widen and exploit with a massed armored thrust up the main road to Rome. The intention was to use Route 6 as the main axis for an advance that would relieve the Anzio beachhead and allow the capture of Rome. The long-term aim was to secure the elusive Pisa-Rimini line. But in accord with Harding's original ideas, the immediate objective of Diadem was the destruction of *XIV Panzer Corps* and hopefully of the *Tenth Army*, thereby forcing the enemy to commit his reserves to Italy and away from France and Overlord.

Diadem was unsubtle but an unexpected bonus was that two crucial German errors of policy and deployment played into the hands of Fifteenth Army Group and left Kesselring's forces exposed and liable to defeat in detail. Kesselring had reckoned that the Allies would not be so crude and unimaginative as to make their main effort on the Winter Line again, and when Diadem opened on 11 May he assumed that the Allied intention was the same as in January – to force him to commit his reserves before a landing was made in the rear. He was consequently caught off balance at the start of Diadem.

His error compounded a more serious error of strategic deployment insisted upon by *OKW*. This arose because of Hitler's determination to repeat the success of the winter, despite the fact that the conditions of fighting had changed considerably in favor of the Allies in the intervening months. Hitler's policy was to continue to stand on the Winter Line and opposite the Anzio beachhead. He failed to realize that his divisions had been exhausted by their earlier exertions. Opposed by an enemy that was always superior, and sustained by a supply line that was always inferior to that of the enemy, Kesselring's armies in the spring of 1944 were in no state to maintain their positions without massive reinforcement and rotation of units, neither of which was possible. Constant Allied attacks had slowly eroded German strength, and as the ground hardened and skies cleared with the lengthening of the days, so German vulnerability grew as Allied supremacy in the air and superiority of armor and artillery in the valleys became ever more pronounced. As Harding had predicted, spring saw the odds lengthen in favor of the Allies, and by insisting on a policy of rigid linear defense at the forward point of contact Hitler robbed himself of flexibility and any chance of securing even a temporary initiative anywhere in Italy.

Without mobility German forces could only conform to any enemy move, with a defense that was sure to be inferior to the enemy. A policy of over-commitment forward, with no armor available for the counterattack and too few divisions to hold the flanks ensured that the front, once broken, could not be repaired. By trying to maintain his position on the Winter Line, Hitler made a fundamental error that ensured German weakness throughout Italy, nowhere more so than on the undermanned Winter Line itself where the Fifteenth Army Group chose to make its effort. In view of these weaknesses, it was ironic that the long-awaited Allied success on the Winter Line came not where it was anticipated (around Monte Cassino and the Liri valley) but to the south. This was the one sector of the front where easy and rapid exploitation of a breakthrough was not possible.

Historical and popular interest in the fight for the Winter Line has tended to focus upon events at Monte Cassino. The months-long struggle for the ruined abbey was an important symbol at the time, but it was across the valley in the inhospitable and largely trackless Aurunci mountains, that the Allies made the breakthrough that turned the Cassino position. The breakthrough rendered the enemy's fallback positions untenable, and broke German communications between the Liri valley and the coast. Here General Alfonse Juin's FEC routed the *71st Infantry Division* with a drive that cut the crucial Itri-Pico road on 17 May. Itri fell on 19 May and Pico, after two days of heavy fighting, on 22 May.

With the last enemy positions in the Aurunci falling to the French before the would-be defenders had time to man them, Kesselring's remaining positions in and to the north of the Liri valley could not be retained. The bloodied Poles secured Monte Cassino as early as May 18, but with the Eighth Army putting so many tanks and vehicles on Route 6 that its rate of advance up the Liri valley was less than that of the French and their mules in the mountains, Kesselring was able to extricate his forces on the right and thereby prevent defeat assuming the dimensions of a disaster. After falling back from Cassino, the Germans were able to deny the Allies control of Pontecorvo until 25 May and then the *90th Panzergrenadier Division* at Ceprano and the *1st Parachute Division* at Arce were able to keep the road to Rome closed until 28 May. Because of these partial successes Kesselring was able to restrict the Allied advance on all routes except along the coast, and his forces registered similar results opposite the Anzio beachhead. Unable to contain an offensive that began on 23 May, the *Fourteenth Army* had to give ground on the left and in the center but not on its right, on the direct route to Rome. On 25 May detached units from II and VI US Corps linked up around Borgo Grappa, thereby raising the siege of the beachhead, but on the same day the Fifth Army amended its earlier orders to VI Corps to develop a dual offensive along Route 7 and, via the Alban Hills and Valmontone, along Route 6. Now VI Corps was ordered to concentrate its efforts along Route 7, where to date its progress had been halting and enemy resistance at its strongest.

By this change, the Fifth Army compounded the earlier Eighth Army failure to develop an offensive rapidly enough to secure the head of the Liri valley in front of the retreating Tenth Army. By directing VI Corps away from Valmontone the Fifth Army passed the chance to get across the enemy's line of support and escape along the direct route between Rome and Ceprano. The result was that Kesselring was able to bring the battered Hermann Goring Panzer and 92nd Infantry Divisions into Valmontone before II US Corps could switch across to Route 6 and therefore was able to hold the Americans on the Albano-Valmontone line until 2-3 June when resistance in the Valmontone area finally collapsed. Rome was entered and secured on 4 June, and while at the time the capital seemed the great prize of the Italian campaign, real victory had eluded the Allies.

The British failure to take Ceprano and Arce and the American failure to secure an undefended Valmontone provided Kesselring with the time he needed to pull his force back along Route 6 or eastwards, across the line of the Allied advance, into the hills that led down to the Aniene valley and thence to the defensive fastness of Umbria. Because of their failure to make a clean break through the enemy defenses or to develop a deep encirclement, the Allies could not prevent a skilful German withdrawal over the minor roads and tracks and their own advances were subjected to inordinate delays caused by the thorough demolition programmes with which the Germans covered their retreat. The mechanized character of the Allied armies told against them in these circumstances, and the Allied air forces, split between strategic and tactical tasks, were unable to win the battle of annihilation that the ground forces could not win for themselves.

Yet even on 4 June when Rome fell, Allied forces stood north of the Tiber while most of the *Tenth Army* was to the south of the river and on the wrong side of bridges that had been demolished prematurely. A battle of encirclement still did not appear impossible, but by the third week of June German formations that two weeks before had seemed in imminent danger of annihilation were established on an interim defense line that straddled Lake Trasimeno, and were conducting a slow and deliberate withdrawal to positions even then being prepared in rear areas. Between 16 and 23 June the Allied forces on the west coast advanced a mere 20 miles, and in the following three weeks advanced only another 25. This was not the rate of advance needed to achieve a clear-cut or annihilating victory. The inadequacy of this performance at this crucial stage of the Italian campaign can be gauged by the fact that in what should have been Diadem's exploitation phase (5 June to 15 August) the

Fifth Army took only 16,969 prisoners – of whom more than 2,000 were Soviet 'volunteers' from the *162nd Turkoman Infantry Division* – compared to its haul between 12 May and 4 June of 11,316. Despite all their advantages, the Allies failed to turn the German retreat from the Winter Line to the Pisa-Rimini position (the Gothic Line) into anything more than an orderly withdrawal. This fact was lost to view both at the time and later because this phase of operations coincided with a revival of the Anvil argument, and this in its turn became the center of much discussion when it became entangled with the much-vaunted Vienna option in the course of the postwar inquest on Allied strategic policy.

THE FACTS BEHIND THE VIENNA OPTION

The Anvil question was raised as early as 17 May by Wilson because he needed to know for what eventuality he was to prepare over the coming weeks. He set out the various options facing the Allies in the Mediterranean for the CCS and five days later warned Alexander that Fifteenth Army Group could expect to lose divisions in June if the CCS decided to proceed with a landing operation outside Italy. Wilson's preference was to go ahead with Anvil, and this was the JCS attitude. It had always wanted Anvil, it had promised the Soviets at the Eureka Conference in Teheran in November 1943 that Anvil would go ahead, and it was still somewhat disillusioned with Italy in particular and the Mediterranean in general. It saw no reason to change its attitude at this time, and after Overlord had succeeded in establishing Allied forces ashore in northern France, the British service chiefs were prepared to go along with the JCS. After an unusually harmonious CCS meeting in Britain and visit to Normandy, the Chief of the Imperial General Staff, General Sir Alan Brooke, noted:

'Now at last we had . . . the south of France operation in its right strategic position. By the time we had reached the Pisa-Rimini line the Italian theater should have played its part in holding German reserves away from northern France. We could then contemplate landing in southern France . . . to co-operate on the southern flank of Overlord operations.'

That was not quite how the Americans saw things, but such a difference of view paled into irrelevance compared to the disagreement that emerged after 17 June when Alexander formally proposed a landing at the head of the Adriatic, the aim of which was to develop an offensive through the Ljubljana Gap towards Vienna. Initially the American and British service chiefs regarded the proposal in much the same light. Both thought that when it came to

48

the Trieste-Vienna road Alexander made light of difficulties little different from those he had failed to resolve properly thus far in the Italian campaign, and they considered Alexander's claim that 'neither the Apennines nor even the Alps should prove a serious obstacle to (Allied) enthusiasm and skill' as facile and unrealistic.

The British service chiefs were sympathetic politically to the Vienna option, but regarded it as impractical. It called for the commitment of 18 divisions (with another six in reserve) to a narrow-front offensive over difficult and restricted terrain after enemy resistance in northern Italy had been ended. The British chiefs of staff could see the obvious objections that doomed such a proposal – that victory in Italy remained to be won, and that there were signs that its winning might prove more difficult than Alexander imagined; that Fifteenth Army Group would have to be further reinforced; and that the Vienna option would spell an end to Anvil. In real terms, the Vienna option called for a force equivalent to the entire British Army of 1944 fighting its way along a single road through the mountains to Ljubljana – and the British service chiefs knew exactly what their American opposite numbers would make of that.

Strategically and politically, the Vienna option was a nonstarter. It contradicted the basis on which Anglo-American policy was founded. The CCS had agreed that the Mediterranean was or would be a secondary theater of operations and that the Allies could not contemplate two major land offensives in Europe. The Vienna option called for an Allied effort in the Mediterranean greater than anything thus far made in the theater, and such an attempt could be made only if the Americans cut Anvil or reduced the build up in Normandy or both. The whole of Allied policy had been built around the primacy of north-west Europe over all other theaters, and this was not a reality that could be casually discarded by some sudden and ill-considered enthusiasm for an adventure into central Europe. The American high command was not interested in reducing the commitment in the main theater of operations in order to maintain and expand the commitment in the secondary theater. The Vienna option was out of the question but the Allied problem was that Churchill could not see this.

CHURCHILL'S JUDGEMENT IN QUESTION

For some months past Churchill had been something of a champion of lost causes. He had tried to test the water in the eastern Mediterranean; had opposed Allied bombing policy in France; had sought to maintain the independence of Bomber Command at a time when Eisenhower wanted it under his own direction during the run up to the landings in northwest Europe; and caused problems over a number of command appointments. But in May and June a seeming indulgence in obstruction became more pronounced, with Churchill apparently intent on backing any policy as long as it was unacceptable to the American high command. At this stage he argued variously in favor of a continuation of the Italian option, landings in the Adriatic and the invasion of *southwest* France.

He was frustrated on all counts by an American constancy of purpose that insisted upon Anvil as Overlord's travelling companion. Even if the JCS had proved unreasonable on the question of Anvil in the past and was wilfully obstinate at this stage of proceedings, there was a basic simplicity and correctness about American priorities with which Brooke agreed. Moreover, Eisenhower supported the JCS view. Alexander's proposals coincided with the infamous Channel storm of 19-22 June that wrecked the American harbor facilities on the Colleville-Vierville (Omaha) beach, after which Eisenhower entertained an overriding but exaggerated fear that without the ports of southern France and with nothing more than existing lines of communication the Allies might not be able to match the German buildup in northern France. Under these circumstances Eisenhower wanted a landing on the Riviera coast as quickly as possible. He had little interest in landings either in southwest France or at Séte and an advance via the Carcassone Gap and Toulouse to Bordeaux. He had no interest either in a 270-mile foray from the head of the Adriatic to Vienna. The Rhone valley had few attractions, scenic or otherwise, but as far as Eisenhower was concerned it held out better hope of ultimate victory than any of the more fanciful routes under consideration by the various Allied commands in the summer of 1944.

It was a sign of Churchill's continuing poor judgement that he persisted with his opposition to Anvil after Eisenhower revealed his hand, and on 28 June and again on 1 July he appealed directly to Roosevelt for support against the JCS. It was only when these entreaties had been rejected in a somewhat dismissive manner that he conceded temporary defeat with as much poor grace as he could muster. Indeed, Churchill continued to snipe at Anvil until 8 August, just one week before the operation was carried out. But the directive that settled Anvil for 15 August was issued on 2 July, and in this there was an ironical comment on Alexander's earlier optimism.

By then the Fifteenth Army Group was having to conform to an increasingly successful German defense in northern Italy, and the fact that Kesselring's command could exhibit such rapid powers of recuperation after its mauling of the previous six weeks suggests that a drive on Vienna would have been a mistake. If the Fifteenth Army Group could not win in Italy in June with a nominal two-to-one advantage in a fluid battle, it was unlikely to win a battle at the head of the Adriatic when the extra closeness to the *Reich* was almost certain to provoke a more violent enemy reaction than in northern Italy.

The reality of flawed success in Italy in May and June was missed at the time and then obscured in postwar analyses of the campaign as attention concentrated on the question of whether and how Soviet hegemony in eastern and central Europe might have been forestalled by an 'alternative strategy' on the part of the western powers in the last two years of the war. As hostility between the Soviets and the other allies intensified, the obvious target for criticism was Anvil and the removal of VI US Corps and the FEC from Italy at the very time when opportunities for better things allegedly presented themselves.

Much of this criticism stressed two points: first, that the removal of seven divisions, nearly 20 artillery battalions and a number of crucially important service units hamstrung the offensive against the Gothic Line, just as the withdrawal of units the previous autumn had stymied the attack on the Winter Line. And second, that a landing in Istria and a drive through the Ljubljana Gap to Vienna to forestall a Soviet arrival in the area would have been possible. Although superficially attractive, the first point is a half truth and the second is spurious.

Twenty Allied divisions could not be expected to defeat an enemy with 26 divisions operating in and behind a series of strong field fortifications. But responsibility for such a situation lay less with a high command that took divisions away for a successful operation elsewhere than with a local command that had failed to win a battle of encirclement and annihilation in the heat of summer and then undertook an offensive in the mountains and autumn rains without sufficient artillery, engineers and infantry to ensure success. If Fifteenth Army Group could not win on the plains, when the enemy was in flight, when it possessed overwhelming advantages and in dry weather, it was not going to win a close-quarter battle in the rain against an enemy in positions of the kind that had defied the Allies for seven months in the south.

The Vienna option, on the other hand, was never more than a will o' the wisp, an old man's pipe dream. It was an example of journalistic generalship, wall-map strategy, that in its inability to relate the aim to what was practical was as outrageous as the worst of Hitler's follies. The idea of a drive on Vienna would have been as successful as the attempt to force the Rhine, surround the Ruhr and bring the war to an end with an advance along a single road that did not even reach Arnhem. The various attempts at a retrospective vindication of Churchill have served only to show the shallowness of vision and his behavior at this time in opposing Anvil conformed to the so-called De Gaulle Syndrome – a penchant for increasingly divisive and irresponsible action in response to a declining ability to influence decisions and events to one's own advantage. In June 1944 Churchill chased the illusion of victory while Alexander saw its substance slip through his fingers.

ROME AND AFTER

June in Italy opened with the initiative firmly in Allied hands and the fall of Rome assured, but it was not until 7 June that a directive was issued for pursuit of the enemy north of the capital. Under its terms the original Diadem directive of 5 May and the disposition of forces observed since 11 May – the Americans on the left in the coastal area and the British on the right in the foothills and mountains – was to be maintained as the Fifth and Eighth Armies advanced into northern Italy. The 5 May instructions had envisaged Fifth Army advancing with first Civitavecchia and Viterbo and then Leghorn as its objectives. With two major roads available for an advance, after the fall of Rome the Americans intended to comply with these orders by pushing VI Corps along Route 1 and II Corps along Route 2. The Eighth Army was under instructions to advance into Umbria along Routes 3 and 4, the two roads that straddled the Tiber, but such orders presented it with obvious problems. On 5 June it was conducting an advance with three corps over minor roads through the mountains between Routes 6 and 5 with I Canadian Corps around Anagni, XIII British Corps at Alatri and X British Corps near Sora. These formations were on the side roads and Eighth Army problems in large part stemmed from Fifth Army being ahead of it on roads that the Eighth needed if it was to get its forces on to Routes 3 and 4.

The previous three weeks' fighting had produced a situation whereby the enemy was now stronger in the mountains than he was in the more important coastal area. Diadem and the breakout from Anzio shattered the *71st*, *92nd*, *94th* and *715th Infantry Divisions* and mauled the *Hermann Goring Panzer*, *65th* and *362nd Infantry Divisions* – in effect the *Tenth Army's XIV Panzer Corps* and the *Fourteenth's LXXVI Panzer Corps*. But the latter, plus divisions from army and army group reserves, had been expended in covering the withdrawal of the *Tenth Army* from the Winter Line, and its efforts allowed *XIV Panzer Corps* to pull back through Rome into *Fourteenth Army*'s area of responsibility while *LXXVI Panzer Corps* was forced to conform to the *Tenth Army*'s movement into the mountains. The result was that *Fourteenth Army* – now with *XIV Panzer* and *I Parachute Corps* under command – retained the bulk of the exhausted divisions in the most open sector of the front while the Eighth Army, operating in more difficult terrain, faced the better organized *Tenth Army*. Thus to comply with its orders the Eighth

Army broke up I Canadian Corps, directed X Corps to develop a supporting offensive along the Arsoli-Orvinio-Rieti axis, and placed XIII Corps in the van of its advance.

The intention was for the latter to advance on two axes with a single reinforced armored division on each. The Fifth Army thereupon obliged the Eighth by halting its own advance in order to let the 6th South African Armoured Division move through Rome to Route 3, and on 6 June this formation was able to take advantage of a rare enemy lapse in leaving the defile into Civita Castellana unguarded. An advance of 33 miles in the day brought the South Africans control of the town, but the destroyed bridge over the Tiber at Borghetto ensured that they could not develop their offensive against Terni. To the east the 6th British Armoured Division established itself on Route 4 on 6 June with an advance from Tivoli to Monterotondo that was opposed by what remained of the *Hermann Goring Panzer Division*, while further to the east its flank was secured by the 4th British Division's successful advance along the Palombara-Montelibretti road in the face of opposition from rearguards of the *1st Parachute* and *15th Panzergrenadier Divisions*.

The directive of 7 June confirmed and elaborated basic objectives. The Fifth Army was instructed to secure the Pisa-Lucca-Pistoia region while the Eighth was ordered to develop an offensive into Florence-Ribbiena-Arezzo area. In the Adriatic sector V British Corps, with the ill-assorted 4th Indian and Utili (Italian Liberation) Divisions under command, was ordered to confine itself merely to following up an enemy withdrawal, the expectation being that the *Tenth Army* would be forced to pull back its left flank to conform to events west of the Apennines.

The directive indicated that if in the course of a withdrawal the enemy proved obstinate around Ancona, II Polish Corps was to take the port with an attack from the west out of the mountains. In the west both X and XIII Corps found that their axes of advance had been shifted from the north to northwest. The X Corps now found that it was to secure Terni, while XIII Corps was to pass well to the west of its former objective on its way to a new objective, the old papal city of Orvieto. From its position astride a volcanic plug, Orvieto dominated the critically important junction of Routes 71, 74 and 79, and it was this fact that led the Germans to occupy the city on 9 June with troops from the *90th Panzergrenadier Division* and later the *356th Infantry Division* as part of the process whereby Kesselring over the next four days moved units from the north into positions from which they could oppose the advance of the Fifth Army's right flank.

It was on 9 June that X and XIII Corps completed a transfer of forces and settled their common boundary, but from the time that the

7 June directive had been issued its twin implications had been clear. First, notwithstanding the proviso concerning Ancona and the Poles, there was to be no attempt to encircle the enemy center and left (ie the *Tenth Army*) or to advance with a drive through the Pennines against Ascoli Piceno, Ancona or Fano. Any Allied advance from the west to the Adriatic could come as a result of German resistance in the east and not as the means of preempting it.

Second, the frontage of the Eighth Army was extended westwards, and this was not simply the result of ground and the configuration of the road system. There were a number of reasons why the Eighth Army should take over part of the Fifth's front, but the main one was that the latter was now called upon to shed formations in readiness for a landing operation outside Italy. Between 9 and 11 June, II and VI Corps were relieved by the FEC and IV US Corps respectively, II Corps passing temporarily into reserve while VI Corps began to prepare for a new career in northwest Europe with the US Seventh Army. Thereafter, divisions earmarked for southern France were withdrawn from the front individually; the first American formation to be stood down leaving on 17 June and the first of the French one week later, on 24 June.

EARLY GAINS THEN THE PACE SLOWS

Thus the fall of Rome ushered in a week of change within the Allied military establishment as it tried to resume the offensive on 6 June after the capture of Rome. The most spectacular early gains were made by VI Corps operating along the coast. Advancing with tanks from the 1st Armored Division supporting the 34th and 36th Infantry Divisions, VI Corps secured Civitavecchia and Bracciano on 7 June. The next day II Corps, advancing with the 85th and 88th Infantry Divisions in the van, took Sutri and Caprarola, but was denied Viterbo when its advance was halted to allow the South Africans to extend their frontage westwards.

With the *26th Panzer Division* established at Orte and the road to Narni closed, the Allied intention was to move against Orvieto by directing the South Africans across the grain of the land from Route 3 to Routes 2 and 11. In the event, halting II US Corps on the evening of 8 June cost the advance little because the Germans abandoned Viterbo that night with the result that the mediaeval walled town, along with Tarquinia, Tuscania and Vetralla, was secured on 9 June by the Americans.

Despite the rotation of formations within the Fifth Army that took place at this time and the arrival in the area of the first enemy reinforcements – the *20th Luftwaffe Field* and *162nd Infantry Divisions* – from the north, the pace of the advance was maintained with Montalto di Castro, Canino and Tessanano falling on 10 June.

On the following day the Germans made a determined stand in front of Orbetello and forced the Americans to commit four infantry battalions in a set-piece attack, but on 12 June the Germans broke off the action and continued to withdraw. Albinia and Latera were taken and the lower Albegna forced the day after, and Magliano was secured on 14 June after vicious street fighting in the little town. Grosseto, the immediate American objective on Route 1, was occupied two days later.

Thereafter the pace of the advance in the coastal sector slackened, Paganico being denied until 20 June. The drag of logistics – despite the opening of Civitavecchia to LST traffic on 12 June and to Liberty ships two days later – and stiffening enemy resistance combined to produce what seemed to the Allies at the time to be nothing more than a temporary respite for the enemy along Route 1.

Events revealed that the check the Americans suffered on the Ombrone had a significance that went unrealized at the time, in part because it came at a time when attention west of the Apennines switched from the coast to the offshore islands of Pianosa and Elba. It had been suggested that their capture (Operation Brassard) should coincide with the start of Diadem, when the seizure of the two islands was certain to have a major impact on the enemy's conduct of the battles to the south, but in the end Brassard was postponed until the time when it ceased to have any real value.

By 17 June, when Brigadier-General Joseph Magnan's 9th Colonial Infantry Division came ashore on Pianosa and Elba, the Fifth Army was almost level with the islands and their capture no longer represented any significant achievement or gain. Be that as it may, the French success on Elba was emphatic if costly. Both islands were secured by 19 June with the 2,700-strong enemy garrisons totally eliminated. The French took 2,000 prisoners and 60 artillery pieces, but in the course of this single operation the 9th lost as many men as the New Zealanders had lost during each of its three-month periods in the line on the Sangro and at Cassino.

On the other side of Route 1, in the foothills and along Route 2, Juin's FEC had entered the line at the time that Viterbo had been taken and thereafter encountered persistent and growing opposition. The French secured Valento and Montefiascone on 11 June, the 3rd Algerian Infantry Division advancing to the west of Lake Bolsena while the 1st French Motorized Division tried its hand on the main road to the east. The latter, however, was to be denied Bolsena itself until 14 June, and continuing enemy resistance both along Route 2 and to the west in the Mont' Amiata area ensured that French progress was both slow and hard earned. In fact, French progress came to a halt along the line of the Orcia on 20 June, the last major French success for the moment being the capture of Radicofani – the highest point on the road between Rome and Florence – on 18 June.

To the east, the progress of the corps in the British part of the front was fitful and very uneven. In the center, June opened with the 2nd New Zealand and 8th Indian Divisions painfully struggling along minor roads towards Route 5, the complete antithesis of fast-moving pursuit forces intent on the encirclement and annihilation of the enemy. The experience of the Indians around Guarcino was typical of the difficulties the two divisions encountered in trying to reach the Via Valeria. Unable to deploy off the road, the Indians had to build a triple Bailey bridge to get into Guarcino, make good a slip that had taken away 50 yards of the road, and then build another bridge to get out of the town. Faced with such difficulties, it was small wonder that it was not until 6 June – when the American 34th Infantry Division was on the point of entering Civitavecchia – that the Indians secured Subiaco and the New Zealanders Balsorano. It took the former three more frustrating days to work their way down the remaining 12 miles of the Aniene valley to Arsoli, while to the east the New Zealanders, advancing up Route 82 and the Val Roveto, were unable to capture Avezzano until 10 June. Thereafter progress was a little quicker. Popoli was occupied on 12 June while Aquila, so similar to Ljubljana (both are dominated by their castles and the distant ring of mountains that surround them) was taken on 14 June.

THE POLISH ADVANCE

Further east, in the Adriatic sector, the long stalemate that had settled on the Sangro front was broken on the night of 7 June when the *278th Infantry Division*, as if responding to that day's directive from Fifteenth Army Group, began to abandon its defensive positions around Ortona. This allowed V Corps, in position between Palena and the sea with the 4th Indian Division holding the coastal sector, to register a number of gains as the startline for a possible two-prong advance to the north. On 8 June the Indians secured Tollo and one end of the minor road to provide the axis of the advance on Chieti. The next day the villages of Orsogna (scene of New Zealand heartbreak and failure during the winter campaign), Guiliano and Guardiagrele were taken, and on 10 June the Indians secured Chieti, crossed the River Pescara, and then drove into the town of the same name. By taking Pescara the 4th Indian Division paved the way for a northwards advance along Route 16, while by securing Chieti they had an alternative axis of advance over the mountains to Teramo and Ascoli by courtesy of Route 81.

But by the time Allied patrols approached Teramo on 17 June to find that Italian partisans had secured the town the previous day and had prevented the Germans from demolishing the bridges over the Tordino, the advance was no longer being conducted by V Corps and its main thrust was along the coast and not over the mountains. On 12 June the advance had been halted to allow the Polish 3rd Carpathian Division to take over from the 4th Indian Division. This was completed on 15 June and two days later, with the bulk of forces halted on the Penne-Atri-Pineto line but with patrols already in Guilianova, II Polish Corps assumed responsibility for the Adriatic sector with V British Corps passing into army reserve at Campobasso. Thereafter the pace of events along the coast quickened considerably. In the Allied camp the Poles were probably unequalled in their willingness and determination to get to close quarters with the enemy, and by 20 June they were not merely the masters of Pedaso and clear of the Aso but were established at Fermo and had obvious designs on Ancona. On the following day the Poles forced no fewer than three river lines only to find, like some of the compatriots three months later in more famous circumstances, that this was one river too many. A strong enemy counter-attack drove the Poles back over the Chienti and their command came to the reluctant conclusion that nothing less than a set-piece attack by the corps was likely to reopen the road to Ancona. Because of the speed of their advance – 60 miles in four days – and the low priority afforded their sector, the Poles found themselves unable to contemplate an offensive over the Chienti before 4 July. The accuracy of this calculation was never tested: standing on this particular river for two weeks while the Allies prepared for an attack was certainly no part of German plans.

Unyielding defense was not yet Kesselring's order to his forces, and on 29 June a very deliberate and orderly withdrawal in the east was resumed to such effect that Polish hopes of a breakthrough were dashed as the Germans relinquished Osima only as late as 6 July and Ancona 12 days later. Such was German success in this phase of operations that they did not cede Fano until 27 August. But unyielding defense had been the predictable and unrealistic order that Kesselring had received from Hitler on 9 June. At that time Kesselring did not have the means to repair his front. West of the Apennines, the ground was too open for the exhausted *Fourteenth Army* to have any chance of holding Allied forces on any of the incomplete defense or phase lines that had been designated by the German high command.

Hitler's orders were prompted by the consideration that the much-vaunted Gothic (or Green) Line was some seven months away from completion – a massive indictment of German foresight and planning – and that in any event its positions held few advantages over equally unprepared lines to the south: the Dora Line (Orbetello-Rieti-L'Aquila), the Frieda or Trasimene Line (Piombino-Chiusi-Perugia-Foligno-Porto Civitanova), the Arrezzo Line (Cecina-

Arezzo-Recanati), and the Arno Line (based on the Arno and Matauro rivers). The first of these positions fell before the Germans could put together a defense but by the third week of June German resistance was beginning to harden along the second of these lines, the Trasimene Line. It was this Line that the Poles unknowingly transgressed on 21 June and on which the Fifth Army had been brought to a halt the previous day.

GERMAN TACTICS IN RETREAT

German success in achieving some measure of stability in Italy by the second half of June was the result of their success in slowing the enemy advance, particularly in the mountains; the fact that the front was relatively constricted with the Allies able to lead with only five divisions west of the Apennines; and Hitler's willingness, even at this stage of the war, to massively reinforce *Army Croup C*. In the aftermath of defeat on the Winter Line the training schools of the *Reich* yielded three divisions that were to have headed east but which found themselves given the numbers of the ruined *71st, 94th* and *715th Infantry Divisions*, while from various parts of Hitler's empire came the *16th SS Panzergrenadier Division*, the *19th* and *20th Luftwaffe Field Divisions* that were soon to be merged, and the *34th Infantry* and *42nd Light Divisions*. Various detached battalions, totalling perhaps the equivalent of a reinforced corps, also made their way to northern Italy and increasingly difficult lines of communication duties.

This influx of forces allowed the Germans to put up an increasingly effective resistance that exerted an increasingly disruptive influence on Allied arrangements after mid-June. In the second half of June the *Tenth Army* was able to recreate its front between Route 3 and the sea. In that sector *LI Mountain Corps* had the *144th Light, 5th Mountain, 71st* and *278th Infantry Divisions* in the line, while to the west *LXXVI Panzer Corps* deployed the *Hermann Goring Panzer, 1st Parachute* and *334th Infantry Divisions* to the west of Lake Trasimeno and the *15th Panzergrenadier, 305th, 94th* and *44th Infantry Divisions* to the east. West of the Apennines the Fourteenth Army still had a fragile right but more substantial left. Opposite the French it deployed *I Parachute Corps*, which had under command three proven formations – the *29th Panzergrenadier, 26th Panzer* and *4th Parachute Divisions* – with which to steady a relative newcomer, the *356th Infantry Division*. On the right a reconstituted but still weak *XIV Panzer Corps* deployed the *19th Luftwaffe Field, 162nd Infantry, 3rd Panzergrenadier* and *20th Luftwaffe Field Divisions*. The events of the next few days and weeks showed that in this their most vulnerable sector the Germans were to be saved from defeat at the hands of IV US Corps by a combination of the timely arrival of the *16th SS Panzergrenadier Division* on Route 1 and the fact that the *90th Panzergrenadier Division* had been retained as corps reserve.

Over most of its length the Germans could not fight from prepared positions on the Trasimene Line but had to rely on the natural roughness of the terrain and the strength of local village stone to slow the Allied advance in this the widest part of the peninsula. Both commodities were amply available in the center of the Line, on either side of Lake Trasimeno itself. West of the Lake was the fertile Val di Chiana which carried the main railway line and road between Rome and Florence and Bologna. This valley was criss-crossed by a myriad of drainage canals and guarded at its southern exit by a hill that reared nearly 350 ft above the road from Orvieto. On this hill stood the town of Chiusi. To the east of Lake Trasimeno stood an even more imposing natural obstacle. More than 1,000 ft above the surrounding countryside and resting in the west on the Tiber and in the east on the Chiasco, was the Ripa Ridge. Just as Chiusi dominated Route 71, so the Ridge dominated the road that followed the Tiber up to Umbertide and Citta di Castello; the road to Scheggia, Route 3 and Fano; and the road to Fossato, Route 76 and Ancona. The one major road that escaped domination by the Ridge, Route 75, led from Perugia along the eastern shore of Lake Trasimeno to Riccio and Route 71.

South of the Chiusi-Perugia line the Germans, intent on delaying the enemy rather than retaining ground, withdrew behind an effective scorched earth programme and occasional fierce rearguard action. Such was the effectiveness of German measures that the 6th South African Armoured Division alone was to rebuild 50 major bridges, mark out 40 detours and fill in 111 craters on its main axis of advance in this single month, but despite this the period between 9 and 20 June was one of steady Eighth Army advances that more or less kept pace with that of the Fifth Army to the west. Only at Bagnoregio between 11 and 13 June did a major action flare, the South Africans finding their advance opposed successively by elements from the *356th Infantry*, *4th Parachute* and *Hermann Goring Panzer Divisions*. This, of course, was on XIII British Corps' front where the Eighth Army had the South Africans and the 78th British Division in the line.

THE BRITISH DRIVE ON

To the east X British Corps, with the Neta valley closed to it and Rieti downgraded to secondary status, chose to drive on Terni on the direct route over the mountains from the Passo Corese-Monte Libretti area. The 6th British Armoured Division secured Torrita and

Cantalupo on 11 June, the 8th Indian Division Montopoli on 12 June and Montasola and Confignio on the following day. At the final village all pretence of a two-divisional advance on axes less than two miles apart was finally abandoned in favor of a single drive that resulted in the capture of Terni on the morning of 14 June – at the same time as XIII Corps took Orvieto without a fight. Thereafter X Corps chose to develop a three-pronged drive on Perugia with British armor pushing up the Tiber valley, Indian infantry advancing over the mountains via Massa Martana and Bevagna, and a flank guard moving along the Spoleto-Trevi road. Acquasparta and Todi (along with Bramante's famous church) were both secured on the first day of the advance, 15 June, as was Massa Martana. Bevagna, Foligno and Spello were taken on 16 June, and on the following day Assisi was occupied and the Indians secured a bridgehead over the Chiasco at Bastia. But Perugia itself remained beyond the reach of X Corps until 20 June because of the effectiveness of German mining, demolitions and booby-trapping, and by the time the city was finally secured battle had been joined on the Ripa Ridge.

It was the original British intention to repeat the previous pattern of the advance after the capture of Perugia – the British armor on the left, the Indians moving to secure the British flank before developing their own offensive on the right (in the Tiber valley) while the designated flank guard drove on Fabriano. The 8th Indian Division, however, ran into trouble on the Ripa Ridge. It cleared Civitella d'Arno and Ripa village itself on 18-19 June but could not reduce the enemy strongholds in Bosco, Belvedere and Pianello. Moreover, British armor coming upon the scene found that while the enemy had abandoned Perugia, he remained just to the north of the city with his artillery. It was not until 26 June that *LXXVI Panzer Corps* was forced to abandon its positions in these sectors, and then its withdrawal was not the result of intolerable pressure being exerted upon it by X Corps. Drawing back the left flank was the result of the need to straighten its fronts as defenses west of Lake Trasimeno crumbled in the face of incessant attacks by XIII Corps.

The latter Corps came up to the German defenses in front of Chiusi on 20 June, and in three days of very confused fighting it managed to establish a toe-hold in the town before a German counter-attack overran South African positions inside Chiusi on 23 June. Thereafter the pace of battle in this particular sector slackened, but with the South Africans securing Sarteano on 24 June and the 78th British Division levering open the German positions at Vaiano and Sanfatucchio (between Lakes Chiusi and Trasimeno) the German position on Route 71 became untenable. Chiusi itself was secured by the South Africans on 26 June, the same day as the Eighth Army attempted to switch the main thrust of its offensive by moving the 6th British Armoured Division to XIII Corps and replacing it in the line by the 10th Indian Division, hitherto X Corps' reserve. Thereafter XIII Corps secured Chianciano on 28 June and Montepulciano, Acquaviva and Castiglione del Lago on the following day, but their successes could not disguise two matters. First, after Chiusi the South Africans (repeating the mistakes in the Liri valley after Diadem) failed to maintain contact with the enemy as he withdrew from the Trasimene Line. Second, from this time the effective frontage of Eighth Army was once more that of a single corps – and that of Fifteenth Army Group, three corps, one of which was making ready to leave the line.

The difficulties of II Polish, X and XIII British Corps on the Trasimene Line after 20 June were shared by the Fifth Army, though most of its initial problems were shouldered by the FEC on the Orcia and Ombrone rather than by IV US Corps on the coast. In the hills the French found their advance blocked by *I Parachute Corps* and elements from the *20th Luftwaffe Field Division* in a series of prepared positions that covered both river lines, and it took the FEC until 25 June to force the Germans back from the Orcia after a series of untidy actions that cost it a thousand casualties. In the coastal sector, IV Corps' problems were reserved for the Arezzo Line rather than further south, but even as it advanced on its bridgehead over the lower Ombrone after 20 June its difficulties mounted as stiffening German resistance slowed the momentum of the American attack. Still unable to reform a continuous front in this sector, the *Fourteenth Army*'s policy was to try to delay the Americans either by committing forces up to battalion size in rearguard actions and even counter-attacks, or by holding the front in sufficient strength to force the Americans to mount time-consuming set-piece attacks that would then be dodged by a timely resumption of the withdrawal. Such tactics could be costly. On 24 June alone the 1st Armored Division took more than 800 prisoners from nine different regiments that in their turn came from no fewer than seven divisions. That same day IV Corps secured Follonica and then took Piombino the following day. Thereafter, however, its advance slowed as German resistance hardened and it, like the FEC, began to shed formations in readiness for Anvil. By 29 June it had reached within a mile of Cecina, but then became entangled in a series of vicious battles with the *16th SS Panzergrenadier Division* for control of the town and its port, Marina del Cecina. By the time the port was secured on 2 July, IV Corps had run into trouble in the center where it suffered a sharp local defeat in its attempt to secure Carsole d'Elsa. It was not until 4 July – and its eighth attack – that IV Corps secured this tiny hill-top village, and then it was to take another three days before it was able to break enemy resistance along Route 68. By then the FEC had recorded its last major success in Italy, its capture of Siena on 3 July.

Thus the month of June in Italy ended with a rather curious situation that reflected the ambiguity, confusion and difficulties that had characterized both sides' conduct of operations over the previous 12 months. By the end of the month Allied momentum had been largely lost, never to be regained, and Allied hopes of registering an emphatic clear-cut victory over the enemy in the field had faded. However, success had been real and substantial, although overshadowed by the invasion of northwest Europe and the fall of Rome which tended to reduce subsequent events to the status of an afterthought or postscript. Allied success in Italy in May and early June forced the Germans to commit the equivalent of three corps to *Army Group C* at the very time when Fifteenth Army Group was planning to send two of its corps out of the theater. Indeed, this partial success had been anticipated by the fact that Allied plans never envisaged an advance along Route 5.

By the end of June the German forces in Italy had largely recovered their balance after their defeats of the previous eight weeks, but the price of such success, and for continuing to keep the Allies at arm's length from the Po valley, proved to be a heavy one. In the last year of the war German formations in Italy consistently outnumbered those of the Allies – by 26 divisions to 20 in August 1944; by 27 to 19 at the end of the year; and by 23 to 17 at the time of the final Allied offensive in April 1945. Such a drain on German resources in a secondary theater of operations was a continuing Allied success, but it is ironic that despite American insistence that this theater should be a backwater, American strength in Italy after August 1944 grew, while that of the British declined. The Americans were forced to pick up the bill for their successful advocacy of Anvil, and this resulted in the number of their divisions in Italy rising from five in August 1944 to six in December and to seven in April 1945 while the number of British and imperial divisions in Italy fell from 13 to ten to seven over the same period.

But at the end of June 1944 these matters remained for the future, and what was apparent on the ground was an unfolding of events that seemed to be similar to those developing in Normandy at the same time. In both theaters the front seemed to be stabilizing and a rough balance emerging, if not of forces then of exhaustion. In Italy the initiative apparently rested with the Allies whereas in Normandy it was disputed. In reality, the circumstances of Italy and Normandy were dissimiliar and deceptive. In Italy the Allies were continuing to advance, but were being forced to conform increasingly to German moves and intentions: in Normandy the reverse was the case. In Italy the apparent balance of forces actually concealed substantial German superiority whereas in Normandy the Allies had a superiority of numbers and firepower that in the end proved overwhelming. Despite appearances, at the end of June 1944 the Allied armies in Italy were on the threshold of stalemate that was to stretch throughout the winter. In Normandy they were poised midway through a campaign that ended with the greatest defeat ever suffered by the German army other than those incurred in the final days of the war.

CHAPTER 3

OVERLORD AND ITS AFTERMATH

With the passage of time, German defeat in the summer of 1944 has assumed an inevitability not apparent at the time. Hindsight suggests that in 1944 the Wehrmacht in the west, like the French army in 1940, was beaten before the first shots of the campaign were fired, but before Overlord neither side believed that a German defeat was a foregone conclusion. On the Allied side a general confidence that the enemy would be overcome rubbed shoulders with the uncomfortable awareness that an assault on a coast held for four years by an enemy of formidable reputation was certain to be hazardous. On the other side, the awareness of Germany's increasingly serious situation and the knowledge that the Allies would not move before they thought success was assured, had not given way to despair. Fatalism belonged not to spring 1944, before the Allied landings, but to the autumn, after *Heeresgruppe B* had been annihilated west of the Seine and the *Wehrmacht* all but driven from French soil.

In the spring German forces awaited an Allied invasion in the knowledge that on its outcome would rest Germany's fate. This they had been told by Hitler and there was no reason to disbelieve him. Few however shared his welcoming of a landing (that he could no longer prevent) on the grounds that its defeat would free Germany of the need to divide her attention between two major fronts.

GERMAN PROBLEMS IN THE WEST

This was certainly not a view that commanded unquestioning support amongst German commanders in the west. Conscious of their forces' weaknesses, they were aware that the *Wehrmacht* had to operate under four sets of circumstances that made defeat likely. These were: a lack of naval and air power sufficient for effective reconnaissance, much less for battle; a command structure that was cumbersome and confused; a tactical doctrine that was disputed even after the Allied landings; and no clear perception of the threat that was presented by the Allies in the west.

Long gone were the days when the *Kriegsmarine* and *Luftwaffe* commanded parts of the Channel. By spring 1944 the former was barely able to provide for its own defense and to ensure that exits from its bases were clear of mines. Between Bayonne and Ijmuiden in May 1944 the navy deployed a total of 11 destroyers and torpedo-boats, 34 MTBs, some 300 minesweepers and 116 patrol vessels of all descriptions. Even with the 49 U-boats earmarked for anti-invasion duties, this was an insignificant force compared to the 105 destroyers, 284 escorts, 291 minesweepers and minelayers, and 495 patrol vessels assembled by the Allies for Neptune, the assault phase of Overlord. Hopelessly outnumbered and outclassed, the *Kriegsmarine* lacked the means to defend the French coast or to contest the passage of an invasion force, even to conduct effective reconnaissance in the Channel and carry out weather reporting duties in the eastern Atlantic.

Similarly, the power of the *Luftuwaffe* in the west had been broken by this time, though the eclipse of the air force was less precise than that of the navy because aircraft, unlike ships or divisions, could be moved over hundreds of miles in a matter of hours as long as their airfields and command structure remained intact. By mid-1944 perhaps a nominal 400 fighters and a similar number of bombers, reconnaissance aircraft and transports remained to Field Marshal Hugo Sperrle's *Luftflotte 3*, but this command was increasingly beset by declining pilot standards and growing shortages of manpower, spares and fuel. Moreover, most of the fighters were in effect committed to the defense of the homeland and Luftflotte Reich rather than to close-support duties in the west. By the spring of 1944 the *Luftwaffe* had lost control of the skies of western Europe, and *Luftflotte 3* had only a minimal defensive and offensive capability. It could no longer withstand the overwhelming strength deployed against it by the Allies, and it lacked the means to conduct effective reconnaissance over the enemy's main bases in southern England.

The command problems that beset the *Wehrmacht* in the west stemmed partly from long-standing weaknesses that plagued the German armed forces as a whole, partly from various arrangements peculiar to *OB West*. Both, however, derived primarily from Hitler and the nature of his regime. The price of his leadership was a command system centralized in his person which lacked a proper joint services planning and supervisory authority, a competent organization to run and coordinate civil and military affairs, and the ability to run a war as opposed to a campaign. Suspicious of his professional subordinates and intent on asserting his personal authority over the *Wehrmacht*, Hitler insisted on a rigid delineation between the armed services and deliberately weakened the unity and cohesion of the army, the only state institution that had the means to threaten his dictatorship.

To counter an ideologically unreliable army, Hitler raised private armies and created organizations within the army itself that owed their existence to him. Reichmarschall Hermann Goring's *Luftwaffe* had been given responsibility for the army's flak defenses as long ago as 1935, and since these included the famous 88-mm gun the air force came to exercise a large measure of operational control over the army's anti-tank arrangements. After 1938 the *Luftwaffe* controlled airborne forces, an elite infantry afforded priority over the army's line formations. In the course of the war the *Luftwaffe*'s ground forces increased in almost inverse proportion to German effectiveness in the air, and by 1945 the *Luftwaffe* had raised two armored, 11 airborne and 22 field and static divisions, a paper strength only slightly below that of the Nazi Party's own praetorian guard, the *Waffen SS*. The 43 divisions that this organization raised came under the administrative control of Reichfuhrer Heinrich Himmler, and like the Luftwaffe's formations enjoyed precedence in claims on recruits, equipment, petrol and training facilities because of their political acceptability to the regime and the patronage afforded their chief.

Hitler had ensured his personal domination of the army not only by his inspired leadership of the early years but by a careful policy of manipulation and divide and rule. Lavish promotions and personal benefits tied many senior commanders to him even while he demeaned them and their profession by becoming after December 1941 the army's commander-in-chief – in addition to being head of state government, party and the *Wehrmacht* – and in 1942 appointing as chief of the general staff an officer who had begun the year as a colonel. He had also extended his personal control of the army's armored, mechanized and assault artillery arms by the creation in 1943 of an inspectorate that raised, equipped and trained these formations outside the administrative jurisdiction of the general staff. Reporting directly to Hitler, this inspectorate was headed by the politically reliable General Heinz Guderian.

Such confused arrangements were reflected within *OB West*. In theory this was the supreme command in the west, but it had no standing in internal security matters, no authority over civil administration, and no direct administrative control over one-third of the divisions in the west. In May 1944 the *Wehrmacht* had nine armored, one mechanized, two airborne, 13 infantry, 33 static and four *Kriegsmarine* security divisions in the west.* The navy was responsible for the ports designated as fortresses and on which considerable resources were lavished in an effort to ensure that their early fall would not provide the Allies with the harbor facilities deemed essential to any invasion attempt. Naval shore installations and coastal batteries came under the local naval command, Admiral Theodor Krancke's *Navy Group West*, and thence to *Oberkommando der Marine* and not *OB West*. The *Waffen SS* provided one

*The term 'in the west' covers The Netherlands, Belgium, France and the Channel Islands, and future reference to German strength in France should be taken to mean France and the Channel Islands.

mechanized and three armored divisions, the Luftwaffe one infantry, two airborne and three static divisions.

Thus 14 of the nominal total of 62 German divisions in the west and seven of the 25 first-grade formations were not part of the army. What made this situation worse for *OB West* was the fact that the quality of its army divisions had suffered in part because of the priority that had been afforded to nonarmy divisions. The impressively large number of static (or coastal) divisions in position in mid-1944 had been obtained mainly by taking away the third infantry regiment and cutting the artillery establishment of those divisions already *in situ*; and the proliferation of command headquarters and divisions, creating a dangerously misleading impression of an increase of fighting power.

Moreover, the natural strains imposed upon an army embarking upon its sixth summer campaign exacerbated this weakness, since these second-grade divisions drew increasingly upon the over-aged, the extremely young, nonGerman nationals, the convalescents and medically dubious, to fill out the ranks. By the beginning of 1944 one in three German soldiers was aged 34 years or more, and the very nature of German commitments in the first half of the year – a passive front in the west and disaster in the east – ensured that *OB West* had more than its fair share of formations with heavy concentrations of second-grade or foreign troops. Indeed, in the Normandy sector alone the German army had nearly 30,000 nonGerman troops in the line, and of the 42 army divisions in France in May 1944 *OB West* wrote off five as unfit for operations.

But if *OB West* suffered from the dubious quality of certain army divisions, its greater problems arose because of disputes over the threat it faced and its subsequent deployment. In May 1944 *OB West* was nominally divided into two subordinate commands. The Netherlands, Belgium and France north of the Nantes-Tours-Geneva line came under the authority of Rommel's *Heeresgruppe B*, but in effect The Netherlands was excluded from Rommel's area of responsibility because *Armed Forces Netherlands* was administered directly by *OKW*. Southern France was the area of responsibility of General Johannes Blaskowitz's *Armee Gruppe C*. Differences of command status and commanders' relative ranks reflected German priorities. Both commands had two armies, but the bulk of German forces were in the north because the high command anticipated an Allied landing in northern rather than southern France. At one time it suspected simultaneous landings in the two areas, but in the first months of 1944, the decline of Allied radio traffic in the Mediterranean and its increase in Britain convinced the German high command that the Allies would make their effort where geography ordained – in northwest Europe. Thus only 17 of the 49 divisions in

France were with *Armee Gruppe G's* *First* and *Nineteenth Armies*. The latter, with one armored, three reforming infantry and six static divisions under command, guarded the Mediterranean littoral. Its companion, with two armored, one mechanized, one rag-tag infantry and three static divisions, watched the Atlantic: it hardly had the means to defend the Biscay coast.

PLANNING FOR D-DAY – THE GERMAN PROBLEM

In Belgium and northern France *Heeresgruppe B* had under command Colonel-General Friedrich Dollmann's *Seventh Army* and Colonel-General Hans von Salmuth's *Fifteenth Army*, their common boundary being the Caen-Argentan-Le Mans-Saumur line. The *Seventh Army* in Brittany and Normandy had under command one armored, two airborne, five infantry and seven static divisions; the *Fifteenth Army*, in Belgium and northeast France, five armored, four infantry and 14 static divisions. But while the *Fifteenth* was much the stronger of the two armies in overall terms but particularly in armor, the geographical distribution of the two armies of Rommel's command reflected German uncertainty about where the Allies planned to land. Between the Franco-Belgium border and the Seine the *Fifteenth Army* had two armored, three infantry and ten static divisions in position, but beyond the Seine *Heeresgruppe B* had three armored, two airborne, five infantry and seven static divisions, and eight of these formations were in position on the coast between Le Havre and Cherbourg. Perhaps surprisingly in view of the generally-held assumption that the Allies would make their effort in the Pas de Calais, *OB West* had more divisions west of the Seine than in north-east France.

The difficulties in deciding where the enemy would land lay at the heart of German problems concerning deployment and doctrine in the first half of 1944. The orthodox staff appreciation was that the landings would have to be made between the Loire and the Scheldt, and that in effect this narrowed the options down to a straight choice between Normandy and the Pas de Calais. The general German view was that the Allies would make their effort in the more obvious Pas de Calais. While this conviction wavered frequently during the spring, German assessments constantly refocused on this area as the likely setting for Allied landings for three reasons. First, it had a number of major ports that once captured could sustain an enemy offensive. Second, landings in any area other than the Pas de Calais would force the Allies to fight across hundreds of miles of France before reaching Belgium and Germany, whereas a landing in the Pas de Calais would provide direct access into the *Reich*. Third, the Allies were unlikely to invade at the limit of the range of British fighters. Accordingly, the Germans believed that the Allies would make their effort in the Pas de Calais, and made this area the cornerstone of their defensive system in the west. But in fact it was not the Allied intention to attack the strongest part of the German line.

What made the Pas de Calais option so obvious to the Germans made it unattractive to the Allies. The Allied choice of landing site, however, had not been determined by the Calais-Boulogne complex having three times as many guns and emplacements as the entire Normandy sector. Far more immediate and practical considerations shaped Allied intentions, and chief amongst these was the fact (recognized by *OB West*) that only the ports of central southern England had the capacity to handle the vast concentration of shipping needed for an invasion. More than 5,300 warships and amphibious vessels were to be assembled for Neptune, and only the Portsmouth-Southampton area could stage an operation of this scale and then only with the smaller harbors along the south coast providing a flow of traffic into the center. Moreover, only by staging from the central ports could Britain's west and east coast ports provide a flow of support shipping over the days and weeks that followed a landing. Such a flow was more easily arranged if directed into the central Channel than if despatched to southeast England. This consideration dovetailed neatly with two others involving calculations of searoom and distance.

The Straits of Dover were narrow and thus afforded a short sea crossing for an invasion force directed against the Pas de Calais, but they were also restricted and shallow. They lacked searoom that would allow thousands of vessels forming the support, escort, bombarding and assault forces to assemble in prescribed order for an invasion. Moreover, the Straits were too far from the most distant embarkation ports of southwest England for there to be realistic hopes of any force from that area making an undetected passage up the Channel to the Pas de Calais.

D-DAY – THE ALLIED PROBLEM

Thus the port facilities of southern England and the configuration of the Channel pushed Allied planning towards Normandy rather than the Pas de Calais, and examination of the topography of the northern coast of France reinforced this tendency. This revealed that contrary to German calculations, the Pas de Calais was not the obvious area for a landing, because the two major ports north of the Seine, Le Havre and Antwerp, were both outside any possible landing area. An invasion effort in this area therefore had to involve a commitment to secure either or both of these ports, neither of which was likely to fall intact into Allied hands.

This simple fact forced Allied planners to consider the otherwise unthinkable option of maintaining armies over open beaches, and if this was to be done the assault beaches had to meet stringent logistical requirements. They had to be gently sloped with firm sand, large enough for a divisional assault and big enough to handle the supply of a corps. They had to be relatively sheltered and provided with good exits. On all counts the beaches of the Pas de Calais failed to measure up to requirements. They were dominated by steep chalk cliffs through which there were few exits inland from small exposed beaches. Those of the Bay of the Seine, on the other hand, were swept by fierce tides and currents, but they were gently sloped, had firm sand and in most cases good exits, and were protected by the Cotentin peninsula from the worst of the Atlantic weather.

Thus the Allies settled on Normandy rather than the Pas de Calais as the site for an invasion attempt, and this decision pointed to the Americans, concentrating in southwest England, forming the right wing of the assault while the British, gathering in the south and southeast, took up positions in the center and on the left. This arrangement thus envisaged a natural demarcation once the breakout from Normandy took place – the Americans being left to clear first the Cotentin and then Brittany in order to develop their own lines of communication across the Atlantic; the British to establish lines of communication across the eastern Channel with which to sustain an advance into the Low Countries and Germany. The subsequent situation on NATO's central front, whereby the Americans form part of Central Army Group in southern Germany and the British part of Northern Army Group in the north, stemmed directly from the decision of the Allies to land in and then fight across western Europe with the British on the left and the Americans on the right.

The fact that the Allies and Germans disagreed on the question of where the Allies were to land in France, lay at the heart of a month-long struggle before and during June 1944 between the rival intelligence services. The German aim was to see through the various ploys with which the Allies tried to conceal their intentions while the latter tried to confirm and reinforce the Germans in the mistaken belief that the landings would come in the Pas de Calais. In this struggle the Germans labored under a triple handicap.

First, as noted already, they lacked an adequate reconnaissance capability in the Channel and over southern England. In the two months before invasion the *Luftwaffe* managed just over 120 reconnaissance missions over Britain, and on the day before the invasion five, none of which contacted any invasion force. Second, as a result of this weakness, German intelligence had to rely for most of its information on agents and sigsint – with very little chance of obtaining corroborating evidence for any conclusion from reconnaissance. It had no means of knowing that all its agents in

Britain were working under British control. Third, the German intelligence effort was fragmented, and in any event professional evaluation was always going to count for less than Hitler's intuitive judgement in determining German strategic deployment.

The fact that its assessments were more than likely to be set aside if they did not accord with Hitler's current opinions did not prevent German military intelligence from making some good guesses about Allied intentions – amidst its more numerous misappreciations. On 8 May *Luftflotte 3* set out the view that the Allies would land in Normandy, and on 12 May army intelligence set down an exact appreciation of Allied intentions, that invasion would come in Normandy and be accompanied by feints across the Straits of Dover. But in the midst of a deluge of conflicting evidence German intelligence never held to any conclusion for any length of time until the second half of May, and then it settled on the Pas de Calais option.

AN INTELLIGENCE SMOKESCREEN FOR D-DAY

Because the German high command seemed so intent on misleading itself, the Allies began the intelligence battle with a very great advantage tempered by two considerations. First, because of the element of irrationality within the German decision-making process there could be no guarantee that even the most rational and successful of deception efforts would produce the intended result. Second, the Allies always ran the risk of making too obvious or too oblique an effort or of using a compromised source, with the result that their effort miscarried. Moreover, there was always the ever-present risk of accidental compromise or that the enemy might happen upon the truth, as did German army intelligence on 12 May. But the Allies tried to ensure that these things did not happen by implementing at different times what amounted to a triple deception effort, at two levels.

A carefully regulated bombing effort in the spring of 1944 and a skilfully orchestrated campaign using radio intelligence and agents, saw British intelligence embark upon first a double deception after March and then a second deception effort in June.

The first involved the suggestion of landings in northern and southern Norway at the end of June (Fortitude North) and in the Pas de Calais (Fortitude South). For a time the two ran in harness, the British calculation being that when Fortitude North was allowed to fail the Germans would swallow the Pas de Calais bait on the basis that the Allies could hardly have mounted two contradictory deception efforts at the same time.

British reasoning was correct. The Germans concluded that Fortitude North was the cover for an invasion of the Pas de Calais and that the Allied predilection with this area was genuine and not the cloak for an effort in Normandy. Thereafter with the Germans caught on the Pas de Calais hook, British intelligence continued its deception with what must have been one of its most audacious coups of the war. On the morning of the Normandy invasion it fed its opposite number the complete Allied order of battle along with the information that this landing was only a feint, intended to draw the *Fifteenth Army* over the Seine and thereafter vulnerable to the real Allied effort that would be made once the German grip on the Pas de Calais was relaxed.

This information was passed to German intelligence by its most trusted agent in Britain, and from 6 June he provided the German high command with a series of reports that were crucial in convincing the German high command not to commit von Salmuth's divisions to the fighting in Normandy until after the battle had been lost. It was a measure of the finesse with which this deception was practised that even after the summer campaign German intelligence continued to place absolute trust in this agent's inaccurate reports.

Allied success in deliberately convincing the German high command that the long-awaited invasion would come in the Pas de Calais, stemmed largely from their ability to convince the Germans that there were many more divisions in Britain than was the case, and that most of these were in the southeast in Lieutenant-General George S Patton's mythical First US Army Group. But alongside this deception went a very real campaign largely planned to reinforce the impression that the Allies intended to make their effort in the Pas de Calais. This particular effort was made by the strategic and tactical air forces in Britain, and between 1 April and 6 June this effort cost them no fewer than 1,616 of their bombers, 763 of which were from Major- General James H Doolittle's 8th US Air Force and 523 from Air Chief Marshal Sir Arthur Harris's Bomber Command. Such losses represented a less than 1 per cent attrition rate on the 144,800 bomber missions flown in preOverlord support operations but overall a loss of 30 per cent of Allied bomber strength at any one time in this period. It is a well known fact that on 6 June, 1944 Allied, German and civilian losses in, off and over Normandy were less than those incurred by the British army on the first day of the relatively obscure battle of Loos in 1915. Less well known is the fact that while the Allies lost about 10,000 dead, wounded and missing, the various Allied air forces lost nearly 12,000 killed and missing in the course of their preOverlord operations.

OPERATION CHATTANOOGA CHOO-CHOO
This campaign, devised by Leigh-Mallory, envisaged a systematic offensive in the weeks preceding Overlord against the transportation

system of western Europe as the means of preventing the enemy's timely and effective redeployment of his ground forces to meet a landing. It incorporated an interdiction effort after 21 May when Operation Chattanooga Choo-Choo was begun. This involved up to 1,000 fighters and fighter-bombers being let loose over western and central Europe – and even beyond the Oder – in the search for opportunity targets.

But its main features were a series of raids on the bridges over the major river and canal lines of western Europe and on the stockpiles, workshops, yards and sidings that sustained the railway system, the Allied aim being to inflict cumulative damage that would prove to be irreversible. The Meuse and Albert canal bridges were attacked after 10 May, those over the lower Seine, after one false start, after 26 May. Major-General Lewis H Brereton's 9th Air Force was in the vanguard of this particular effort, and it was also responsible for most of the early attacks on German coastal and radar installations in northern France, strategic bombers joining this particular effort after 25 May.

At least three in five of all attacks on northern France were directed against the Pas de Calais, and herein lay the element of deception that reinforced Fortitude South. The scale and intensity of Allied air attacks convinced the Germans that the Allies intended to land in the Pas de Calais and to seal off the area from reinforcements. The real Allied intention was to create such an impression but also to ensure that the enemy could not move forces quickly and effectively from this area into Normandy. In this second intention the Allies were successful because in the weeks before Overlord rail traffic in France as a whole declined by over 60 per cent while traffic in the north fell by three-quarters. The decline of rail traffic within Normandy was assessed at 30 per cent but this rose dramatically beyond the 75 per cent mark after the Allied landings freed the air forces for unlimited opportunist attacks west of the Seine. Moreover, other success came the way of the Allies as a result of this air offensive. By 6 June Allied air power had neutralized all German airfields within 130 miles of Normandy, and had accounted for about 500 of the 1,868 aircraft lost to the *Luftwaffe* between 1 April and 5 June.

In effect, the Allied air offensive preceding Overlord secured air supremacy over Normandy in advance of the invasion, thereby confounding one of the major objections leveled against Leigh-Mallory's plans by the bomber barons, Harris and Lieutenant-General Carl Spaatz, commander of the US Strategic Air Forces in Europe. In the course of the arguments that preceded their commands being placed under Eisenhower's direction in readiness for Overlord, both had protested against the 'misuse' of air power in support of an 'unnecessary' invasion of France. Both had urged that since their forces could not provide effective support for Overlord, they be left alone to win the war in their own inimitable manner, Harris by burning German cities to the ground and Spaatz by razing the *Reich*'s oil installations. Indeed, on 5 March Spaatz guaranteed a German collapse within six months if allowed to develop such an offensive. He warned that diverting the heavy bombers from the struggle over Germany would give the *Luftwaffe* time to recover from the mauling it was then undergoing, with the result that the fight for air supremacy would have to be resumed during the summer over Normandy. Events proved the latter claim to be as unfounded as most German assessments of the likely impact of Allied air power on a land battle in western Europe.

ROMMEL'S APPOINTMENT

The various German assessments of the situation caused much of the confusion that existed within the German high command and its subordinate authorities in the west. This arose because the command structure of OB West institutionalized the argument about the impact of Allied air power and the tactics that had to be employed by German ground forces in the face of enemy air supremacy. The crucial element in this confusion stemmed from Hitler's decision at the end of 1943 to appoint Rommel as inspector of defenses in the west. In this role Rommel was to examine the establishments, state of training, defenses and installations of the forces in the west, and to make recommendations on deployments and operational doctrine. Moreover, Rommel was to prepare plans for the conduct of the defense and to take command of a land battle, irrespective of where the Allies might land. Thus even though *OB West* incorporated an operational command in the shape of *Heeresgruppe D*, Rommel's *Heeresgruppe B* was fixed into the chain of command below *OB West* and over the *Seventh* and *Fifteenth Armies*. It had direct access to Hitler and *OKW* and had orders that, had it not been for the subsequent creation of *Armee Gruppe C*, would have meant its assuming control of forces in southern France if by chance the Allies landed there before landing in the north. It had no control of the theater reserve whatsoever.

At the beginning of June Rommel held the *2nd Panzer Division* at Amiens, the newly-raised *116th Panzer Division* at Rouen, and the *21st Panzer Division* at Caen as his own command reserve. But the theater reserve, *Panzergruppe West*, was not under his command, and nor was it under the command of von Rundstedt. Originally *Panzergruppe West* had been raised under the command of Lieutenant-General Leo Freiherr Geyr von Schwappenburg in order to train all armored formations in the west and, in effect, provide *OB West* with a reserve. But on 26 April Hitler reconstituted *Panzer Lehr* and the *1st* and *12th SS Panzer* and *17th SS Panzergrenadier Divisions* as *I SS Panzer Corps* and *OKW*'s reserve in the west. With this single decision Hitler placed the most powerful assault divisions in the west under the administrative control of the *SS* and took them away from von Rundstedt without giving them to Rommel. Denied the right to move without Hitler's express permission, these divisions remained unconcentrated throughout the spring.

At the end of May the *1st SS Panzer Division* was outside Brussels, *Panzer Lehr* and the *12th SS Panzer Division* were west of the Seine at Chartres and Evreux respectively, and the *17th SS Panzergrenadier Division* was near Tours. None were in the *Seventh Army*'s area of responsibility. Since all the armored formations but the *21st Panzer Division* had recently arrived in France and most were the worst for their recent experience on the Eastern Front, the state of German armor in the west was uncertain and its deployment reflected an irresolution within the German high command as to where the Allies might land and how they were to be countered.

GERMAN HESITATIONS

The traditional German view of the conduct of the defense in the west had been that the much-vaunted Atlantic Wall would be sufficient to defeat any invasion attempt. However, this had always been more formidable on paper than in reality. In fact the Atlantic Wall had never done anything more than protect Hitler's conquests just as long as they were unthreatened. Once the Channel ceased to be an obstacle to but an avenue for the Allies, and once the Americans concentrated in Britain on a scale that made the threat of invasion a real one, the Germans were left with an almost impossible dilemma: whether to continue to base their hopes on fixed defenses, on a battle on the beaches, in the immediate hinterland or in the interior.

The German problem was that they lacked sufficient forces to hold the front in strength, and they lacked the means to assemble strong mobile reserves to cover all the eventualities open to the Allies. Even in the high-priority Pas de Calais *Fifteenth Army* divisions had to contend with 50-mile frontages, and to the west those of the *Seventh Army* averaged 100 miles. The Germans lacked the means to do more than cover a coastline they had to defend, but the German high command knew that the enemy would be at his most vulnerable while on or in the water and on the beaches. It was also aware that if Sicily, Salerno and Anzio were any guide, armor unable to move directly into an attack on enemy forces on the beaches were unlikely to be given a chance to do so. At Salerno forces just three miles from the coast had been unable to counterattack because of Allied naval gunfire, and at Anzio massed German armor had been stopped dead by Allied artillery and air power. The German high command was well aware of the fact that at the moment of invasion the defense had an opportunity which was unlikely to be repeated.

For this reason von Salmuth favored an all-out defense of the beaches, even though this was a course of action open to the obvious objection: that forces committed forward would, like static defenses, be rendered useless by a single breakthrough in any other area. Inadvertently von Salmuth provided the corrective to his own recommendations, since his advocacy of forward defense was matched by his certainty that the Allies would land in the Pas de Calais. But his tactical ideas were shared by Rommel who had experience of the effectiveness of Allied tactical air power. He was convinced that the defense would never have the chance to bring up reserves from the interior in order to mount effective counterattacks. As far as Rommel was concerned, armor had to be in positions covering the beaches because it could never be assembled and committed quickly enough to be effective if it was dispersed inland.

Such ideas were opposed by Guderian, von Rundstedt and Geyr though they disagreed on what should be put in their place. Von Rundstedt had little faith in coastal defenses since he believed that the Atlantic Wall could never defeat an invasion. He saw coastal defenses as the means of breaking the cohesion and momentum of an assault, the invader having to divide his forces in order to come around in-depth defenses and thereby rendering himself liable to defeat in rear coastal areas by mobile reserves held back for just this eventuality. Such orthodoxy ignored the nub of von Salmuth's argument, that such reserves – if they were available – would never have the chance to get into the battle. In one respect, however, von Rundstedt, von Salmuth and Rommel were in some measure of agreement. Though divided on exactly where and how the battle was to be fought, they envisaged a forward campaign and the *Luftwaffe* being committed to battle at the outset against the naval bombardment forces that could devastate the armored divisions. In this they differed from Geyr who placed even less reliance on coastal defenses than von Rundstedt. Geyr envisaged coastal defenses imposing as much delay and loss on the enemy as possible but the outcome of an invasion being decided not on the beaches but in the interior. By channeling an Allied attack, Geyr hoped to hold along the line of the Seine and the Loire and to subject the enemy to the type of massed armored counter-attack in which the German army had long excelled. According to such a scenario the would not be committed to the coastal struggle but would make its effort during the mobile phase of the campaign.

Geyr's ideas attracted little support, since any plan that

contemplated not giving battle until the full strength of the Allies had been deployed, ran the risk of battle not been given until there was a certainty of its being won. In any case any defensive campaign that involved a voluntary withdrawal, even one designed to lure the enemy into a killing zone, seldom enjoyed sympathetic consideration from *OKW*. Hitler was usually adamantly opposed to any idea of mobile defense conducted in depth over vast tracts of conquered territory.

In the spring of 1944 Rommel offered him the kind of strategy that he understood and which was ideologically to his liking. An all-out unyielding defense at the point of contact, as an expression of determination, was psychologically well-tailored to Hitler's own views, but at this time Hitler was incapable of deciding between conflicting arguments. He hesitated to preposition armor before he was certain of where the Allies would land. In fact at the beginning of May he singled out Normandy and Brittany, and particularly Calvados and the Cotentin, as the places where the enemy would land, but in that spring Hitler could no more settle on a single conclusion than his intelligence services.

At various times throughout the spring virtually every stretch of coast from North Cape to the Aegean was deemed to be the likely area for an Allied landing. In any event Hitler's guess of Normandy was coupled with the belief that a landing there would be the prelude for an invasion of the Pas de Calais once the *Fifteenth Army* was lured from its positions. At different times Hitler inclined towards the Rommel-von Salmuth tactical thesis, and in May Hitler's concern for Normandy resulted in no fewer than three armored divisions being deployed within an hour of the beaches on which the Allies were to land. But without the means to determine the future point of contact, Hitler shrank from any irrevocable decision and chose to hold *Panzergruppe West*'s divisions inland and unconcentrated, thereby tacitly hoping that the Atlantic Wall and the static divisions would rise above their combined weaknesses. Faith in the Atlantic Wall was dependent on distance from it and since it was little more than gaps held apart by the occasional position outside the main fortresses, such hopes were illusory. With the fact that the *Seventh Army* was equipped with 92 different guns firing 252 different types and calibers of ammunition to serve as a yardstick of German problems, German deployment and doctrine incorporated the worst of most eventualities.

THE DAY OF RECKONING APPROACHES

The Allied intention was to take advantage of German difficulties and irresolution with a plan of campaign that envisaged Anglo-American forces securing a beachhead astride the Vire estuary. This would be developed into a lodgement area from which main force operations directed into Germany could be developed. Allied planning incorporated five assault landings and individual beachheads being consolidated into one and given a depth of at least eight miles, if not on the day of the landings then over the next day or so. Thereafter with the eight divisions that were to be landed on D-Day growing to 13 on D + 1 to 17 on D + 3 and to 21 on D + 12, this foothold was to be developed until on D + 25 the Allies stood on the St Malo-Rennes-Laval-Alençon-Argentan-Lisieux-Deauville line. Subsequently the Americans, with two armies in the line, would clear Brittany before the full strength of the Allies drove for the Seine. Planning suggested that this river line might be reached by D + 90, by which time the Allies would have 39 divisions in France and further reinforcements would be arriving in Europe at the rate of five divisions per month.

The initial landings, made by three airborne and five seaborne divisions, were to be carried out during the hours of daylight on a day when there would be two low tides between dawn and dusk after a night when there would be a full moon. Such requirements were laid down by the Allied naval and air commands and adopted despite the objections of a military that would have preferred to land under the cover of darkness. Charged with the safe delivery of the assault force, the naval command insisted on landings beginning at least 40 minutes after nautical twilight so that the final approach to the beaches and the supporting naval bombardment could be conducted in growing light.

Similarly, the air command wanted a daylight assault to allow American heavy and medium bombers to join a bombardment that naval forces could not complete unaided. Both commands wanted a moonlit night to ease the navigational, station-keeping and target-identification problems of their formations. This was a particular concern of an air command that had to stage two quite separate operations during the hours of darkness: airborne landings at either end of the intended beachhead and a massive raid by more than 1,500 bombers on communications and enemy positions in Normandy and the Cotentin.

Such were some of the considerations that determined a plan of campaign that envisaged assault landings being carried out on a rising tide around sunrise. German preparation of beach obstacles below the high water mark forced the Allies to plan to land about one hour after low tide. By landing at such a time the assault vessels would not foul the defenses and those that beached could
get off under their own power without waiting for the next tide. Moreover, by landing on a rising tide at dawn the distance the infantry would have to cover across open beaches would be kept to

a minimum and the assault engineers would have the daylight to clear the beaches before reinforcements arrived. It was clearly desirable to carry out landings simultaneously, but there was a tidal time difference of 60 minutes between the eastern and western beaches.

In any event Neptune plans had to include a proviso whereby they allowed a minimum period of 30 minutes and a maximum of 90 between nautical twilight and the first of the landings. With suitable tidal conditions existing on only three days in every fortnight and the combination of tidal and moon requirements coming together three days in every month, the Neptune plans had to be flexible enough to take account of day-to-day variations of tide and sunrise in order to avoid a month's postponement. In fact Eisenhower intended to avoid this by executing Neptune on the first possible opportunity after the target date of 31 May. Faced with a choice between 5, 6 and 7 June, on 8 May Eisenhower chose 5 June as the date for an operation that was to open with attacks on the Fontenay, St Martin de Varreville and Merville coastal batteries by British bombers shortly before midnight. Bomber Command was to mount further attacks between 0315 and 0500 against la Pernelle, Maisy, Pointe du Hoc, Longues, Mount Fleury, Ouistreham and Houlgate batteries. The division of this effort into two phases was because the first batteries to be attacked were in or next to areas in which airborne forces were to land soon after midnight – the others being attacked as part of the general softening-up process preceding the seaborne assault.

OVERLORD'S AIR SUPPORT

Some 20 minutes after midnight pathfinders were to be dropped in two areas, north of Caen and on the neck of the Cotentin. They were to mark dropping and landing zones for main force landings. In the east approximately 450 transports were to drop almost 8,000 members of the British 6th Airborne Division's two parachute formations between the Orne and the Dives. The 5th Parachute Brigade, supported by a reinforced company from the 6th Airlanding Brigade in six gliders, was to secure the bridges over the lower Orne and the Caen canal plus the high ground around Ranville that overlooked Ouistreham beach. The 3rd Parachute Brigade in the meantime was to take the Merville battery and destroy the bridges over the lower Dives across which any proposed German counter-attack on the Allied left bank would have to be launched.

Because of German obstructions on possible landing zones and a general shortage of towing transports, the British planned to bring the balance of the 6th Airlanding Brigade into the bridgehead during the remainder of the day after the other formations had secured and cleared the area. The British also planned to reinforce the 6th

Airborne Division with a marine brigade that was to be landed from the sea with the 3rd British Division at Ouistreham.

At the other end of the front the Americans planned to use almost 1,000 transports and gliders to drop and land a total of about 15,000 troops from the 82nd and 101st Airborne Divisions in eastern Cotentin behind Utah beach where the 4th US Division was to come ashore. The 101st, with the 501st, 502nd and understrength 506th Parachute Infantry Regiments under command, was to be dropped behind the causeways leading from Utah beach and also astride the routes over the lower Douve into the peninsula. The 82nd was to be dropped on either side of the Merderet, the 507th and 508th Parachute Infantry Regiments to the west and the 505th, tasked to secure St Mere-Eglise, to the east.

The task of the 101st was to secure the rear of Utah; to ensure the security of the 4th Division's left flank as it established itself ashore; and to establish bridgeheads over the Douve from which operations to take Carentan and link up with forces east of the Vire could be conducted. The task of the 82nd was to provide depth to the beachhead; to secure the right flank of the assault force against attack from the north; and to secure a springboard for an advance that would reach across the peninsula to the other coast and lead to the capture of Cherbourg by D + 15.

Like their ally, the Americans planned to reinforce their airborne formations both by air and sea during D-Day. The 101st's 327th Glider Infantry Regiment (GIR) was to be landed with the 4th Division, and gliders were to land other reinforcements at dawn and dusk on D-Day and the following day if necessary. The American problem was German flooding of low-lying areas and extensive obstruction of possible landing zones in the Cotentin and along the Aure. Nevertheless, even without reinforcement the American landings constituted the largest single airborne operation of the war to date.

The airborne landings were to be carried out at the same time as more than 1,300 Fortresses and Liberators, 300 Marauders and 150 fighter-bombers took to the air to add some 4,200 tons of bombs to the 5,000 tons Bomber Command was to have dropped on enemy positions in the course of the night. The American targets were roads and bridges in and around Caen, batteries and beach obstacles. While most of the fighter-bombers were to be detailed to seek out enemy transport on the Cotentin, the heavy bombers of the 8th Air Force were to concentrate their efforts between the Vire and the Orne, and the medium bombers of the 9th against Utah alone. Most of the ordnance was instantaneously fuzed to avoid severe ground cratering.

The American attacks were to be concentrated in the 45 minutes before touchdown, ending not later than ten minutes before troops came ashore. As the last air attacks ended, 305 support landing craft moving into the attack with their various assault forces would take up the bombardment with assorted artillery, howitzer, mortar, rocket and automatic fire. These support landing craft were divided between five assault forces, each lettered after their landing beach and supported by a single bombarding force. Thus Force U consisted of the formation that was to land on Utah beach under the guns of Bombarding Force A: Force O was to come ashore on Omaha with Bombarding Force C in support: Force G, supported by Bombarding Force K, was to come ashore on Gold beach: Force J was to assault Juno with the help of Bombarding Force B: and Sword beach was to be softened up by Bombarding Force D in readiness for Force S.

The Allied timetable envisaged loading the assault forces between D-6 and D-4 and embarking troops on D-2. The bombarding forces were to leave the Clyde and Belfast on D-2 and they, the assembled assault forces, and other shipping involved in Neptune, were to use the normal swept channels along the coast. They were then to follow four channels into the main assembly area – known as area Z or more colloquially as Piccadilly Circus – some eight miles southeast of St Catherine's Point. Thereafter they were to follow the 245 minesweepers that formed the vanguard of the invasion force down five marked channels assumed to be free of mines. South of latitude 50°N, where the Germans were known to have concentrated their defensive mining, the minesweepers were to clear and mark a fast and a slow lane for each assault force. These were to lead to transport areas where assault craft would be lowered and the various amphibious vessels arranged into attack formation.

Because of the danger presented by converging fire from two adjacent coasts, the American transport areas were to be 11 miles offshore compared to the seven miles of their British opposite numbers. This extra distance ensured that American assault vessels would need about three hours to make their approach compared to the two hours required by the British, and this in its turn meant that American assault forces had to begin to assemble in the transport areas about four hours before touchdown, compared to the three hours of the British. In this time between assembly and assault the minesweepers were to clear lanes for the bombarding forces and the assault vessels.

US ORDER OF BATTLE:
UTAH AND OMAHA

The American landings on Utah and Omaha were timed for 0630, but one of the little known aspects of D-Day is the fact that the first seaborne landings of the day were made some two hours earlier by an American detachment on the offshore Isles St Marcouf. The American concern was that the enemy might have positions on the islands that would interfere with the forces sweeping past to attack Utah. Landing operations in the American sector were to be entrusted to Rear Admiral Alan G Kirk's Western Naval Task Force (TF 122) with Rear Admiral Don P Moon's Force U (TF 125), Rear Admiral John L Hall's Force O (TF 124) and Commodore CD Edgar's Force B (TF 126) under command. Force U, loaded in Plymouth, Salcombe, Dartmouth and Torquay and then concentrated off south Devon, was to land Major-General RO Barton's 4th Infantry Division on Utah. The latter, from Major-General J Lawton Collins's VII US Corps, was to lead with the reinforced 8th Regimental Combat Team (RCT), one battalion landing on Tare and another on Uncle, each having a single unit in immediate reserve. The 22nd and 12th RCTs formed the reserve with the 359th RCT from the 90th Infantry Division and the 327th GIR assigned as the Initial Follow-up Regiments. The 90th's two remaining regiments, the 357th and 358th RCTs, constituted the Follow-up Formations, the 9th and 97th Infantry Divisions being detailed to complete the corps order of battle.

Force U was to be covered by Rear Admiral Morton L Deyo's cosmopolitan Bombarding Force A which had under command an American battleship, a British monitor, a Dutch gunboat, one British and two American heavy cruisers, two British light cruisers and eight American destroyers. Force O, loaded at Portland and Weymouth and then held in those ports and at Poole, was to land Major-General Clarence R Huebner's 1st Infantry Division and two Ranger battalions on Omaha. The 2nd Ranger Battalion, with the 5th in reserve, was to come ashore at the Pointe du Hoc and around Vierville-sur-Mer on Dog beach. The 116th RCT, detached from the 29th Infantry Division and placed under Huebner's command, was to divide its attention between Dog and Easy beaches while the 16th RCT, with the 18th in reserve, was to divide its strength between Easy and Fox. Both the 116th and 16th were to lead with single assault battalions on each beach, their third unit being held as reserve.

With no Initial Follow-up Regiments on hand, the reinforcements that were to come ashore on Omaha were the balance of the 1st and 29th Divisions plus specialist troops from Major-General LT Gerow's V US Corps. These were to be constituted as Force B and represented the first part of a buildup that was to include the 2nd Infantry and 2nd Armored Divisions. Force B was to be loaded at Falmouth and Plymouth. Rear Admiral CF Bryant's Bombarding Force C was to watch over Omaha and the progress of Force O. Bryant had under command two American battleships, one British and two Free French light cruisers, and eight American and three British destroyers. The reserve for the two assault forces was to be a solitary British light cruiser, plus destroyers from convoys as required. Kirk's own flagship was to be a heavy cruiser, one destroyer being attached.

BRITISH ORDER OF BATTLE:
GOLD, SWORD AND JUNO

The British landings on Gold and Sword were timed for 0725 and those on Juno between 0735 and 0745, staggered to take account of the tidal differences and to allow time for a suspected rocky outcrop on Juno to be covered. Rear Admiral Sir Philip Vian was in command of the Eastern Naval Task Force. Vian, with a light cruiser flagship and a battleship, light cruiser and designated destroyers as reserve, was to have Commodore CE Douglas-Pennant's Force G, Commodore GN Oliver's Force J and Rear Admiral AG Talbot's Force S under command. Force G, loaded at Southampton and assembled there and in the Solent, was to land Major-General DAH Graham's reinforced 50th (Northumbrian) Division on Gold. The 50th was to lead with two infantry brigades, the 231st on Jig and the 69th on King. The 231st was to attack with two battalions with another two in reserve while the 56th Infantry Brigade, tasked to secure Bayeux, was to be held as reserve. On King the 69th was also to lead with two battalions, but was to have just one unit in reserve while the 151st Infantry Brigade was constituted as reserve. Reinforcement for the 50th Division was to consist of the 7th Armoured Division and the 153rd Infantry Brigade from the 51st (Highland) Division. Constituted as Force L and embarked at Tilbury and Felixstowe, these formations were to be landed on the second tide of D-Day after a sea passage that was to involve the first transit of the Straits of Dover by large British transports since 1940. Following them were to be the 49th (West Riding) Division and the independent 33rd Armoured Brigade. Covering proceedings on Gold were to be four British light cruisers, a Dutch gunboat, and one Polish and 12 British destroyers of Captain EWL Longley-Cook's Bombarding Force K. Force J, also loaded at Southampton and assembled there and in the Solent, was to land Major-General RFL Keller's 3rd Canadian Division on Juno. It was to lead with two of its infantry brigades, the 7th Canadian dividing its attention between Mike and Nan while the 8th Canadian, backed by the 9th Canadian Brigade, concentrated solely on Nan. In support of operations on Juno were to be the two British light cruisers and 11 British, Canadian, Free French and Norwegian destroyers of Rear Admiral FHG Dalrymple-Hamilton's Bombarding Force E. Force S, loaded and assembled at Portsmouth, Shoreham and Newhaven, was to land

Major-General TG Rennie's 3rd Infantry Division on Sword.

Unlike any other assault division, the 3rd British was to restrict its efforts to a single sector of its designated beach, and it planned to attack Queen with the heavily reinforced 8th Infantry Brigade. With two battalions in the vanguard the 8th was to hold a reserve of one infantry and five marine units, three of the latter being earmarked as reinforcements for the 6th Airborne Division. In immediate support was to be the 185th Infantry Brigade with the 9th constituted as divisional reserve. Because the 3rd British and 3rd Canadian Divisions both formed part of Lieutenant-General JT Crocker's I British Corps, Sword and Juno were equally liable to be the landing beach for the Follow-up Formations, though the intention was to land the balance of the 51st (Highland) Division and the independent 4th Armoured Brigade on Juno rather than Sword.

Proceedings on Sword in the meantime were to be watched over by Rear Admiral WR Patterson's Bombarding Force D, one of the most powerful of the support groups. It had under command two battleships and a monitor, one heavy and four light cruisers, and 13 destroyers. The strength of this particular force was determined by the presence on the disengaged flank of enemy coastal batteries that could interfere with the landing force both in the transport area and during the assault phase. Because of the difficult approaches to Sword and Juno both were to be marked by midget submarines despatched in advance of the invasion fleet.

SUPPORT FORCES FOR THE D-DAY LANDINGS

The Allied naval commander, Admiral Bertram H Ramsey, was to retain a general reserve of one battleship, but providing cover for his invasion fleet were to be task groups from the Plymouth, Portsmouth and Dover commands. To counter the possibility of German submarine and surface attacks in the west, Plymouth was to provide three destroyer task groups, one to cover Force U's passage, a second to patrol in mid-Channel and the third to patrol off Ushant. Coastal vessels were to supplement the two latter groups and also to provide close support for the assault forces while they were in mid-Channel coming south. Further afield, six escort groups, drawn from Western Approaches Command were to be about 130 miles west of Land's End to deal with any German submarines trying to break into the Channel from the Atlantic. Fewer and weaker task forces were to be in the eastern Channel where the waters were restricted and the threat was less immediate than in the west. In the eastern sector, however, distant cover was provided by the three fleet carriers, three battleships and six cruisers that formed the nucleus of the Home Fleet.

In the air, cover was to be provided by RAF Coastal Command,

Air Defence of Great Britain (formerly Fighter Command), and the Allied Expeditionary Air Force. RAF Coastal Command, with 1,070 aircraft in 49 squadrons, was to conduct its normal patrols over home waters, around Iceland and into the eastern Atlantic, but it was to concentrate its efforts in the western Channel. With help from the US Navy, Coastal Command was able to saturate this area, the American effort alone involving the patrolling of the Swanage-Cherbourg-Ushant-Scilly Isles line with Liberators at 30-minute intervals. ADGB was to cover all shipping and convoy routes to a range of 40 miles from the British coast, and thereafter responsibility for the protection of the invasion force fell to 69 of the 171 fighter squadrons that the Allies were to assemble for D-Day. The Americans were to maintain five squadrons permanently over the swept channels and another five as high cover for the beaches; the British were to have five squadrons providing low cover for the ground forces.

The Allied plan of campaign and order of battle was to be completed by the arrangements covering the supply of the assault forces, the improvization of port facilities and the implementation of deception plans for D-Day designed to squeeze the last possible advantage from German uncertainty. The first two matters were obviously related since they shared three calculations: that eight convoys a day would be needed to sustain and build up the invasion force; that the Allies were unlikely to take a port quickly and intact; that the rail system of any liberated part of France was unlikely to be operational before D + 90, by which time the Allies envisaged their being on the Loire and Seine.

These calculations were dealt with in four ways. First, on D-Day Allied troops were to come ashore with two days' rations; all vehicles were to be issued with an emergency petrol supply; and barges laden with up to 4,000 tons of ammunition were to be beached as an immediately available reserve. Even with such improvization the ammunition situation remained potentially precarious, and overall ordnance margins for Overlord were never much more than 6 per cent of those observed by the Americans in Pacific landings. Second, 15 transports, 74 oceanic merchantmen and 200 coasters were assembled before D-Day to form the first resupply and reinforcement convoys into the beachhead. Third, the armies that were to be put ashore were to be fully mechanized. Though the long-term intention was to supply the armies by pipeline, road, rail and air, the feature of Allied resupply in the first months of the campaign was its ability to maintain rapidly expanding field forces solely by road. In the first 87 days after the landings the Allies put ashore 3,098,259 tons of stores, 2,052,299 men and no fewer than 438,471 vehicles, and in doing so they touched upon the fourth, last and most impressive single part of the supply effort, the Mulberry project.

GOOSEBERRIES AND MULBERRIES

To ensure continuity of supply when it was probable that they would not be able to secure an intact port, the Allies planned to take two of their own with them. All five assault beaches were to be provided with breakwaters, known as Gooseberries, behind which merchantmen could shelter and unload, but on Gold and Omaha the blockships that made up the Gooseberries were to be supplemented by hollow caissons known as Phoenix. Blockships and caissons alike were to be sunk on the 15-ft line, but the latter were to be extended shorewards to provide an enclosed area with two entrances. Inside this harbor floating steel roadways were to reach out to pierheads at which shallow-draught ships and lighters could unload directly into vehicles.

Built to accommodate seven oceanic merchantmen, 20 coasters and up to 400 tugs and 1,000 lighters and assorted ancillary craft, the Mulberry harbors were to incorporate an unsuccessful feature. These were floating breakwaters, known as Bombardons, moored some 1,000 yards to seaward on the ten-fathom line that were supposed to offer shelter for other deep-draught vessels. These various arrangements were designed to ensure that 7,000 tons of stores could be handled daily by each harbor in addition to any supplies that were landed over open beaches and through captured ports. This whole project involved an enormous engineering and transportation effort. The largest of the caissons displaced 6,000 tons on dimensions of 200 x 55 x 60 ft, and the overall programme called for 2,000,000 tons of reinforced concrete and ten miles of steel roadway to be formed into the 213 caissons, 93 bombardons, 23 pierheads and the roads that had to be towed across the Channel and sited on or off a coast in tides that ran at 22 knots. The towing operation alone was to involve more than 10,000 men and 160 ocean-going tugs.

The Phoenix were assembled off Selsey and Dungeness and in the Thames, while the pierheads and roads were gathered together in the Solent and off Selsey. They began their passage to France on D-Day itself, five days after the 54 merchantmen marked down for self-immolation as blockships set out from Oban in Scotland. All units were to use three channels reserved for them, and the blockships were to begin scuttling themselves in position on D + 2. The Gooseberries were to be completed by D + 5 when the first of caissons and breakwaters were to arrive. It was planned that the Mulberries would be completed and begin to function in the second week after the invasion – before Cherbourg was captured. In the event things did not work out quite how they were intended, though the Allies were to enjoy a small bonus in the fact that the tiny harbors of Courseulles-sur-Mer and Port-en-Bessin were to be opened on D + 6 and handled some 15,000 tons of supplies in the following week.

THE INTELLIGENCE SMOKESCREEN THICKENS

Deception measures intended to ensure tactical surprise completed Allied arrangements. These consisted of a dual effort in support of the airborne landings and a four-fold undertaking intended to protect Neptune. The first involved attempts to blind German radar during the approach by the highly vulnerable transports and gliders, and to cause maximum confusion to enemy ground forces with a number of real and dummy parachute landings in rear areas. The initial effort involved Stirling medium bombers covering the American approach by dropping Window across the Gulf of St Malo while a force of 29 Halifax and Stirling bombers did the same around Le Havre and east of Caen. Then these same bombers were to drop dummy paratroopers, thunderflashes and pyrotechnics in an effort to simulate firefights that would force the Germans to commit their reserves to futile chases around an unfriendly countryside when they needed to concentrate for the counter-attack. But complementing the dummy landings astride the Le Havre-Rouen road (southwest of Caen and west of St Malo) were real ones made by teams from the Special Air Service. These were dropped near Le Havre, around Lisieux and Evreux and in western and southern Cotentin in the area roughly bound by Lessay, St Lo and Avranches.

The second effort was to involve Operations Big Drum, Taxable and Glimmer, plus a simulated heavy bomber raid along the line of the Somme. The latter involved 29 ECM Lancasters and Fortresses that were to blind German radars with Window and then to find and jam Luftwaffe fighter-control frequencies. The other parts of this effort involved a combination of measures designed to conceal the approach of the Allied invasion force and to feed the Germans false and misleading information on the landings. These measures were to begin where air raids on German radar stations ended, the initial Allied ploy being to overwhelm the whole of the German radar system east of the Seine by aerial jamming. But because a total jamming of enemy radars was certain to draw a response from the Luftwaffe's night reconnaissance aircraft, the Allies planned to leave two gaps off Cap d'Antifer and Cap Griz-Nez into which the German radars could continue to see.

In these gaps the Allies were to create radar images of forces clearly intent on landings in the Le Havre and Boulogne areas. Initially this spectral activity was to be carried out by bombers – Lancasters off Le Havre and Stirlings over the Straits of Dover – engaged in tight-formation precision-flying while dropping Window at five-second intervals. By using Window, cut to reflect the frequencies of German shore-based radars, these bombers could simulate the outline of a convoy advancing on an eight-mile front. Thereafter the second part of this effort would come into effect. In both areas the Allies were to have nine coastal craft and launches equipped with radar reflectors tailored to the shorter frequencies of enemy airborne radars, ensuring that any Luftwaffe aircraft approaching under the cover of dark would confirm the mistaken impression gathered by shore-based radar.

By these various measures the Allies intended to convince the Germans that invasion forces were moving in any direction except towards Normandy. In the early hours of D-Day the Allied high command and its intelligence services had the immense satisfaction of knowing that the Taxable convoy off Le Havre had attracted Luftwaffe attention throughout the night and that the Glimmer convoy had drawn radar-directed gunfire from coastal batteries near Boulogne. The real convoys, on the other hand, were to have no fewer than 262 of their ships equipped with radar-jamming devices to ensure their undetected crossing, and they also had the benefit of a modest deception effort involving four launches – Operation Big Drum – directed against Barfleur.

But the one thing that the Allies could not disguise was the sound of thousands of propellers in the Bay of the Seine, and on the morning of D-Day German hydrophone operators at Cherbourg detected the approaching Allied invasion forces long before they were visible. Yet this availed the *Wehrmacht* little because the discovery came too late to dispel the mounting confusion that gripped the German high command before dawn on D-Day.

OVERLORD'S MOST IMPRESSIVE ASPECT

Radar failures, the false contacts in the Channel and in the air, the dummy landings in the Pas de Calais and throughout Normandy all combined to paralyze the German decision-making process, and herein lay the most impressive single aspect of Overlord.

This was to be the greatest amphibious operation in history. It was to include in its order of battle about 11,500 aircraft, 200,000 sailors and soldiers in the first wave alone, and no fewer than 713 warships, 4,216 assault vessels, 805 merchantmen, 59 block- ships, 736 auxiliaries, plus the two artificial harbors. The five assault forces alone had to be mustered into 59 separate convoys and then had to be organized to land in the correct sequence. The minesweeping effort had to be arranged so that minesweepers operating at $7^1/_2$ knots did not outrun invasion forces advancing at 5 knots. As the invasion forces formed up in the transport areas, the minesweepers had to continue to sweep and maintain formation in the dark as the tide turned.

However, the prior concentration of forces in southern England, the postponement of Overlord after the first assault forces had set out across the Channel (and when minesweepers were 40 miles off the enemy coast) and then the approach of so massive an invasion force, unfolded without the Germans becoming aware that the long-expected invasion was upon them. The vanguard of an invasion force that ultimately totalled about 7,000 ships was to come within artillery-range of the Calvados coast without the defenders realizing what was happening, and even then the latter fumbled away crucial hours as they tried to put together a response to Allied moves. By any standard, the Allied success in concealing their intentions was remarkable, though the Germans should have been able to deny the Allies at least some of their success because Overlord's security had been compromised.

Despite all Allied precautions, German army intelligence had been able to gain some insight into the possible timing of an invasion through an agent within the French Resistance. It knew that British Special Operations Executive had prepared and primed resistance groups for a sabotage campaign in support of Overlord, and it had long been aware that the BBC was to broadcast two suitably cryptic warning orders to the French Resistance when invasion was imminent. The first was to be made on the first day of the month when the invasion was scheduled; the second was to indicate that landings would begin in the next 48 hours. On 1 June, the BBC put out the initial warning – the first line of Paul Verlaine's *Chanson d'automne* (*'Les sanglots longs des violins d'automne'*) – and during the evening of 5 June it broadcast the next line (*'Blessent mon coeur d'une langueur monotone'*) – thus warning the French Resistance and German radio monitors with the *Fifteenth Army* that Allied landings were less than two days away.

The Germans responded to developments speedily but with less than their normal efficiency. Not for the first time that spring, von Salmuth placed his army on full alert and informed *OKW* and *OB West* of what was apparently afoot. Warning orders then went out to the *Kriegsmarine* and *Luftwaffe* though both discounted the possibility of landings at this time, partly because tidal conditions were 'wrong' but mainly because of the storm that even then was sweeping up the Channel. Rommel, convinced that the Allies could not invade in a storm that confined German surface units to harbor and prompted the cancellation of reconnaissance on 5 June, had left northern France for south Germany. At all other levels within the German high command the *Fifteenth Army*'s information and action were regarded skeptically. *OKW* inclined to treat the whole affair as yet another false alarm, and initially *OB West* and the naval and air commands in the west casually discarded von Salmuth's warning.

It fell to one of von Rundstedt's officers to make the famous remark that the Allies were hardly likely to announce their arrival in France in advance over the radio. It was not until the night wore on and German forces made contact with a variety of real and imagined enemies that the high command slowly and hesitantly realized that it was dealing with a full-scale attack. It then found it had to operate with failing communications and under conditions rendered more difficult than they need have been by a combination of two unfortunate sets of circumstances. First, Dollmann's *Seventh Army*, in position along more than half the northern coast of France, was not included on the addressee list of commands and formations notified of the *Fifteenth Army*'s suspicions and actions. Second, and compounding so amazing an omission, the formation holding the Normandy sector, the *7th Army's LXXXlV Corps*, had arranged for senior divisional officers to attend a war game at Rennes on 6 June, the subject being Allied airborne and seaborne landings in Normandy. Late on 5 June *LXXXIV Corps*, suddenly concerned that so many senior officers would be away from their posts at the same time, ordered its gamers to delay setting out for Rennes until after dawn, but by then many had already left.

The result was that many formations in the threatened sector lacked their commanders when Allied landings took place. There was grim irony in the fact that one of those at Rennes who set off for his command when word of enemy landings was received, was killed en route by soldiers from the 82nd Airborne Division. It was doubly unfortunate from the German point of view because this officer, Lieutenant-General Wilheim Falley, was commander of the *91st Light Division*, one of the strongest formations in the Normandy sector and the *7th Army*'s reserve.

Thus the Allied landings fell upon a *Wehrmacht* in confusion and disarray at all levels. It had no settled policy or tactical doctrine. It was surprised. It lacked its local army group commander and many of its senior divisional commanders and officers in the sector under attack, and its overall chain of command and communications in the battle area were at best uncertain. Over the previous 18 months the *Wehrmacht* had demonstrated its resilience in the face of adversity and its tactical superiority over all its enemies on numerous occasions. It remained to be seen whether it could once more meet a new challenge in the theater where, almost four years earlier to the day, it had secured Compiègne in the course of its most successful campaign.

CHAPTER 4
JUNE IN FRANCE

For the best part of 450 years perhaps the most significant single factor in world history was that it was easier to go around continents than across them; that maritime communications were superior to those overland. The development first of railways and then motor transport shifted the balance of power away from the maritime states of western Europe in favor of continental powers of great size and resources, neither of which had been realizable assets until the development of modern means of communication.

These means of overland communication theoretically provided Germany with her best hope of avoiding defeat in France in 1944. An assault landing from the sea is generally acknowledged to be perhaps the most complicated, difficult and hazardous of all military operations, but it is one that if properly conducted gives the attacker an initial and potentially very marked advantage over the defense. Surprise, the concentration of force at the point of contact, plus air and naval supremacy are the automatic prerogatives of an assault force and both the prerequisites and guarantees of its success. But the advantages of choosing when, where and in what strength to mount an assault are assets that are cashed in at the moment of landing because the defense, suddenly freed from the need to continue to deploy defensively, is thereafter able to use overland communications to converge against a restricted enemy beachhead. Given the modern superiority of overland communications to those by sea and the concentration of resistance around a cramped area into which the attacker must channel his strength, the aftermath of a landing is that the defense should compete with the attack on a minimum basis of equality.

No such equality should have existed in Normandy after 7 June despite the excellent road and rail system of northwest France. The very real advantages that the Allies enjoyed on the previous day should have been the basis of increasing superiority over the following weeks, and for two very obvious reasons. First, as the head of the Armed Forces Operations Staff General Alfred Jodl noted as early as the previous February, what should have been Germany's greatest single asset, her ability to operate along interior lines of communication, was no more because the Allied capacity to land anywhere prevented the concentration of a reserve. Second, Allied air power destroyed the assured superiority of road and rail communications over those by sea. Thus, after 6 June the *Wehrmacht* had no strength outside France on which to draw for reinforcements, and within France its formations could not move with the speed and cohesion of those of an enemy moving by sea to the beachhead. But events did not unfold in so neat and simple a manner as this imbalance suggests.

THE FLAW IN OVERLORD

A rough equality settled on the Normandy battlefield after 7 June for three rnain reasons. The first of these was the formidable standard of training and professionalism of the German ground forces and the superiority of the individual German soldier in good defensive positions over an attacking enemy. It is perhaps worth noting that even at this desperate stage of the war the German army spent longer on basic training than does the British army at the present time. The other two elements that combined to produce a seven-week 'stalemate' in Normandy were the German ability to concentrate a surprisingly high number of divisions against the Allied beachhead despite overwhelming enemy air supremacy and fearful confusion of strategic and tactical priorities on the part of the high command; and the fact that the Allies possessed a flawed plan of campaign.

The Overlord plan had been overwhelmingly concerned with two matters: the assault phase and creation of the beachhead, plus the provision of forces for the subsequent campaign in northwest Europe. Relatively little attention had been paid to the question of how operations were to be conducted once Allied forces were established ashore. This omission was natural, but unfortunate.

The basic idea was that the British should spearhead the advance in the open rolling country around and behind Caen. In his pre-invasion briefing, Montgomery had set out his intention to penetrate rapidly and deeply inland with the Second British Army, taking Caen itself on D-Day thereafter pressing into the Falaise area. There was little chance of so emphatic an exploitation as a prelude to battle. German defensive positions in front of Caen were extensive and a part of the coastal defenses. Also resistance was certain to be strong on the British sector of the front. It represented a direct threat as it was that part of the Allied position closest to Paris and the crossings over the lower Seine. Moreover, as many American commanders suspected, the divisions that represented Britain's last manpower reserves could not be expected to show the aggressiveness needed to record the advances envisaged by Montgomery.

The slenderness of national resources could only induce caution on the part of British commanders, and the Americans believed that unless the Germans uncharacteristically collapsed in Normandy they, with their much greater reserve of killable manpower than the British, would have to play the shock role. This was the catch. The Allied plan of campaign called upon the Americans to clear the

Cotentin and secure Cherbourg before turning their attention to the possibility of an advance into the interior, but the Americans were on that part of the Allied front least suited to mobile operations. In the area before St Lo, but particularly to the north of St Mère-Eglise, the Americans found themselves beset by the *bocage*, a murderous labyrinth of sunken roads and thick hedgerows tailor-made for defense and guaranteed to show up every American tactical and technical failing and none of their strengths. Also, and in a cause-and-effect relationship, the presence of the *bocage* and the unlikelihood of their being able to make rapid progress inland prompted the Americans to cut back on the armor and transport that was to come ashore on D-Day in favor of infantry and ammunition.

The result was that for the first month of operations in Normandy the Americans were ill-placed, both geographically and in terms of mobile striking power, to play the role of main assault force. Indeed, whereas on D-Day the British planned to land three times as much armor as their ally and to bring ashore the equivalent of more than two armored divisions, the second American armored division to arrive in Normandy did not come ashore until 24 June.

Many historians have claimed that the basic principle underlying Allied strategy in Normandy was to draw and hold main enemy formations on the eastern or British sector to allow the Americans to break out in the west – 'to exploit the American competence in extremely rapid mobility' – and it is indeed undeniable that German strength was drawn to and for the most part held down on the British part of the front. On 15 June, for example, the British were opposed by 43 infantry battalions and 520 tanks, and over the next fortnight German strength on this sector rose by almost 50 per cent to 64 battalions and 725 tanks: the comparative figures for the German front were first 63 battalions and 70 tanks and then the same number of infantry units but 140 tanks.

What is not so frequently noted by historians is that initially the Americans were not assigned the assault role, and that in any event the terrain was decisively against their being able to carry out such a role. The German armored concentration against the British sector was achieved only at the price of a corresponding concentration of Allied armor in the same sector. As we shall note, however, there was to be one crucial and all-important difference between the German armored deployment and that of the Allies.

THE GERMAN COUNTERATTACK IN PREPARATION

Alongside this basic weakness within the Allied plan of campaign went the one matter touched upon in the Allied beachhead during June. This was the formidable German achievement by 30 June of concentrating no fewer than 22 divisions or *kampfgruppes* in a combat zone where on 6 June there had been nine divisions, and this increase in strength takes no account of those divisions stricken from the order of battle as a result of their losses in the first three weeks of their being trapped in Cherbourg when the port finally fell on 29 June.

At that time six of the nine divisions that had been in position between the Seine and the west Cotentin coast on 6 June were still in the line. These were the *1st Panzer*, *Panzer Lehr*, *12th SS Panzer*, *91st Light*, *352nd Infantry* and *711th Divisions*. By 30 June they had been joined by the *9th* and *10th SS Panzer Divisions* from the Eastern Front; the *2nd Panzer*, *1st SS Panzer*, *16th Luftwaffe* and *346th Divisions* from north of the Seine; the *3rd Parachute* and *77th*, *275th* and *353rd Infantry Divisions* from Brittany; and the *2nd SS Panzer*, *17th SS Panzergrenadier* and *271st*, *272nd*, *276th* and *277th Infantry Divisions* from *Armee Gruppe C*, though the *271st* and *272nd Infantry Divisions* were in fact detailed to the *Fifteenth Army* and defense of the lower Seine.

This gathering of German strength in Normandy was achieved in the face of such Allied superiority in the air that on D-Day alone the various Allied air commands flew as many sorties as *Luftflotte 3* flew between 6 and 30 June. Whereas *Luftflotte 3* flew about 250 sorties on D-Day and 13,289 between then and the end of the month, the various Allied commands flew more than 14,000 sorties of all types on D-Day and no fewer than 67,223 offensive and 37,281 defensive sorties in direct support of the beachhead between D-Day and the end of June. These latter totals exclude all sorties flown against other targets in France and northwest Europe.

German movements into Normandy during June convey a very misleading impression unless certain qualifications are made. Though some formations such as the *77th Infantry Division* were able to come against the beachhead quickly and in good order, most were slow to arrive and somewhat the worse for wear by the time they reached the front because of the attention they received from Allied fighter-bombers during their advance to contact. Many examples of the experiences and losses suffered by German formations moving up to the front are well known. *Panzer Lehr*, for instance, on 7 June alone lost 84 half-tracks, prime movers and self-propelled guns, 40 fuel bowsers, 90 soft-skinned vehicles and five tanks as it made its way from Le Mans to Caen; and likewise *Kampfgruppe Heintz*, a very powerful formation of nine reinforced battalions drawn mainly from the *275th Infantry Division*, needed eight days to complete a journey of 140 miles from Redon to Montmartin-en-Graignes. It arrived piecemeal, exhausted, and without much of its equipment and one of its battalions that had been annihilated *en route* without getting anywhere near the FEBA.

The German reinforcement of Normandy with divisions from outside the area of responsibility of *LXXXIV Corps* was not matched by any flow of replacements that could cover the losses incurred by the various divisions once they were in contact with the enemy. Between 6 and 25 June German losses in Normandy (excluding the northern Cotentin) totalled 47,070 officers and men. Inevitably though, with only 6,000 replacements arriving at the front between 6 June and 12 July the downgrading of German divisions as their effectiveness became permanently impaired was never less than inevitable. The whole of *I SS Panzer Corps* was experiencing mounting difficulties by 23 June and was in desperate straits by 27 June, partly because of its losses of men and equipment but also because of worsening shortages of fuel and ammunition and the growing exhaustion of men too long at the front. Similarly, the 260 tanks with which *Panzer Lehr* began the campaign had been reduced to about 100 by the time the battles around Villers-Bocage died away by 18-19 June.

By that time its earlier losses amongst its supporting arms could only compound the inroads being made into the formation's effectiveness. What made this situation ever more serious for the Germans was the simple fact that by the third week of June they could not milk *Armee Gruppe C* of any more divisions because there were no more to be had, the *9th* and *11th Panzer Divisions* existing in no more than name with the former deploying just four tanks and an infantry only partially motorized. Of course there were other divisions, but herein lay the final qualification that must be made about German arrangements and effectiveness: the element of strategic and tactical confusion that engulfed the German high command after the Allied landings took place. In this there was an irony that probably passed unnoticed and most certainly would not have been appreciated at the time. The Allied landing should have put an end to the doubts and confusion about Allied intentions and the countermeasures that would be needed. Instead, German confusion was even more pronounced after the invasion than it had been beforehand.

CRISIS IN THE *WEHRMACHT*

The Allied descent on the Normandy coast impaled the German high command on the horns of a dilemma. To be precise it presented the Germans with four sets of concurrent alternatives, none of which could be decided easily and quickly. First and foremost, the Allied invasion amazingly did nothing to resolve the *Wehrmacht*'s Pas de Calais or Normandy quandary. Second, it presented the German high command with the dilemma of whether to concentrate against the British or the Americans. Third, it forced the Germans to decide between accepting the loss of Cherbourg and trying to extricate their forces from the Cotentin or making an all-out effort to prevent the fall of the port. Fourth, it presented the German commanders with the impossible problem of trying to hold the front but at the same time keeping their armor concentrated and intact for the counter-attack.

The German difficulty was that the existence of so many gaps along the front forced them to commit their armor piecemeal and defensively. Herein lay the crucial difference between Allied and German armored deployment referred to earlier: Allied deployment was deliberate whereas that of the Germans was forced upon them, with the result that almost from the start the defense was obliged to fight the wrong type of battle. It was in trying to resolve these various dilemmas that the Germans let slip their few and fleeting opportunities for success, their best chances probably coming on D-Day itself and then between 10 and 13 June at the time of the struggle for Carentan and the area between the Douve and Vire.

On D-Day itself the Germans came within measurable distance of success only in two sectors, and in one of these sectors the effort made by the defense on D-Day and D + 1 left it unable to offer any coherent and effective resistance over the next five days, with obvious repercussions for the stability of the front. On Utah the Americans suffered fewer casualties than they had incurred in the famous incident during the exercise off Slapton in April, when German MTBs had managed to get amongst a practising assault force. On Juno and Sword, British success was equally emphatic and there was no difficulty in XXX Corps linking its Gold and Juno beachheads on 6 June.

On Omaha, however, and the extreme western part of Gold where the invaders encountered the first-class *352nd Infantry Division*, the Allies came within measurable distance of defeat. At the end of the day, the 1st US Division was described by its army commander as digging in on the beach with its fingernails. Roughly half of all American casualties incurred on D-Day were suffered on this single beach where the enemy was strong and sited in commanding defensive positions, where the air and naval bombardment failed to do its job, and where armor was lacking because of accident and miscalculation. On the evening of D-Day the furthest the Americans had penetrated inland was 1,900 yards, and in places opposite the main landing sites the Germans still remained within 1,000 yards of the beaches.

Further to the east the British had no such crisis that threatened the security of a whole beach (and which for a time prompted the Americans to consider unloading Omaha's reinforcements on the flanking beaches) but they had problems of their own. These came in the shape of the only armored counter-attack of D-Day, when the *21st Panzer Division* drove to the sea down the open Juno-Sword boundary. Like that of the *352nd*, this effort by the *21st Panzer Division* failed because of lack of support. Losing roughly half its armor to fighter-bomber and artillery attack, the *21st Panzer Division* was not backed by sufficient infantry to maintain the gap between the 3rd Canadian and 3rd British Divisions, and the Germans thereafter lost the chance to deal with Juno and Sword separately. The result was that the following day's counter-attack by the *12th SS Panzer Division* had to be directed not against an open flank but against the two leading brigades of the 3rd Canadian Division, and by then the German moment had gone. On 7 June Juno and Sword tied in their flanks and with the Canadians holding firm, the Germans found themselves increasingly obliged to conform to Allied moves as pressure along the whole of the second British Army's front began to mount.

To the west the German situation opposite Omaha was no better because on 7 June the 1st and 29th Divisions gradually gained the upper hand and on the following day tore both of the *352nd Infantry Division*'s flanks from their positions on the coast. In the west the 5th Rangers aided by the 116th Infantry and 29th Division, relieved the beleaguered 2nd on the Pointe du Hoc and thereafter secured Grandchamp, while the 175th Infantry unleashed a drive to and then along Route 13 that resulted in its easy capture of Isigny during the night of 8-9 June.

On the other flank, American and British forces linked up behind Port-en-Bessin early on 8 June, but they could not close the trap behind them and catch the *726th Infantry Regiment* between Route 13 and the sea. Nevertheless, this regiment's withdrawal from its positions on the upper Aure was the first voluntary withdrawal by any German formation; in the event it availed the *352nd Infantry Division* and *LXXXIV Corps* little. The *352nd* had been so mauled in the course of the fighting between 6 and 8 June that it proved unable to withstand a three-division assault – by the 1st, 29th and just-arrived 2nd Division. This took V Corps from the Isigny-Canchy-Formigny-Tour line on the morning of 9 June to Caumont and the line of the Elle by the 12th. In fact during this offensive the front on either side of Caumont was all but undefended over ten miles of its length. Perhaps one of the real tragedies of the Normandy campaign was that the Americans lacked the armor that alone might have enabled them to exploit their hard-earned success.

Nevertheless, the real point behind these events and Allied success was that it forced the German high command to define its priorities, and its failure to do so reflected the continuing influence of Fortitude South. By 7 June Hitler was sufficiently concerned by the Allied landings to have released *Panzer Lehr* and the *12th SS Panzer Division* from the reserve; to have authorized the transfer of the *2nd Panzer*, *1st* and *2nd SS Panzer* and *17th SS Panzergrenadier Divisions* to Normandy; and to have approved the move of the *3rd Parachute* and *77th Infantry Divisions* to the front.

This was the first stage of a much wider redistribution of forces in the west that was put into effect in the two weeks after the Allied invasion, but it was no more than a partial reorganization because Hitler shrank from a general redeployment of forces into Normandy. The idea that the Allies had to land in the Pas de Calais had become so much a part of German strategic thinking that over the next few weeks a concern for the long-term security of this area prevailed over the increasingly desperate and immediate claims of the Normandy front. Even as late as the last week of July, by which time the *5th Panzer* and *Seventh Armies* in Normandy were in extremis, the official *OKW* view was that enemy landings in the Dieppe area could be expected and had to be forestalled.

Given the existence of such an opinion at that late stage of proceedings, it was hardly surprising that in early June Hitler rejected the view that the German army had to deal with enemies ashore rather than take precautions against those that might never arrive. To Hitler, and it would seem the weight of opinion within the army except that part engaged in Normandy, the Pas de Calais retained its importance as the cornerstone of the German defensive system in France even (perhaps especially) after enemy landings in Normandy.

There was an additional reason for Hitler's concern with the Pas de Calais. After months of elaborate and costly endeavor, the start of the V-1 offensive against London was just one week away when the Allies came ashore in Normandy, and the launching sites for this attack were of course in this area. The first flying bombs aimed against southern England were launched on the morning of 13 June, and by the end of the month 2,049 had been fired of which 1,557 had crossed the coast of southern England and 783 had hit London. Because of his faith in his new weapons, Hitler deemed the holding of the Pas de Calais to be essential. The fact of the matter was that Hitler's fixation with and faith in his secret weapons projects were misplaced, and both efforts were at best irrelevant to German needs since neither could ever compensate Germany for her increasing inferiority in the air. Like the guided weapons used by the Luftwaffe for the first time in 1943 and the jet interceptors that came into service later in July 1944, the V-1 programme inadvertently proved if proof was needed, that there was no effective substitute for conventional air power.

ALLIED INTELLIGENCE ACTIVITY AFTER D-DAY

It was this concern with the Pas de Calais that Allied intelligence hoped to reinforce during June in order to forestall any possibility of a major German move into Normandy that might yet tip the scales against Montgomery's Twenty First Army Group. At the end of the month, when the meteorological conditions of 6 June repeated themselves, a series of feints and offshore and air bombardments were staged against the Pas de Calais, but it was immediately after the Allied landings that the British were able to build on the success of Fortitude. In response to a German request for more information of the kind that had been supplied on the morning of 6 June, the British through their double agent presented the enemy with 'the big lie' – the old idea of the more implausible the story the more likely it was to be believed.

On the morning of 9 June the British fed the Germans the suggestion that the very scale of the Normandy landings was proof enough that it was only the deception part of the grand design and that the balance of some 715 divisions in Britain remained to be thrown against the Pas de Calais. The *OKW* record indicated that the bait had been at least nibbled if not accepted since there were supposedly signs that the enemy intended to land north of the Seine.

Nearly two weeks later there was proof of the extent to which the Pas de Calais illusion had taken hold and was too deeply entrenched to be changed. The German army intelligence summary of 22 June indicated that perhaps 24 enemy divisions were in France and that a further 12 remained in reserve in Britain, along with possibly as many as 32 more divisions with Army Group Patton. Under these circumstances it was inconceivable that the German high command could consider relaxing its grip on the Pas de Calais. Nevertheless, the failure to crush the Allied landings in their infancy, the mounting pressure exerted along the whole of the *Seventh Army*'s front, and the impossibility of challenging the enemy's superiority in the coastal belt added up to a crisis that even *OKW* had to recognize on 10 June. By then a counterattack on the Orne bridgehead had begun badly, while a planned attack on the Canadians by the *12th SS* and *21st Panzer Divisions* had not begun at all. The command entrusted with this attack, *Panzergruppe West*, had been devastated by an air attack that killed every member of its operations staff, killed or wounded almost every officer except von Schwappenburg, and destroyed virtually all the command's signals equipment.

In the west the German positions in Carentan were coming under mounting pressure, and at the same time the whole of the front north of Caumont disintegrated. On 11 June von Rundstedt and Rommel both warned Hitler that the battle was being fought the wrong way and that means had to be found to force more infantry into the fight and to keep the armor away from a close-quarter battle. That same day Hitler ordered the *9th* and *10th SS Panzer Divisions* of *11 SS Panzer Corps* to return to France from the Eastern Front, and five days later – when the *2nd SS Panzer Division*, fresh from adding to German laurels at Oradour-sur-Glane on 10 June, arrived on the scene – the direction of Hitler's thinking became evident. With the decision to reinforce the *Seventh Army* with forces from the Netherlands and from the *Fifteenth* and *Nineteenth Armies*, the *Fifteenth Army* in return receiving reinforcement from Norway and Denmark. At the same time Hitler ordered preparations to begin for an all-out counter-attack by no fewer than seven armored divisions that he intended to concentrate with *I* and *II SS Panzer Corps*. Hitler planned to make this effort against the Americans.

HITLER MAKES HIS MOVE

The reasoning behind this decision was that the British were too strong to be attacked frontally and that the panzers had to eliminate the Americans before turning to settle accounts with the British. It was a decision that begged some very obvious facts, not least the constraints of terrain and a pattern of road communications that ensured that any division arriving at the Normandy battlefield from the north or east would be automatically drawn to the British rather than the more distant American part of the front. Nevertheless, this decision was in accord with the emphasis placed on the retention of Cherbourg and the earlier attempt to keep VII and V US Corps divided by holding on to the neck of land between Douve and the Vire.

But even by 11 June, when Hitler made his initial decision on the employment of *II SS Panzer Corps*, it was becoming clear that denying the Americans either or both these desirable pieces of real estate was likely to be beyond the *Seventh Army*. Indeed, during the early hours of the previous day, 10 June, it had been unable to prevent the first tentative link-up of elements from the 101st Airborne and 29th Infantry Divisions around Auville-sur-le Vey. During the rest of that and the next day Carentan's garrison, drawn mainly from the *6th Parachute Regiment*, became increasingly exposed as successive American attacks threatened to outflank and encircle the town.

On the night of 11-12 June the Germans quietly evacuated the town that on 9 June Rommel had deemed was one of two places that had to be held if the defense was to prevail. Thereafter the Americans moved tanks from the 2nd Armored Division into this area as both sides prepared to resume the stuggle for the Carentan-Auville-Montmartin area with new arrivals, the Germans with the *17th SS Panzergrenadier Division* and *Kampfgruppe Heintz* and the

Americans with XIX Corps. Activated on 14 June with the 29th and 30th Infantry Divisions under command, Major-General Charles H Corlett's corps was given the task of consolidating and expanding the American position between the Douve and Vire and thereby secure the flanks of both VII and V Corps during the next phase of operations.

By the time that the Americans tightened their grip on Carentan in readiness for the inevitable counter-attack mounted by the *17th SS Panzergrenadier Division*, the American front presented a curiously lopsided appearance. The Carentan position obviously lacked depth and was disputed for the moment, but after its bad beginning on Omaha, V Corps had effectively destroyed the enemy that had opposed it on the beach and had carved out for itself a reasonably deep beachhead. On the other hand, VII Corps, after a relatively easy time coming ashore on Utah, in the course of the next week failed to make any significant territorial gains except on the lower Douve and around Carentan; and it encountered increasingly serious difficulties as it tried to improvize a time-saving attack to secure Cherbourg. By 13 June it was still held up on positions that had been responsible for most of the few problems it had encountered during the landings on 6 June, and it may be that in trying to extemporize VII Corps took longer than necessary to secure Cherbourg.

THE IMPORTANCE OF CHERBOURG

The slowness of VII Corps' progress was certainly the result of difficult terrain and effective resistance, but its attempted improvization probably stemmed from an awareness of how important the speedy capture of Cherbourg was to the Allied cause. Certainly the need to take the port quickly was impressed upon VII Corps at ever higher levels during 7 June when Bradley, Montgomery and then Eisenhower reviewed progress to date, reassessed earlier priorities and reconfirmed Cherbourg as the main objective in Collins' area of responsibility.

An awareness of who was looking over his shoulder could have been at least part of the reason behind Collins' subsequent decisions to mount a frontal assault towards Cherbourg along the main road without waiting either to tie in his flank with V Corps or to seal off the Cotentin with a drive to the west coast. But on the day when Collins was made aware of the views of three levels of command above him, his forces were not going very far: it was then that the Germans in the northern Cotentin made what turned out to be their supreme effort in defense of Cherbourg.

While a regiment from the *91st Light Division* tried to clear the west bank of the Merderet of scattered groups of American paratroopers and then to establish itself over the river, the Germans made their main effort down Route 13 from Montebourg with what was a *kampfgruppe* of three infantry and three artillery battalions drawn from the army reserve, the *91st Light* and *243rd Divisions*. This attack carried to the very edge of St Mère-Eglise and the positions of the 82nd Airborne Division before being broken up by some 60 tanks from two armored battalions that the 4th Infantry Division pushed forward to help the paratroopers. The German attempt to overrun at least the enemy airborne forces on 7 June thus failed, but the day did not end without the Germans recording some useful defensive successes. First, the German attacks prevented the 82nd establishing itself in jumping-off positions over the Merderet – these were essential to the success of any attack to the west Cotentin coast. Second, despite having their own attack broken by enemy armor, the Germans were able to bring another *kampfgruppe* (this time from the *243rd Division*) to stabilize the front, and herein lay the key to the fighting of the next six days. With the Germans able to choose the pick of the ground over the five miles back to Montebourg and also along the Quinéville ridge, the 4th Infantry Division proved unable to clear the coast below Quinéville, secure the village and get astride the ridge until 14 June. Even then, Montebourg itself did not fall to the Americans until the morning of 19 June at the start of the final offensive that was to carry VII Corps to the edge of Cherbourg's landward defenses.

One other partial success came the German way at this time. Because of American inability to seal off the Cotentin, German formations were able to move towards the neck of the peninsula and into positions in front of the beachhead. This, however, posed a problem for the German command because it then had to decide whether its forces should enter the peninsula in order to stand between Cherbourg and the enemy or stand to the south, seal off the peninsula and thereby ensure that they in their turn were not trapped by an enemy's advance.

Hitler and Rommel instinctively and correctly sought to defend Cherbourg. Like the Americans, they did not believe that an Allied invasion could succeed without the facilities of a major port. Cherbourg was the second of the two places that on 9 June Rommel determined had to be retained if the invasion was to be defeated. Von Rundstedt, on the other hand, clearly regarded the defense of Cherbourg to be doomed because on 10 June he ordered the garrison to begin the demolition of the city's civil and port facilities. If this was indeed tacit admission that Cherbourg was as good as lost, von Rundstedt's foresight had been anticipated: the garrison had set about the destruction of the port as early as 7 June. In the end, however, most of the German decisions regarding the defense of Cherbourg were to be made for them.

On 9 June, with little sign of a German collapse on Route 13 and VII Corps' beachhead still not much larger than it had been on 6 June, Bradley ordered Collins to revert to the original plan of campaign to capture Cherbourg. This involved isolating the port from the outside by sealing the neck of the Cotentin and then advancing the length of the peninsula to take the fortress. Collins thereupon reorganised his forces and placed the 90th Infantry Division in the vanguard of the attack towards the west coast. Four days of indecisive fighting later, with the Americans still unable to secure a bridgehead around the confluence of the Douve and Merderet, Collins dismissed three of the senior commanders from the 90th, relegated the division to flank guard, and pushed the elite 9th Infantry Division into the line with orders to secure its own bridgeheads and to advance the 20 miles to the west coast.

Supported on its left flank directly by the 82nd Airborne Division and indirectly by VIII US Corps which was activated on 15 June to protect the flank and rear of VII Corps during this and subsequent operations, the 9th Infantry Division sliced its way across the peninsula to reach the sea at Barneville late on 17 June and just before the 77th Infantry Division was able to get clear of the closing trap. In fact this formation should have escaped from the Cotentin. As the American offensive reached across the neck of the peninsula and it became clear that any German forces to the north not withdrawn immediately would soon be lost to the defense, Rommel tried to have the largely-intact *77th Infantry Division* pulled back to positions on the southern flank of the American advance.

But a confusion of priorities within a chain of command that involved Hitler, Rommel, the *Seventh Army*, *LXXXIV Corps*, and two local commands in northern Cotentin, ensured that the *77th*, despite having been able to keep clear and in front of the 9th Infantry Division during the initial phase of the American advance, did not begin its breakout attempt until the VII Corps' front had begun to harden across its line of withdrawal. The result was that on 18 June the 9th Infantry Division encircled and annihilated the *77th*, just two battalions being able to escape from the *débacle*. The outcome of this unfortunate sequence of events for the Germans was that the defense south of the Cotentin was deprived unnecessarily of the services of most of a division, while in the north the defense of Cherbourg had to be entrusted to remnants from the *91st Light* and *243rd* and *709th Divisions*.

GERMAN FAILURE IN PERSPECTIVE

The isolation of Cherbourg and the destruction of the *77th Infantry Division* marked the end of the first and very distinct phase of the battle. It is a somewhat curious feature of the Normandy campaign that it tends to divide into very convenient phases marked by major decisions on both sides that were taken at roughly the same time. Thus the period between 6 and 18 June was really one of failure for both sides at the end of which Allies and Germans alike redefined objectives and policies, and then settled down to a phase of operations remarkably similar to the first. This in its turn was brought to an end on 30 June – 1 July with a series of decisions on both sides that marked a most definite shift in policy and the conduct of operations for both the Germans and Allies.

The German failure in the opening phase of the Normandy campaign was much more obvious and significant than that of the Allies. The Germans failed successively to prevent, defeat and contain an enemy landing, and by the time of the famously inconclusive Margival meeting on 17 June (when Hitler met with von Rundstedt and Rommel in the command bunker near Soissons built in 1940 in readiness for the invasion of England) the Germans had been forced on to the defensive along the length of the front.

In the east their attacks on the Orne bridgehead between 10 and 12 June had narrowly but decisively failed, and they had been unable to make any headway against the Canadians. In the first week after the Allied landings they had been unable to make a single armored counter-attack anywhere along the American part of the front, and they had been ejected from virtually every one of their defensive positions opposite American formations. The British had been halted in front of Caen, but German success in this area had been dearly bought in terms of a loss of initiative and any chance of securing superiority at any point because of the defensive deployment of their armor.

In the center their forces had secured one very notable success on 13 June when an attempt by the 7th Armoured Division to come around the supposedly unsecured left flank of *Panzer Lehr* was shattered by a single company of four Tiger tanks which destroyed a total of 53 British tanks and armored vehicles in little more than five minutes.

This single action annihilated the British vanguard, and was largely responsible for denying the British the village of Villers-Bocage until 4 August. But this was just one small action, and its follow-up proved very costly to the Germans. Herein lay the crucial problem that confronted the German high command: every successful German defensive effort was all but certain to consume proportionately greater resources than the Allies would expend in an attack, and even the most successful defensive effort would automatically use up reserves and resources quicker than they could be replaced. Because the Allies could be certain of the arrival of a growing flood of American reinforcements, they had only to avoid total disaster to be assured of total victory: by the same token no amount of local German success could ultimately stave off final and general defeat, unless there was a major shift of German strategic policy.

This was the issue that was dodged at Margival and which, being evaded, ensured that the conference had to be indecisive in that its only outcome could be confirmation of the 'same-as- before' formula. With control of the battle slipping from its grasp and its forces steadily losing the battle, the German command was confronted with pressing tactical problems in Normandy. In the end though, its main difficulties were strategic. It had to contend with problems caused by enemy air supremacy and naval gunfire, failing logistics, immobility, the misuse of the armor, and many other local troubles.

In the final analysis, however, it had to decide how, where and with what it was to make its effort. It could try to maintain its present positions despite previous failures and rely on the forces even then making their way to Normandy to swing the battle in Germany's favor. It could attempt to withdraw to a shorter, more easily-defended line, less vulnerable to naval gunfire and better supplied by shorter lines of communication, thereby securing for the defense some measure of freedom of action denied at the present time in Normandy. It could, as a last resort, adopt a policy of voluntary withdrawal on all the secondary fronts, to ignore the risk of any further Allied landings and to concentrate everything on one single attempt to win a deciding strategic success in the west. Of course the alternative to success in such an effort was obvious – Ludendorff's *'Dann muss Deutschland eben zugrunde gehen'* ('Then Germany must inevitably be ruined') of the previous war – but that was the alternative in any event.

It was this solution, risking everything on a single roll of the dice, that Jodl proposed on 13 June after he had originally proposed stripping the Italian theater to counter the Normandy landings. But with Hitler pathologically averse to almost any withdrawal, acceptance of so radical a proposal was out of the question, and it was probably too late in the day to put such a policy into effect. Thus Margival ended with nothing more than local or tactical decisions: instructions to the *Kriegsmarine* to neutralize enemy naval forces; and to shift more forces from what was by now the almost non-existent *First Army*. It was only after the conference had ended and its participants dispersed that any change of strategic policy was recorded, and then it was exactly the opposite of what was needed. In response to American success at Barneville and in subsequent operations in the Cotentin, Hitler instructed that the planned assault on the Americans in the St Lo-Caumont sector should be widened to include an attack at the base of the Cotentin peninsula. The least that could be said about these various decisions is that they hardly constituted the kind of inspired leadership that the *Wehrmacht* needed at this particular time.

CHERBOURG AND CAEN:
THE OBJECTIVES REAFFIRMED

The Allied situation, on the other hand, also contained failure, but it had the ingredients of success because disaster had been avoided at the outset. The most conspicuous feature of the campaign to date was the contrast between partial success in the western sector and failure in the east. The British failure to secure Caen and the lack of progress along the whole of the British front was in sharp contrast to the gains that had been made behind Omaha and were being recorded on the Cotentin. The initial British intention to rush Caen had never materialized, and subsequent attempts to mount converging attacks on or around the city had all been forestalled.

By the middle of June there was clearly an element of uncertainty about the best course of action open to the Second British Army. On the American sector the momentum that had taken V Corps to Caumont had been lost, and with the *2nd SS Panzer Division* taking up defensive positions in front of St Lo there was little chance that it might be regained. Only on the Cotentin were events unfolding in a satisfactory manner. Under these circumstances Montgomery's policy was strangely similar to Hitler's: namely more of the same. With the reserves that could ensure long-term success, on 18 June Montgomery redefined Cherbourg and Caen as the Allies' objectives in the next phase of operations.

It is difficult to see what options were open to the Allies at this stage of proceedings other than to reconfirm Cherbourg and Caen as the twin Allied objectives in the next phase of operations. But in the countless memoirs, biographies and histories that have subsequently refought this campaign, this was one of the decisions that came to be bound up with the various national and personal rivalries that bedeviled the question of Montgomery's command of operation during the campaign.

Settling this question has never been helped by Montgomery's own insistence that this and every battle in which he exercised command developed along lines that had been foreseen and anticipated: that everything unfolded to an end that had been approved and ordained. By claiming such an omniscience (that even deemed the battle of Arnhem to be 90 per cent successful) Montgomery denied himself any claim to such attributes of generalship as flexibility, imagination and a willingness to improvize that equal perception, far-sightedness and clarity of thought as the essential requirements of a great commander. Montgomery showed all these latter qualities in the planning, preparation, and the conduct of the landing and initial phase of Overlord, and he was to show the others at the end of June when, with his offensive stalled, plans were recast and new objectives defined. The subsequent switch in emphasis set in motion the breakout from Normandy and the overwhelming Allied victory in northern France in late July and August. But this flexibility was not present in the orders of 18 June, though their terms did allow one very important improvization to be incorporated into the Allied plan of campaign even before the end of the month.

Because American operations directed to the capture of Cherbourg were in hand at the time Montgomery issued his orders to the two armies under his command, Bradley's First US Army was able to comply with instructions before Dempsey's Second British Army was able to mount Operation Epsom. Indeed, Bradley had been able to anticipate orders with a reorganization of his forces in readiness for the advance on Cherbourg. With the 82nd and 101st Airborne and 90th Infantry Divisions under command, VIII Corps was to defend the rear of VII Corps as the latter advanced on Cherbourg with its full strength – the 9th Infantry Division, the 4th Cavalry Regiment, and the 79th and 4th Infantry Divisions – committed to the offensive across the length of the front. The unlikelihood of serious opposition allowed the Americans to dispense with a reserve and to plan to use only the 9th and 79th in the assault on Cherbourg itself, but in the event the 4th Division was to take part in the final attack on the city and to become its garrison after its fall.

CHERBOURG FALLS – AND NEPTUNE ENDS

The American advance on Cherbourg began on 19 June, the 9th Division making very rapid progress on the left at first only to slow on 20 June and 21 June when it came up against the enemy's main line of resistance some three or four miles short of Cherbourg. In the center and on the right the Americans encountered much more substantial opposition on 19 June, and neither the 79th nor the 4th was able to record much headway on either side of Valognes. In fact the Americans had missed what had been probably their best opportunity to turn German positions on the main routes into Cherbourg when, on 17 June, they failed to realize that the *77th Infantry Division*'s initial movement towards the west left the Brisquebec-Valognes position undefended. Nevertheless, the crumbling of the right- flank in the face of American pressure forced Major-General Karl-Wilhelm von Schlieben, initially commander of the *709th Division* and then the whole Cherbourg garrison, to pull back his center and left on 20 June. This allowed the Americans to close up to Cherbourg's defenses on all sides by the evening of 21 June.

With a call to surrender disregarded by von Schlieben, the Americans on 22 June began a series of concentric attacks that were joined on 25 June by a task force of three battleships, two heavy and two light cruisers and 11 destroyers. This force attacked German positions around Querqueville and Fermanville at either end of Cherbourg's defenses, and while its bombardments did little physical damage they appear to have brought home to the German garrison the hopelessness of its position.

Von Schlieben and his naval counterpart, Rear Admiral Walter Hennecke, were captured at St Souveur on 26 June, and the following day all organized resistance in Cherbourg itself ceased. The last of the fortresses on the breakwaters did not surrender until 29 June, and German forces held out on the Cap de la Hogue for another 24 hours. A total of 45,000 prisoners were taken by VII Corps in the last four days of an offensive that cost the Americans 1,800 dead and a total of some 15,000 casualties, but it was appropriate that the clearing of the Cotentin should coincide with the official end of Neptune.

With the Allied armies securely established ashore, German naval power in the Channel effectively neutralized despite the first U-boat successes since the landings on 25 and 29 June, and with the call on naval firepower slackening as more artillery came ashore, Neptune was ended on 30 June. This was the same day that the British chiefs of staff bluntly advised Churchill to drop his opposition to Anvil. In fact, the need to provide Anvil with more naval support was one of the reasons why Neptune was brought to an end. The American battleships *Arkansas*, *Nevada* and *Texas* and the heavy cruisers *Quincy* and *Tuscaloosa* were amongst the units that were to be transfered from British home waters and Neptune to the Mediterranean and the Allied landings in southern France.

The end of both Neptune and the battle for the Cotentin coincided not merely with the Anvil argument coming to a head but the 30 June revision of Allied priorities by Montgomery. This, in its turn, took place in the aftermath of two Allied failures: the inability of XIX US Corps to develop an offensive in the Villers-Fossard area to the northeast of St Lô and, more seriously, the failure of XXX, VIII and I British Corps to secure Caen in the course of Operation Epsom.

Originally Epsom was planned as a pincer attack that would begin on 22 June with a drive by I British Corps from its Orne bridgehead around the east of Caen while the main effort was made to the west by the newly-arrived VIII Corps. Supported by XXX Corps on its right flank, VIII Corps was to drive from a start line around the upper

Mue, across the Odon, Orne and Laize to stand across the main roads coming south from Caen. But an awareness of the shallowness of the Orne bridgehead and then the delays caused to the buildup of reserves and supplies by the 'Great Storm' of 19-22 June led to Epsom's being first modified and then postponed. The plan for a corps attack from the north was abandoned in favor of a local offensive by the 51st Division. The aim of this was to secure St Honorine and thereafter tie down enemy forces in this area as the main attack unfolded on 26 June. But by the time XXX Corps opened its supporting attack on the 25th the Allied high command was aware that at least part of the *1st SS Panzer Division* was over the Seine and that *II SS Panzer Corps* was on the Franco-German border with its leading elements already around Alençon and orders to move against the American sector.

Through its signals intelligence the Allied high command was also aware even before Montgomery's orders of 18 June that the Germans were packing their front around Caen and that at least six high-grade divisions other than the panzers were on their way to the beachhead. Herein lay the element of opportunism within Epsom that was to give rise to so much confusion. The aim of the offensive was to secure Caen but also to destroy enemy divisions by drawing the Germans into a close-quarter battle, where German qualitative superiority in armor would be discounted and where the Allies would be able to bring superior numbers and firepower to bear in a battle of attrition. Confusion surrounded the various inquests that followed this battle, not least because Montgomery disingenuously claimed, after a battle that ended with Caen still firmly in German hands, that he had never intended to take the city in the first place. Even allowing that he could not admit before the battle that recourse was being made to a strategy of attrition, this was not true, though it was undoubtedly the case that the desire to wreck German plans and timetables by dragging *II SS Panzer Corps* into the mincer around Caen was incorporated as one of the main aims of this operation.

LAUNCHING EPSOM

Epsom began well enough before first light on 23 June when a surprise attack by the 51st Division overran St Honorine and thereby secured a slightly improved defensive perimeter that withstood counter-attack by the *21st Panzer Division* later that day. On the morning of 25 June Operation Dauntless (the supporting attack by XXX British Corps) began with the 49th Division securing the village of Fontenay but only with great difficulty in the face of opposition from both *Panzer Lehr* and the *12th SS Panzer Division*. The 49th proved unable to clear the critically important Rauray ridge on 25 June, and it could not improve upon this situation the next day when XXX Corps' artillery joined that of I Corps in providing a massive bombardment in support of VIII Corps' drive to the Odon. XXX Corps did manage to secure the village of Rauray itself, and with the right flank still held by the Germans, VIII Corps made slow progress in the face of resistance from the *12th SS* and the *21st Panzer Divisions*.

The opening attack by the 15th (Scottish) Division very quickly bogged down in a series of untidy and costly actions around Cheux, but by the evening of 26 June the 15th had been able to drag itself to positions within striking distance of the Odon, even though the ground that it had conquered during the day was very far from being occupied effectively. During the night a German counter-attack carried to Cheux before being turned back, and during the following day the British secured an intact bridge over the Odon at Tourmauville and immediately pushed armor across the river in order to form a bridgehead to exploit this success.

By this stage, however, the tide of battle had begun to turn against VIII Corps. The failure of XXX Corps to clear the Rauray ridge and Noyers, left it if not in the classically vulnerable position of a narrow-front vanguard with trailing flanks back to a much wider start-line, then certainly in a narrow salient held on three sides by an alert and powerful enemy. VIII Corps was indeed able to advance some six miles on a two-mile front on 26 and 27 June. However, with all semblence of traffic and staff control collapsing amid the ruins of Cheux and the armor and infantry not properly tied in together, the Germans proved able to reinforce their forces' positions around the British salient more quickly than the British could feed armor forward to the Odon.

Despite Allied air supremacy the Germans were able to thin their Orne front and use units from the *21st Panzer Division* alongside a battle group from the *12th SS Panzer Division* in a spoiling attack on Mouen on 28 June. At the same time they were able to contain the Odon bridgehead from their positions on the forward slopes of Hill 112, albeit at heavy cost to their 88-mm guns. But on this same day the Allied high command became aware that what was intended to be the mightiest assembly of *Waffen SS* armor ever to be concentrated in a single place, was even then gathering around the Cheux salient. With almost the full strength of the *9th* and *10th SS Panzer Divisions* available, the German plan was to attack the British position around Cheux on all three of its sides with *I* and *II SS Panzer Corps* on the morning of 29 June. With the incomplete *10th SS Panzer Division* ordered against the Odon bridgehead the *9th*, with any battle groups that it could acquire from *Panzer Lehr* and the *2nd SS Panzer Division*, was to attack Cheux from the west, while in the east the *1st* and *12th SS* and *21st Panzer Divisions* were to gather their combined strength for a drive against VIII Corps' inner flank.

EPSOM FALTERS – BUT THE GERMANS MISCALCULATE

The crisis day of the battle for the Second British Army should have been 29 June, but while this was undoubtedly the case it was a crisis completely overshadowed by the one that was to engulf the German high command. On 29 June and over the next two days the British were forced to give ground at several points, and on 30 June the situation appeared serious enough to commit Bomber Command to a series of daylight attacks against German armored columns west of Cheux. But the problems that the Second British Army encountered were small in comparison with those of the German high command because between 29 June and 1 July it effectively destroyed the last German hopes of recording a decisive success against the Allied beachhead.

The British had been forewarned of German intentions by their signals intelligence and by an *SS* prisoner captured with his marked map while conducting a reconnaissance on the morning of 29 June. The result was that when it moved into the attack that afternoon the *9th SS Panzer Division* was all but overwhelmed by so intense an artillery fire that the Germans believed that the British were using some new kind of self-loading field gun. The mauling of this formation at this point presented the German high command with its supreme crisis of the Normandy campaign. On the previous day yet another interminable and indecisive *Führer* conference resulted in von Rundstedt and Rommel leaving Berchtesgaden with fresh instructions to continue an unyielding defense at the forward point of contact to confine the Allies to their present beachhead.

Hitler's very real concern at this point was to prevent a mobile battle since the full weight of Allied resources could only result in the annihilation of German forces in the west. But these instructions, plus the confirming orders of 29 June, represented the bankruptcy of Hitler's strategic thinking, since they condemned the divisions in Normandy to the progressive erosion of their strength and to inevitable defeat. Without an attack the Germans had no chance of avoiding defeat, and herein lay the significance of the repulse of *I* and *II SS Panzer Corps* around Cheux on 29 June. For the previous two weeks or so German strategy had rested on the hope that armored forces could be assembled for an all-out attack that would crush the Allies. Now, on 29 June, that attack had been made and effectively crushed before it had the chance to obtain any momentum, still less success. In effect, *II SS Panzer Corps* had represented Germany's last hope of crushing the Allied beachhead because after it had been committed there was no more armored forces that could be fed into the battle.

On 29 June the German command in the west found that this formation, like all the other armored formations that had been in Normandy for any length of time, could not make inroads into Allied positions and was forced on to the defensive and to commit its armor piecemeal. In fact, the whole of the attack of 29 June was mishandled on the German side, the British being able to pre-empt the attempted German armored concentration against the Americans and thereafter force the Germans to fight the battle around Cheux in any way but the one that might have brought them success.

HITLER FAILS TO HEED THE NORMANDY LESSONS

The lessons of defeat on the Odon were not lost upon German commanders in the west. Geyr, back in action as commander of *Panzergruppe West*, and SS-General Paul Hausser, acting commander of the *Seventh Army* since Dollmann's death on 28 June after a heart attack, both urged a withdrawal to positions south of Caen, and Geyr was particularly emphatic in expressing the view that 'a clear-cut choice must be made between trying to cobble together a rigid defense, which leaves the initiative with the enemy, and the adoption of flexible tactics which might allow us some initiative for part of the time'. Such an assessment was thoroughly in keeping with the views Geyr had expounded before the Allied invasion, but it also constituted a massive indictment of Hitler's conduct of the battle and the orders that he had issued to von Rundstedt and Rommel on 28 and 29 June. Hausser, Rommel and von Rundstedt all backed Geyr's views, von Rundstedt taking the opportunity to seek approval for a withdrawal behind Caen and his assuming a tactical discretion denied him thus far in the battle. At the same time Rommel unilaterally placed all *Kriegsmarine* and *Luftwaffe* personnel in northern France under army command.

In a series of reports, therefore, the military command in the west displayed a rare unity in challenging Hitler's strategic and tactical direction of the campaign. Their combined view presented Hitler with a choice that was neatly summarized by Jodl's observation that Geyr's views implied that the Allies could not be defeated but would continue to inflict irreplaceable losses on the *Wehrmacht*. Jodl's own opinion was that Germany was faced with a choice between crushing the Allied beachhead and withdrawing to the shortest possible defensive line on the Franco-German border, but these were the alternatives that the dictator sought to avoid by reconfirming his original instructions of 28-29 June and dismissing von Rundstedt and Geyr.

These dismissals, and clearly the impending disgrace of Rommel after his transgression, represented the end of the second phase of the battle for Normandy since they removed two rational, if increasingly ineffective, influences from the German conduct of operations. Thus far the German high command had been spared from disaster because the professionalism and tactical expertise of its forces could compensate for strategic inferiority and make good the errors of deployment and design.

By the end of June there was deadlock in Normandy, just as there was in Italy. But there were crucial differences between the German situation in Italy and the one that confronted the *Wehrmacht* in the west. In Italy Kesselring's retreating forces were as numerous as their attackers and were falling back into increasingly difficult terrain that was ideal for defensive operations. In Normandy, on the other hand, the terrain behind the German front favored the attacker and the Allies had secured a potentially overwhelming superiority on land to complement their superiority in the air. With 26 divisions equally divided between the First US and Second British Armies, the Allies held a clear and growing advantage over a *Wehrmacht* that at the end of June included in its Normandy order of battle eight armored divisions in various stages of disarray.

By the end of June the Allies had landed 929,000 men in the beachhead and had incurred a total of 61,732 casualties, 8,469 of them fatalities. Thus far success had been bought at a remarkably economical price, but though Epsom at times saw some of the most intensive fighting of the campaign the bloodiest battles in Normandy were to be reserved for July. However on 30 June, when the bouyant Montgomery switched the point of future attacks from the British to the American sector and Hitler stood on the brink of decisions that led to the defeat of *Heeresgruppe B*, the issue had been decided.

The amazing aspect of the subsequent campaign, however, was that on 31 July the front line in Normandy had hardly advanced beyond where it had been on 30 June – yet within another month most of France would have been cleared and German casualties had almost reached the 500,000 mark. Such was the totality of German defeats in July and August, not just in Normandy but on all fronts, that the number of German missing was double the dead and wounded – a clear indication of an army going down to defeat both in the west and in the east, and it is to the latter campaign in Belorussia to which we now turn.

PART TWO

THE EASTERN FRONT

In the Soviet account of the history of the Great Patriotic War of 1941-1945, 1944 was the year of the ten offensives or victories in the course of which Soviet forces cleared their enemies from almost every corner of the homeland and carried the war against Germany into nonSoviet territory for the first time.

These offensives began in January when Soviet forces finally lifted the siege of Leningrad and drove the Germans back as far as Pskov and the old Soviet-Estonian border, and they were then continued into February and March at the other end of the Eastern Front when Soviet armies, breaking from their bridgeheads over the Dnieper, carried the war beyond the 1938 Soviet-Polish and Soviet-Romanian borders. In April and May the main focus of the struggle was in the south, around Odessa but more importantly the Crimea, and in June battle was joined on two quite different fronts: in Karelia and Belorussia.

In July Soviet forces maintained the pressure on the enemy with drives that carried them into the Baltic states and Galicia, and in the following month the Soviets switched the point of their attack away from the North European Plain into the Balkans with an offensive over the Dniester into Romania. In September the Soviets began operations that completed the clearing of the Baltic states except for Courland where about 20 German divisions from *Army Group North* were incarcerated after the Soviet Army's 1st Baltic Front lived up to its name. October saw twin offensives that resulted in Soviet armies breaking into both Yugoslavia and Hungary, and the year ended with Soviet forces still on the attack, clearing German forces from northern Finland and carrying the war into occupied Norway.

In the course of this single year the Soviet high command, the Stavka, displayed a formidable level of flexibility, imagination and mastery of logistics and operational procedure at the strategic level in putting together an impressive campaign. This was characterized by constant switches between its various fronts in successive attempts to take advantage of local enemy weaknesses and to tie down the much-feared German armored formations in readiness for a renewal of the offensive in some other theater. In an unusual reversal of normal military practice, the Soviet high command in 1944 displayed a strategic acumen and skill that was unmatched at the operational and tactical level by the forces at its disposal. The various fronts, armies and divisions under command generally showed little initiative or panache in the course of their operations, yet during 1944 Soviet formations underwent a qualitative improvement that the German army in the field, if not at high command level, could not but acknowledge.

117

THE MECHANIZATION OF THE RED ARMY

The Soviet army in 1944 was a very different organization from the one that had so narrowly survived the first three campaigns in 1941 and 1942 when German mistakes as much as its own exertions proved its salvation. It was also very different from the army that had prevailed in the great defensive battles of Stalingrad and Kursk-Orel and which had gone on to clear the east bank of the Dnieper in the autumn of 1943. The Soviets themselves recognize this and even point to the time when the gradual transformation of the Soviet army was be seen for the first time to have a marked impact on the battlefield.

Indeed, Operation Bagration, the offensive in Belorussia in June 1944 (or, as it is more widely known in the west, the destruction of *Army Group Center* in the White Russian campaign) is known to the Soviets as the first modern offensive of the third phase of the war. According to the Soviets in the summer campaign of 1944 they left behind them the 'strategic defensive' and 'consolidation' phases of the war in which they had first prevailed and then secured the strategic initiative on all fronts and at all times of the year.

By June 1944 the Soviets held this initiative and were embarked upon 'strategic counter-offensive' operations designed to carry the war into the heart of Nazi Germany. All previous Soviet offensives had been characterized by poor and shallow exploitation of breakthroughs; an inability to maintain a forward momentum and lack of deep penetration of enemy rear areas; the maintenance of offensives long after their moment had passed; and a penchant for costly frontal attacks. In June 1944 the Soviet high command put together a plan of campaign that did not consign all these errors to the past but which certainly did show the emergence of an army increasingly formidable in the one area of operations – the offensive – where it had been traditionally weak.

SUCCESS IN BELORUSSIA

The Belorussian campaign was the first occasion when the Soviet army was able to orchestrate massive shock action across a wide front, to shatter enemy formations, and then to follow up with concentrated armor and mobile forces being fed through a number of breaches, in order to destroy enemy reserves and lines of communication in the rear areas.

One account of the Normandy campaign written nearly 20 years after the end of World War II asserted that in June 1944 the German army had to contend with attacks by 'a highly mechanized modern enemy in the West' and 'a horde reminiscent of Ghengis Khan or Attila, . . . a "human sea" of ragged soldiers plodding across country on foot or sweeping forward on horseback, with little transport except farm carts and American lend-lease lorries, and living off the countryside' in the East.

Much of this was true, since the motorization of the Soviet army was by no means complete in mid-1944 or even by the end of the war, but so stereotyped a picture of this latest army to descend from the steppes misses the point. In the course of 1944 the Soviet army was put on wheels – American wheels – with the result that it came into a strategic and tactical mobility that started to compare to that of western armies and which was superior to that of the bulk of the *Wehrmacht*. Soviet accounts of the Belorussia campaign acknowledge the extent to which this growing capacity for large-scale deep penetration was changing Soviet operational effectiveness and contributed to what was perhaps its greatest single victory.

According to these accounts Soviet success was not the result of superior skill or morale at the point of contact or even superiority at the strategic level. In the Soviet view success in the Belorussia campaign was the result of German errors of deployment induced by a masterly Soviet deception effort; the concentration of overwhelming firepower on enemy positions in the first phase of operations from which there could be no recovery; and the effectiveness of what were called at the time 'mobile groups' but which are now termed 'operational maneuver groups' in the breakthrough phase. These were independent formations that enjoyed a degree of mobility superior to that of the remainder of the Soviet army and, more importantly, the German defense. The Belorussia campaign is significant because it was a clash between two military concepts, one stressing defensive action and based primarily on fixed strong points and a mobile reserve, and the other stressing mobility for all aspects of the offensive.

June 1944 was significant not merely because of the changing nature of the Soviet army and its increasing effectiveness in mobile operations. This time was probably the peak of Soviet achievement in the war before Soviet stoicism, endeavor and patriotism gave way to the desperate tiredness and exhaustion of the last months of the war. In the second half of 1944 the Soviet Union drew upon its last physical, moral and manpower reserves for a final effort that left it totally exhausted; and it must always be remembered that the Soviets lost more men in the drive over the Oder and the taking of Berlin than either Britain or the United States lost in the whole of the war.

The Soviet Union lost an average of 15,000 dead or the equivalent of *one western division for every day of her war* with Nazi Germany, and as this struggle entered its fourth year the strain of such staggering losses could not be concealed. But in June 1944 there was both gain to compensate for such losses and danger in the unfolding of events. In that month Soviet forces carried out an offensive that took them deep into pre-war Poland, beyond even the old Curzon Line and the 'amended' Soviet frontier of 1940. In the same month the Stavka and military necessity ensured that the Soviet army would have to overrun most if not all of eastern Europe as an unavoidable part of the process of the defeat of Germany. Herein lay the seeds of future dispute with erstwhile allies because there was never any question of the Soviet Union's relinquishing control of enemies that she conquered or small nations that she freed from Nazi control. As the Soviets made very clear in the immediate aftermath of the Eureka conference, eastern Europe represented a Soviet sphere of influence and was nonnegotiable.

Soviet determination to hold down Germany physically and to seal off an unruly Poland had to foreshadow a momentous political and economic upheaval in eastern Europe as the inevitable consequence of the Soviet Union's search for security. The Soviet Union could only secure her sphere of influence, the buffer zone against further invasion, by using local communist parties to achieve a social revolution in eastern Europe that was possibly without parallel in its history. Probably not even the collapse of Ottoman power in the course of the nineteenth century or the destruction of Hohenzollern, Hapsburg and Romanov power in 1917 and 1918 compare to the social and political transformation that was to be put into effect in eastern Europe after 1945. It was on the brink of this massive upheaval that Soviet forces stood in the summer of 1944.

EASTERN EUROPE AND THE WEB OF ALLIANCES

As we have noted, in June 1944 there were two Soviet offensives, one in Karelia and the other in Belorussia. This naturally reflects the fact that more than one conflict was being resolved in the east though in the end all of Germany's allies and associates were dependent on her success for the little freedom they enjoyed. Italy and Spain had provided forces for the common cause in the east, and one of the little known features of the war was that more Italians were killed fighting for the Axis powers on the Eastern Front than in North Africa. But the Italians and Spaniards who were going home had long since left, and now only the Hungarians, Romanians and Finns remained in the field against the Soviets. The Bulgarians had taken the precaution of never having declared war on the USSR, though this did not prevent a Soviet declaration of war and the invasion of Bulgaria in September 1944 when Soviet forces arrived on the Danube.

By the spring of 1944, the Germans could have held few illusions about their Allies' enthusiasm for the common cause, because by that time Hungary, Romania and Finland had all approached one or more of the Allies in attempts to take themselves out of a war they knew

120

to be lost. Indeed, in March the Germans had sought to guard against an Hungarian defection by physically occupying Budapest and treating it as a guarantee of Magyar sincerity, and in the following weeks Hitler had to concede the principle of equality of command, and place some of his forces in the south under direct Romanian operational control as the price for holding Marshal Ion Antonescu's government in power and Romania in the Axis camp.

Finland remained in company only because the terms that the Soviets had insisted upon as the price of an armistice in July 1943 and again in February 1944 were so onerous that President Risto Ryti's government felt it had no option but to reject them and continue a war not of its making. But the Finns regarded themselves less the Allies of Germany as a people forced to take up arms in their own defense against a neighbor that had attacked them in both November 1939 and June 1941. The struggle that the Finns called 'The Continuation War' was one that they would willingly have ended, but with their troops deep inside Soviet territory and established as far to the east as the Svir and Lake Onega, the Finns were obliged to wait upon events that they knew would ultimately run against them.

They continued to put as much distance between themselves and the Germans as possible, and despite their dependence on Germany for arms and supplies and the presence in Lappland of Germany's *Twentieth Mountain Army*, they were very largely successful. Because of Finland's relative isolation and inaccessibility; because German forces in Finland were outnumbered and qualitatively no match for the Finns; and because the amount of aid at his disposal was limited, Hitler had little hold over the Finns.

Minor allies who used German weakness to exact otherwise unthinkable concessions while displaying a disconcerting ingratitude and unwillingness to sacrifice themselves for Germany were the least of Hitler's problems in the second quarter of 1944. By then Hitler knew that he could not achieve in 1944 the destruction of Soviet power that had eluded him in 1941, 1942 and 1943, when his forces had been stronger. He knew that he was fighting a defensive war in which he would be forced to respond to enemy moves, but he had already decided and acted upon the main features of policy.

Even after the loss of the Ukraine and the Transdniester during the winter and early spring, vast tracts of enemy territory still remained under German control in the east and in these, in the Balkans, Italy and the west, was the space that Hitler could trade for time in his attempt to achieve his primary aim. As fears for German security and the threat from the east became a reality, Hitler sought to divide enemies that he could not defeat. Hitler's aim was to cause his enemies to lose heart, to create the conditions whereby this ill-assorted alliance of imperialists, communists and capitalists would fall to pieces as a result of its own internal contradictions. To do this Hitler sought time in which to complete the process of placing the economy on a war footing and to develop the rockets, jet aircraft and new fast submarines that he believed would regain the initiative for Germany. Moreover, Hitler planned to concentrate against what he believed to be his weakest enemies, the Anglo-Americans. By defeating an Allied landing in northwest Europe Hitler sought to forestall the necessity of having to divide his main forces between two fronts.

To these ends in early 1944 Hitler stripped the Eastern Front of some of its best formations in order to strengthen the *Wehrmacht* in the west, but he did so without corresponding changes on the Eastern Front that were essential if every possible advantage of time and space was to be squeezed from the conquered territories. The reduction of the *Wehrmacht*'s power in the east had to be accompanied by a reduction of its commitments, and this could only involve withdrawals to a shorter defense line that would be more modest in its demands on manpower and resources than the requirements of present positions.

Hitler would not accept the need for withdrawals that were certain to make a bad impression on the neutrals, his Allies and the German people alike, and which would deprive him of the space that was essential to his cause. Nor would he accept the idea of conducting defensive operations in depth across this last belt of captured enemy territory. But good reason and not just wilful obstinacy lay behind Hitler's unwillingness to consider the latter course of action. The German army's overall lack of mobility made the successful conduct of a mobile defense increasingly unrealistic. In any event the rail system east of Brest lacked the carrying capacity for preparing field defenses in depth on any significant scale. Moreover, there was no evading one very awkward fact. Vast areas of the east remained under German control, but in certain crucial areas the front line was beginning to creep close to home, and there was no longer quite the freedom of action that the presence of a buffer zone should have implied.

On 2 April, 1944 the Soviets entered Romania and thereby established themselves in positions that menaced Ploesti and Germany's only major source of natural oil. At the same time the Soviets arrived in the Kovel area, thus coming within striking distance of Lvov and the direct route into eastern Germany via what had been Poland. By establishing themselves along the upper Pripet they also posed a severe threat to the German positions in the Baltic states because their forces in the Kovel-Sarny area were nearer to East Prussia and the Baltic coast at Memel than those divisions of *Army Group North* that remained in northern Estonia. The front, in fact, displayed a curiously lopsided appearance. The Germans had space in the north in which they could maneuver, but relatively little in the center and south. This situation in large part determined German strategy and tactics in the east in the spring of 1944.

HOW HITLER MISREAD THE EASTERN FRONT
As the Soviet winter and spring offensives died away, Hitler determined to hold the Minsk salient where *Army Group Center* had the *3rd Panzer*, *Fourth*, *Ninth* and *Second Armies* under command. The reasoning behind this decision was obvious and could hardly be faulted. The German retention of a position that overshadowed the Soviet re-entrance to the south served to check any Soviet inclination to move against Lvov and into Galicia. With *Army Group North Ukraine* in position between the Carpathians and the Pripet Marshes, *Army Group Center* was well placed to move against the flank and rear of any Soviet attempt to take the direct route via Lvov and Lublin into Germany, and it could even menace any Soviet move against *Army Group South Ukraine* and Romania. Thus in the spring of 1944 Hitler considered the Minsk salient and *Army Group Center* as the cornerstone of the German defenses in the east, and accordingly he took two steps to guard against the possibility of a Soviet breakthrough in this general area.

First, a series of defensive positions were prepared along the Drut, Dnieper, Berezina and Svisloch, and certain of the major towns of Belorussia were designated fortresses and assigned garrisons that were to splinter any Soviet offensive and provide the fixed points from which the Soviets might be fought to a standstill. Slutsk, Bobruysk, Mogilev, Orsha and Polotsk were each accorded a single division for their defense, Vitebsk nothing less than a reinforced corps. Second, in order to guard against the Soviets mounting an ambitious offensive on the weakness of the front (the junction of *Army Groups Center* and *North Ukraine*) with the aim of breaking from the Kovel-Sarny area towards Konigsberg, Hitler stripped the front of most of its armor and even moved *II SS Panzer Corps* from France in order to concentrate a massive strike force of ten armored and mechanized divisions in northern Galicia. It was all very logical and impressive, but also inadequate and faulty.

The most obvious weaknesses of Hitler's plan of campaign was that *Army Group Center* lacked the front-line strength and reserves to withstand major assault. It was spread over 300 miles or one-third of the front, but it had only 34 divisions in its various armies and allegedly only 40 operational fighters in support on 23 June. In most instances the only armor in panzer formations outside Galicia was in their titles, and most of the armies had no more than a solitary division in reserve. Moreover, as the spring fighting around Tarnopol had proved, the idea of fortresses was tenuous to say the least. Divisions surrounded in their fortresses quickly became liabilities that had to be supported by the *Luftwaffe*'s dwindling number of transport aircraft, and in any event they ceased to have any significant role and were effectively lost to the defense if the Soviets chose to mask and bypass rather than besiege them.

Far more serious than these weaknesses however, was the fact that Hitler made a number of errors in trying to divine Soviet intentions, with the result that the prepositioning of armor was faulty and the German anticipation of how the Soviet offensive would unfold was in error. Hitler underestimated the strength available to the Soviets and failed to take proper account of the qualitative improvement of the Soviet army in what was to be its first summer offensive. It was stronger and better than it had ever been, but Hitler kept thinking of it in terms of its 1941 and 1942 performance when its effectiveness, if not its overall strength, had been very much less. Hitler did overestimate the Stavka in one respect, however.

He believed that the Stavka would make its effort around the south of the Pripet Marshes against East Prussia and the Baltic coast – the type of grand sweeping encirclement that had characterized German offensive operations in 1941 and 1942. This was not the Soviet intention. It was at the strategic level rather than at the operational level (of a number of army groups or armies) that Soviet plans were subtle and imaginative. Having seen spring offensives come to grief in both 1942 and 1943 around Kharkov, the Soviet high command was not prepared to adopt an ambitious plan of campaign that might involve a 300-mile advance along a single axis.

Its inclination was towards a series of small offensives that would be built up into a general offensive that would rip not just *Army Group Center* but *Army Group North Ukraine* to pieces. At the operational level the Soviets planned to overwhelm *Army Group Center* with a series of massive frontal attacks and then, with the enemy forced to commit everything he could to closing this breach, to switch the point of attack with an offensive designed to shatter *Army Group North Ukraine*. In the spring of 1944 the German high command failed to grasp the nature and scale of the offensive the Soviets planned for the summer. It could not appreciate that the enemy intended to attack frontally and to run its efforts against the two most powerful German army groups in the east more or less at the same time.

THE BALANCE OF POWER: PERSONNEL AND MATÉRIEL ON THE EASTERN FRONT

In fact, in the spring of 1944 the Stavka planned to achieve much more than the destruction of *Army Groups Center* and *North Ukraine* come the summer. Between 17 and 22 April it brought offensive operations to a halt across virtually the whole front and thereafter ordered its forces to go on the defensive while waiting for the ground to dry, the reorganization of fronts to be complete, and plans for a four-fold offensive to be finalized. The Soviet intention for the summer was nothing less than the defeat of Finland; the invasion of Romania and the Balkans; and a dual attack in the center.

What enabled the Stavka to contemplate this ambitious program was an awareness that the Soviet armed forces at last held very considerable margins of superiority over an enemy estimated to have about 60 per cent of his strength in the east. By Soviet calculations, in June 1944 the Germans had four army groups with 179 divisions and five brigades on the Eastern Front, their various allies contributing another 49 divisions and 18 brigades. With a total of about 4,300,000 men in the east, the Germans were estimated to have about 59,000 guns and heavy mortars, 7,000 tanks and self-propelled guns, and 3,200 combat aircraft at the front. According to the Soviets' own figures, in June 1944 they had a total of 19,000,000 men and women under arms and a total of 133,000 guns, 11,800 tanks, 21,800 aircraft and 207 naval vessels, including 51 surface combatants, with the various armed services. Of these some 6,600,000 soldiers, 98,100 guns, 7,000 tanks and 13,000 aircraft were with the 461 rifle, airborne and cavalry divisions and 21 tank and motorized corps at the front. Such an imbalance of strength, plus the added disparity that resulted from the enforced dispersal of the defending Germans and Soviet concentration on selected axes of advance, was seen by the Stavka to be a guarantee of success.

The Soviet intention was to make its main effort against *Army Group Center* and *Army Group North Ukraine* in the belief that if these were destroyed the whole of the enemy front would be ruined beyond recall, that the destruction of *Army Group South Ukraine* and *Army Group North* would surely follow, and that the war would be carried to the borders of Germany itself. But in drawing up its plans the Stavka determined on a preliminary operation against Finland, the optimistic aim being to confuse the Germans and oblige them to reinforce this front while the more realistic objective was to remove the Finns from the ranks of the Soviet Union's enemies.

This operation was intended for the first half of June while 19 June was selected as the date for the start of operations against *Army Group Center*. This was deliberately changed to 22 June so that Bagration should mark the third anniversary of Hitler's invasion of the Soviet Union, but in the event this timetable slipped by a day. Attacks would then build up until by the end of the month and then into July there would be a general offensive against *Army Group Center* and *Army Group North Ukraine*. Thereafter the tempo of operations would be maintained with an offensive against *Army Group South Ukraine* and the Romanians. (It was to be a sign of Soviet intentions towards her southern neighbor that, despite a declared disinterest in Romania's internal affairs made in April, on 13 June the Moscow-based Romanian Communist Party, acting on the instructions of its Soviet counterpart, began to draw up plans for 'a popular uprising.')

This general timetable of offensives allowed the Stavka less than two months to complete a regrouping of forces that constituted the largest single redeployment of formations thus far attempted by the Soviet armed forces during the war. By stripping the center and south, and in particular the 2nd, and 4th Ukrainian Fronts, the Soviets moved eight combined arms, two tank and one air armies (13 tank, 11 rifle and two cavalry corps for a total of 76 divisions) into positions to strengthen the forces already in the line opposite *Army Group Center*.

By mid-June a total of 251 divisions of all types had been deployed with the fronts opposite *Army Group Center* and *Army Group North Ukraine* with no fewer than 166 of these formations, along with two independent corps and 21 brigades, concentrated with the 20 combined arms and two tank armies that made up the four Fronts committed to the attack on *Army Group Center*. The 1st Baltic, 3rd, 2nd and 1st Belorussian Fronts between them marshaled some 2,400,000 front-line troops, 30,000 guns and 5,200 tanks, and each army had an attached air army – respectively the Third, First, Fourth and Sixteenth – with another, the Sixth Air Army, held in reserve for second-phase operations only.

Between them these five armies had a total of about 6,000 aircraft of which approximately 1,000 were bombers and 2,000 were ground-attack aircraft. In addition, another 1,000 1ong-range bombers under a separate command were deployed to support Bagration. Moreover, the Stavka assigned for itself a reserve of two combined arms, one tank and one air armies. With 645,000 men under command, these mustered 9,500 artillery pieces, 1,800 tanks and self-propelled guns and 2,900 combat aircraft between them.

Even by the most cautious of standards the forces assembled for the offensive against *Army Group Center* possessed potentially overwhelming advantages over an enemy unable to discern the weight, location and direction of the coming attack. Such was the German concern for the Kovel-Lublin-Lvov sector and the Balkans that 24 of the 34 armored and mechanized divisions in the east were south of the Pripet and thus in no position to come immediately to the support of *Army Group Center*'s main forces to the north of the Marshes and in front of Minsk. The Germans had deployed a total of 63 divisions and three infantry brigades with *Army Group Center*, its two flanking armies, on anti-partisan duties and in general reserve behind the front but, as we have seen, only 34 divisions with *Army Group Center* itself. The Soviets enjoyed a minimum 4:1 advantage over the Germans in artillery, tanks and aircraft in the combat zone, but only a 2:1 advantage in manpower.

In the north Soviet margins over the Finns were much larger. To face the Soviets the Finns had 15 divisions and nine brigades, but their 268,000 troops, 1,900 guns and mortars, 110 tanks and self-propelled guns, and 248 combat aircraft were hopelessly outnumbered by an enemy whose ground force of 450,000 men, 10,000 artillery pieces and 800 tanks was supported by 2,000 combat aircraft from the air force and naval air force; and by 300 combat and amphibious ships and craft from the Baltic Fleet and the flotillas on Lakes Lagoda and Onega. These various orders of battle reveal the extent of Axis weakness and the great disparity of strength on the Eastern Front on the eve of the Soviet summer offensive. But the most significant fact is that with 1,350 combat aircraft with the three air fleets on the Eastern Front and 1,200,000 men, 9,500 artillery pieces and 900 tanks under command, *Army Group Center* had only as many guns but fewer aircraft, tanks and self-propelled guns than the Stavka had assembled in its strategic reserve.

THE SOVIETS TURN NORTH

It was partly a sign of grudging respect for the Finns that in drawing up its plans for the attacks in the north the Stavka, in an effort to ensure that the offensives on the Karelian isthmus and in Karelia were conducted with all possible speed, made special provisions that it did not repeat in Bagration. The Soviet high command believed that its forces could defeat the Finns quickly. But the danger of underestimating Finnish toughness had been learnt in the Winter War of 1939-1940, and Soviet concern for speed in the offensive was determined by the need to get behind Finnish forces and thereby prevent their conducting defense in depth in extremely difficult country. The Soviets were aware that on the Karelian isthmus the Finns had prepared defenses over depths of 70 to 110 miles along the main axes of advance. They also knew that the wilderness of lakes, rivers, swamps, forest and granite cliffs of eastern Karelia would be skilfully exploited by the Finns unless the defense was crushed at the outset and not given the chance to escape to its fall-back positions.

In an effort to ensure that the Finns would not be able to conduct a fighting withdrawal either on the Karelian isthmus or in eastern Karelia, the Soviets planned to overwhelm the enemy first-line defenses with a pulverizing artillery and air bombardment, to conduct amphibious operations in enemy rear areas with all three of their naval commands, and to use specially-raised storm units – in

127

Soviet parlance 'shock battalions' – to spearhead the attacks. In a theater of operations where the 41 divisions and five infantry brigades assembled for the offensive were roughly 30 per cent understrength with divisional establishments hovering between the 6,500 and 7,500 marks, these shock battalions were at full strength and drawn from the best and most experienced troops available. Given the obvious nature of their tasks, these units were heavily indoctrinated and in some cases the Party and the Komsomol provided up to 40 per cent establishment.

These units were to be in the vanguard of an offensive that was typically Russian in that it was to build up slowly across a wide front until a number of major formations were involved in a general attack. In the case of the Vyborg-Petrozavodsk operation the major formations numbered two, the Leningrad and Karelian Fronts. On the Karelian isthmus the Leningrad Front of General LA Govorov deployed the Twenty First and Twenty Third Armies, and was supported by General SD Rybal'chenko's Thirteenth Air Army, formations from the naval air force, the Baltic Fleet and the Lake Lagoda flotilla. On the other side of Lake Lagoda was Meretzkov's Karelian Front. It had the Seventh Army (General AN Krutikov) on the Svir between Lakes Lagoda and Onega, and the Thirty Second Army (General FD Gorelenko) in the area of Povenets, slightly to the east of the Murmansk-Kirovsk (Leningrad) railroad and the town of Medvezh'yegorsk. This Front was supported by the Seventh Air Army (General IM Sokolov) with the Lake Lagoda and Lake Onega flotillas detailed to support Seventh Army operations.

These two fronts and six armies were to carry out an offensive that would end on the Lake Tiksheozero-Sortavala-Kotka 'final line of occupation', by which time they would have achieved all Soviet objectives: to protect the northern approaches to Leningrad; to secure Vyborg; to liberate Petrozavodsk, capital of Karelia; to recover all Soviet territory lost since 1941; and to destroy if not the Finnish army then the Finns' will to resist. These objectives were to be realized by a plan of campaign that envisaged General DN Gusav's Twenty First Army opening proceedings and then to be supported by General AI Cherepanov's Twenty Third Army.

THE ATTACK BEGINS

The Seventh and Thirty Second Armies were to join in the attack at a later date, an arrangement that pointed to the simple fact that the success or failure of the operation as a whole was not going to be decided in eastern Karelia but on the Karelian isthmus, in particular on the Vyborg sector. Here the Twenty First Army had been given the task of breaking *IV Corps* on the direct and most important axes of advance into Finland. If the Finns were broken on this the strongest part of their defenses, their positions in the east were certain to become untenable sooner or later. This was a fact to which the Finns were sensitive. Even before the Soviet attack they had decided that in the event of real danger emerging on the isthmus they would draw back their *VI*, *V* and *II Corps* from the east to the River Uksu-Lake Loimola-Lake Tolva line and thereby release at least two divisions into the reserve.

The Soviet intention, as we have seen, was not to allow the Finns time for so deliberate a move, and it planned to overcome enemy resistance on the three defense lines in front of Vyborg with a single set of attacks that would shatter the Finnish formations on the isthmus before they could get back to the defenses of the Vyborg-Kuparsaari corridor. Accordingly, the Twenty First Army was much the stronger of the two armies opposite *IV* and *III Corps* with up to 80 per cent of the supporting arms and services available to the Front under command. Although the latter planned to add a touch of subtlety to proceedings with a plan to have the Baltic Fleet land five of the Twenty First Army's divisions from Orienbaum behind the Finnish front line, its overall intention and plan of campaign was very obvious. With the Twenty First Army at the outset assigned the equivalent of ten infantry and three armored divisions for a double echelon attack on a frontage of just eight miles; and with (in Finnish and German estimation) the Soviets having assembled between 600 and 800 guns for nearly every mile of front, the intention was to flatten opposition with a series of massive air and artillery bombardments and steamroller attacks.

The Vyborg-Petrozavodsk operation began on 9 June with a two-hour preliminary bombardment by the Baltic Fleet and the field artillery. Throughout the day and into the night the Thirteenth Air Army maintained the pressure on the defense with more than 1,100 sorties against enemy positions, most of its efforts being directed against the first two lines of defense that the Finns had thrown up across the isthmus.

The first, roughly matching the old pre-1939 border, was held by three divisions and a brigade, but the main line of resistance was the second line of defenses between Vammelsuu and Taipale. Here the Finns deployed another three divisions, a brigade being assigned labor duties. The Finns' third line of defense was to have run from Vyborg to Kuparsaari and then along the north bank of the Vouksi to Lake Lagoda. One armored division stood on this line at the start of the Soviet attack, but the line itself was incomplete and suffered from two weaknesses crucial to the Finnish conduct of the defense. Only 17 miles separated Vyborg from the upper Vouksi, and the river itself was crossed only by a single bridge at Kiviniemi. Thus while *IV Corps* could fall back along several lines of retreat to Vyborg, *III*

Corps on its left always stood in danger of being cut off before it could get back to Kuparsaari. Its alternative was to use the solitary bridge to escape to the north bank of the Vouksi, but this was a course of action that always threatened to involve the loss of all heavy equipment.

On 9 June the Finns had to contend only with probing attacks by the Twenty First Army, but on the following morning *IV Corps* came under heavy and sustained attack after raids on Starii Beloostrov, the Lake Svetloe position and the Rayayoki station by Soviet air and naval air units and after bombardments of Rayvola and Olila by the Baltic Fleet. Attacking in the center, three Soviet divisions annihilated one Finnish regiment and by noon opened a breach to a depth of six miles that was expanded during the course of the afternoon. Though the Finns attempted to reinforce *IV Corps* with more than a division on 10 June, they could not prevent the Soviets gaining control of most of the western part of the first defense line or from getting across the Sestra and making a general advance of about nine miles in the course of the day. On the following morning the Twenty Third Army also went over to the offensive, but it found progress difficult and had to commit an independent infantry corps to add weight to its attacks even though *III Corps* by 11 June was pulling back in order to conform to the withdrawal of *IV Corps*.

A VERY REAL DEADLINE

By the end of 12 June both formations had the bulk of their forces in the main line of resistance, but on the morning of 13 June the Soviets fought their way into this position and began to exert such pressure on *IV* and *III Corps* that the Finnish high command was obliged to commit two divisions and two brigades to the Vyborg road in order to maintain the front. It was on this day that General Axel Heinrichs, chief of staff of the army, told the Germans of the Finnish intention to pull back from Eastern Karelia and the Murmansk-Kirovsk railroad in the event of defeat on the main line of resistance.

It was also on this day that the Stavka set the Leningrad Front the deadline of 18-20 June for taking Vyborg, and, of course, under the Soviet code of conduct deadlines did have a tendency to take on a very literal meaning. In the course of the Great Patriotic War no fewer than 238 general and flag officers were shot or reduced to the ranks in penal battalions where they were killed for failing to take their objective either on time or at all. For commanders always under a suspended death sentence the lives of their subordinates could not have held very great value, and that may well have been part of the reason for the nature of the next phase of the battle.

With the price of failure – even partial success – well known in advance to any Soviet commander, the Leningrad Front and Twenty

Top: British troops in the town of Cassino in May 1944 after the fight that opened the Liri valley to an Allied advance.

Bottom left: The morning after Rome was liberated, senior commanders from the Fifth US Army tour Vatican city. In the Via Di Consiliazione with St. Peter's Cathedral in the background are Lieutenant-General Mark W. Clark and (behind him) Major-Generals Alfred M

Gruenther (Chief of Staff) and Geoffrey Keyes (Commander II US Corps).

Bottom right: The advance through the mountains of Central Italy, summer 1944. A British self-propelled gun takes a hairraising corner near Mondavio, above the Cesano valley. The awkward Italian terrain called for flexibility and imaginative use of infantry.

Top left: Field Marshal Erwin Rommel, Commander of *Heeresgruppe B*, leading a party of officers from a camouflaged position during a tour of inspection of German defences in the west in spring 1944.

Top right: The Battle for the Hedgerows was fought in ideal defensive terrain. Here scouts from the 5th/7th Gordon Highlanders cautiously explore woodland in the Bois-de-Bevent area, June 1944.

Bottom: The Allied High Command for Overlord: (sitting, left to right) Air Chief Marshal Sir Arthur Tedder (Deputy Supreme Commander), General Dwight D. Eisenhower (Supreme Commander) and General Sir Bernard L. Montgomery (Land Commander); (standing, left to right) Lieutenant-General Omar Bradley (Commander First US Army), Admiral Sir Bertram Ramsey (Naval Commander), Air Chief Marshal Sir Trafford Leigh-Mallory (Air Commander) and Lieutenant-General W. Bedell Smith (Chief of Staff of Supreme Commander).

Top left: American troops on Omaha, 6 June 1944.

Top right: Men of the 'Screaming Eagles', the 101st Airborne Division, pose for the camera with a captured German jeep in Carentan, 12 June.

Bottom: Normandy, 12 June, and the British military leadership tour the beachhead. From the left: General Sir Miles Dempsey (Commander, Second British Army), Field Marshal Sir Alan Brooke (Chief of the Imperial General Staff), Prime Minister Churchill, General Sir Bernard L. Montgomery (Commander, Twenty First Army Group) and Lieutenant-General Richard O'Connor (Commander, VIII British Corps).

Top: A Finnish mortar team head for the front with something less than enthusiasm during 'the continuation war' (1942-45). The man in the foreground carries the base-plate, the next man in line has the barrel, the next the bipod, and the foremost man of the team carries the rounds.

Bottom: Confident in the supremacy of their air cover, these T-34/85 Soviet tanks at the approach to Alitus (Lithuania) are bold enough to advance in single file along the road.

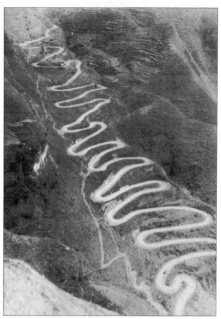

Top left: A pioneer from the *Grossdeutschland Division* engages a T-34 tank with a Panzerfaust Bazooka 'somewhere in Belorussia' allegedly on 30 June 1944.

Top right: The prize of the Salween and Burma Theater: The Burma Road. As one observer has noted, no road ever commanded so much attention and effort to so little purpose.

Middle left: Fit for traffic in fair weather only. This shot of the Tiddim-Torbung Road was taken near milepost 106 and just to the north of Tongzang, which was the scene of a major clash between the 17th Indian Division and the Japanese 33rd Infantry Division.

Bottom: Marine assault wave heads towards the beaches of Saipan. After prolonged bombardment, the first landings were made on Saipan by 2nd and 4th Marine Divisions.

Landing ships, landing craft and the landed – Saipan, June 1944. On the extreme right is an 'Alligator'; a tracked amphibious vehicle able to cross coral.

Top left: The architects of rival strategic policies. 'Pacific-First' Admiral Ernest J. King (Commander-in-Chief US Fleet and Chief of Naval Operaions) with the Allied Supreme Commander in the European Theater of Operations, General Dwight D. Eisenhower.

Top right: Admiral Jisaburo Ozawa, Commander of the 1st Mobile Fleet at The Battle of the Philippine Sea in June 1944 and last commander of the combined fleet.

Bottom: An SBD-5 Dauntless dive-bomber from USS *Lexington*'s Bomber Squadron over the amphibious forces off Saipan (15 June, 1944).

Two days after the last Banzai charge of Saipan, 2nd Marines were still encountering pockets of resistance (9 July, 1944). The defenders were flushed out with flamethrowers and grenades. To move against these positions was to enter an intricate web of sniper fire. Just over three weeks elapsed before the island was secured, and American losses numbered 16,525, of whom 12,934 were marines.

First Army had not hesitated to adjust to the relative slowness of the advance to date by trying to circumvent the main Finnish positions by a move along the coast road. But the narrowness of the front precluded any possibility of maneuver, and on 14 June another massive air and artillery attack, this time of 90 minutes' duration, heralded a set-piece attack by the Twenty First and Twenty Third Armies on well-prepared enemy positions that were covered by extensive minefields and antitank defenses. Soviet histories describe the subsequent fighting as 'ferocious', and given the fact that little fighting on the Eastern Front ever escaped so dubious an epithet, one must presume that the fighting on the Vammelsuu-Taipale position between 13 and 17 June left little to the imagination.

Such a battle, however, could only have one outcome. Though the Finns counter-attacked along various parts of the front, by 15 June the Twenty First Army had managed to break down Finnish defenses across an eight-mile sector between the sea and Kuterselka, and on 16 June the commander-in-chief of the Finnish army, Marshal Gustaf Mannerheim, ordered his forces to pull back to the last positions around Vyborg. On 17 June, however, the Soviets broke through the main line of resistance, but complete command of the second Finnish position continued to elude them until 19 June, and by then they were too late to prevent an orderly withdrawal by *IV Corps* behind Vyborg and *III Corps* to the Vouksi.

It was on this same day that the Finns formally asked the Germans for military and relief aid that had been withheld since their attempt to get out of the war in February. The Finns requested food and weapons for themselves, and asked the Germans to provide six divisions to relieve them in eastern Karelia while they stabilized the situation on the isthmus. Hitler immediately made available the *122nd Infantry Division*, a regiment of assault artillery, and two reinforced air groups from *Luftflotte 1* (behind *Army Group North* in the Baltic states) and *Luftflotte 5* (in northern Finland and Norway). Hitler promised more help which in fact he proved unable to send, but the price that he demanded for assistance was a binding military alliance that committed the Finns not to make a separate peace. Negotiations for such an undertaking lasted seven days until Ryti gave a personal commitment that, as president, he would not allow any Finnish government to begin negotiations or conclude an armistice or peace treaty with the Soviets without German consent.

The Finns regarded this promise as one exacted from them under duress, and they had no hesitation in repudiating it when the Germans proved not only unable to send the various formations they initially promised but intent on securing the return of the few they did despatch. Be that as it may, the Germans came to the aid of the Finns as early as 21 June, when the Twenty Third Army reached the

131

Vouksi and the Twenty First Army occupied Vyborg, the Finns having abandoned the city on the previous day. On 21 June the *Luftwaffe* flew almost 1,000 sorties in support of the Finns – an amazing effort in view of what was happening in Normandy and what was about to happen in Belorussia. Even without any inkling that the promised assault regiment was to arrive in Finland on 23 June and the *122nd Infantry Division* on 28 June, the Stavka could have been forgiven if on 21-22 June it thought that at least a part of its diversionary effort in the north was having its planned and intended effect.

FINLAND AND THE SOVIET UNION STILL LOCKED IN COMBAT

It was inevitable after 21 June that Bagration should overshadow the Vyborg-Petrozavodsk operation, but the start of the Belorussian campaign and the fall of Vyborg by no means brought an end to operations in the north. In fact, 21 June saw the extension of Soviet operations as the Leningrad Front received fresh orders and the Karelian Front went over to the offensive. Reinforced by the arrival of the Fifty Ninth Army, the Leningrad Front was instructed to resume the offensive between 26 and 28 June with the aim of securing the Imatra-Lappenranta-Virojoki line, all of which places were beyond the 1940 border. The enemy was to be cleared from north of the Vouksi – in fact *III Corps* still had a bridgehead to the *south* of the river – and to secure Keksgol'm (present-day Priozersk) and Elisenvaara on the northeast of Lake Lagoda. In the meantime the Karelian Front was to attack with Petrozavodsk as the target of the Seventh Army and Povenets and Medvezh'yegorsk the objectives of the Thirty Second Army.

The Soviet attempt to maintain the Leningrad Front's offensive proved unsuccessful. On 25 June an assault with ten infantry divisions in the Repola area brought a gain of just $2^1/_2$ miles, and by 28 June the Finns had been able to seal off but not eliminate this bridgehead. Along the Vouksi the Soviets made little progress though the Twenty Third Army was able to eliminate the Finnish bridgehead south of the river and to establish one of its own on the far bank. On the western sector the Soviets did little better and suffered a minor defeat in trying to hasten along a Twenty First Army advance that covered just six miles in the first ten days of July. After the seizure of the islands of Linosaari and Tuokkola in the B'yorsky Archipelago (in Vyborg Bay) by the Baltic Fleet at the end of June, the Soviets attempted to establish a beachhead on the far shore of the Bay with an assault landing during the first week of July. This had the misfortune to take place at the very time as the *122nd Infantry Division* was moving through the assault area on its way to the front.

Between the start of the Soviet offensive and mid-July the Finns lost about 36,000 troops, roughly half of these in the 'quiet' phase after 21 June. The Finns themselves attributed their relative success on the Karelian isthmus in this second phase of operations to a combination of three factors: an influx of German bazookas and antitank grenades that for the first time gave their infantry a genuine antitank capability; a very sharp reduction in the performance of Soviet infantry in the course of the battle (despite there being about 23 divisions on the isthmus by 21 June and 30 by mid-July); and a definite down-grading of the Soviet effort during and after the second week of July.

This affected the infantry, the better Soviet formations being taken from the front and replaced by defense units, but more particularly the artillery and air support. The Soviets themselves considered that the effectiveness of these two arms had been the key to their early success, and it was this artillery-air formula that they relied upon for results when the Seventh Army attacked across the Svir at Lodeynoye Pole on 21 June. Backed by a Seventh Air Army that flew 642 sorties during the day, the Seventh Army punched a bridgehead ten miles wide and five miles deep over the river, secured Podporozhie, and confirmed the Finns in their view that they should begin to withdraw *VI* and *V Corps* back to the Uksu.

On the same day the Thirty Second Army advanced ten miles to capture Povenets, but thereafter its advance on Modvezh'yegorsk slowed as the Finns covered their withdrawal (and the despatch of formations from their *4th* and *6th Infantry Divisions* from this sector to the isthmus) by demolitions and tree-felling across the forest tracks. On 23 June, after criticism by Moscow of the speed and conduct of operations, the Karelian Front redefined its two armies' objectives. The Seventh Army was instructed to divide its attention between Olonets and Pitkyaranta in the west, on the eastern shore of Lake Lagoda, and Kotkozero and Krasnaya Pryazha, to the east. The Thirty Second Army was ordered to secure Suvilakhti and Kondopoga. The general aim of the Karelian Front was to mount a converging attack on Petrozavodsk with the Seventh Army advancing from the south, the Thirty Second Army closing in from the north, and the Lake Onega flotilla closing the ring from the east with amphibious landings at Derevyannaya on 28 June.

But 23 June did not pass without some advances and gains. The Thirty Second Army overcame last-ditch resistance on the part of rearguards from the *6th Infantry Division* in Modvezh'yegorsk, and the Lake Lagoda flotilla sought to offset disappointment on the Leningrad Front with an assault landing by the 70th Naval Rifle Brigade between the Tuloksa and Vidlitsa, this operation being timed to coincide with a major effort by the Seventh Army from its bridgehead over the Svir. Though the marines were put ashore safely and were able to cut the track forward to Olonets, the Finns reacted strongly to this landing in their rear and on 24 June the Soviets had to put ashore a second naval brigade to support the hard-pressed 70th. But at this stage such matters were little more than minor inconveniences for the Soviets.

On 25 June the Seventh Army secured Olonets and two days later it was astride the Vidlitsa in pursuit of an enemy now intent on getting *VI Corps* behind the Uksu and *V Corps' 11th* and *17th Infantry Divisions* to the isthmus. On 28 June Petrozavodsk was liberated and the direct Murmansk-Leningrad line cleared for the first time since October 1941. Thereafter the Soviets continued to advance across a roadless waste until 21 July when they arrived on the border. Operations in the area continued until 9 August with neither side really anxious to persist with operations clearly drawing to a close.

On 1 August Ryti had resigned, and by then the Finns had been given the word via the Swedes that they could be assured of a peace settlement that would leave their country's independence and political institutions intact. With Karelia reduced to a backwater and the focus of attention switched away from the north, the Soviet interest was to end a campaign that had been a liability to all concerned and to concentrate on operations in the west and south. The terms that Finland were to be granted under the armistice of 19 September, the peace treaty of 10 February 1947, and the Finnish-Soviet mutual assistance treaty of 6 April 1948 were harsh, but she avoided occupation and reduction to the status of client state of the Soviet Union – a fate that befell every one of Germany's European allies with the single exception of Italy.

BELORUSSIA – THE HEART OF THE MATTER

The Stavka regarded the Belorussia offensive as the key to success in the summer campaign. It believed that the viability of operations planned for late summer and autumn depended on the outcome of Bagration, and, as we have seen, in order to ensure success in this offensive, it assembled a potentially overwhelming superiority of force opposite Field Marshal Ernst Busch's *Army Group Center*.

The Stavka plan of campaign, formally approved on 30 May and issued to subordinate commands the following day, called for an offensive across a 300-mile front between Polotsk and Bobruysk by General Ivan Bagramyan's 1st Baltic Front, General
Ivan Chernyakovsky's 3rd Belorussian Front, General Matvei Zakharov's 2nd Belorussian Front, and General Konstantin Rokossovsky's 1st Belorussian Front. The aim of this offensive was to eliminate the Minsk salient with its enemy forces, to clear

Belorussia, and to advance to the Vistula and the German border. With air force and partisan units allocated vital reconnaissance, interdiction and support roles, Bagration was to be spearheaded by the 3rd and 1st Belorussian Fronts which together were assigned 65 per cent of the personnel, 63 per cent of the artillery and heavy mortars, 70 per cent of the tanks and self-propelled guns, and 73 per cent of the aircraft assembled in the four fronts and five air armies committed to this offensive.

The general Soviet intention was that the 1st Baltic Front should operate as flank guard and that the 2nd Belorussian Front should be in a supporting role between the 3rd and 1st Belorussian Fronts. These latter were to be the two arms of a pincer that were to close behind Minsk. With the Soviets in effect carrying out two separate but complementary efforts, Marshal Aleksander Vasilevsky (chief of staff) was to preside over the operations of the 1st Baltic and 3rd Belorussian Fronts while the Deputy Supreme Commander-in-Chief, Marshal Georgi Zhukov, watched over those of the 2nd and 1st Belorussian Fronts.

The Soviet plan of campaign and general intentions were shaped by the fact that Belorussia was both a natural and man-made wasteland. A region roughly the size of Britain or West Germany, Belorussia had very few roads, almost all of which were poor quality, but a great deal of swamp, rivers and forest. As many as a quarter of its pre-war population of about 8,000,000 had died under the German occupation, and it has been estimated that total industrial and agricultural output in 1944 stood at 5 per cent of its 1940 level. Soviet histories give lists of damage that would seem as endless as the damage itself, suffice to note that it was across this devastated area that the Soviets planned to advance in June-July 1944.

The Soviets drew up their plans in the knowledge that while the Germans had prepared defenses on certain axes over a distance of 170 miles, they only had enough strength for a single echelon defense. Moreover, while they knew that all the main roads would be covered by 'hedgehogs' or 'fortresses' in the major towns, there would still be routes through 'the Fatherland Line' that could be used with adequate sapper support. In addition, the Soviets knew that the Germans had virtually no armored reserve immediately available for the counter-attack. They were also aware from German dispositions that they had misread Soviet intentions.

The Soviets therefore put together a plan of campaign that envisaged the 1st Baltic Front destroying enemy opposition along the Vitebsk-Lepel axis and the 3rd Belorussian Front sweeping aside the Germans on the Vitebsk-Orsha sector. With the right wing of Bagramyan's 1st Baltic Front committed to holding the hard shoulder around Polotsk, his left wing and the right of

Chernyakhovsky's 3rd Belorussian Front were to sweep around either side of Vitebsk and thereby complete the encirclement of the town and the annihilation of its garrison. The main effort of Chernyakhovsky's command, however, was to be on the left in the form of a two-pronged drive against Senno and Borisov. The long-term objective of the 3rd Belorussian Front was Minsk, Molodechno and the road to Vilna, Kovno and Konigsberg. Whereas General NF Papivin's Third Air Army was able to concentrate in support of the single axis advance of the 1st Baltic Front, General TT Khryukin was obliged to divide his First Air Army in order to cover the divergent thrusts of the 3rd Belorussian Front, 11 of his divisions being assigned to the Orsha sector and the remaining six to the north.

In the center, Zakharov's 2nd Belorussian Front, with just three armies under command and assigned to mopping-up duties after the battle of the salient had been won, was to break down the Mogilev position and to press forward to the Berezina, therefore securing the right flank of the 1st Belorussian Front as it set about the reduction of Bobruysk. Rokossovsky's command was to make its effort on the right of its sector from the Rogachev beachhead, and after the capture of Bobruysk it was to divide its effort between the Pukhovichi-Minsk and the Slutsk-Baranovichi axes. As with the forces under Vasilevsky's overall direction, the air armies allocated to the two fronts south of the Orsha-Minsk high road alternatively concentrated and dispersed their forces. General KA Vershuin's 4th Air Army was concentrated in order to help the 2nd Belorussian Front achieve its rather narrowly proscribed objectives, but the Sixteenth Air Army of General SI Rudenko had 13 of its divisions assigned to the Minsk axis and seven to the intended thrust to the west.

REMARKABLE FACETS OF OPERATION BAGRATION

A number of new or notable features were incorporated into this plan of campaign, but only two of them were directly related to ground force practice. First, as we have noted, Bagration saw the first large-scale employment of 'mobile groups' that were intended to develop the offensive by operations deep in the enemy rear areas. Such groups consisted of two corps, one armored or mechanized and the other horsed. Their relatively small size ensured flexibility, and in the rough terrain of western Russia the cavalry proved very effective throughout the war. Second, whereas the 1st Baltic and 3rd Belorussian Fronts were afforded a single creeping barrage that was to last between two hours and 140 minutes, the 2nd and 1st Belorussian Front were granted the privilege of the first double creeping barrage ever carried out by the Soviet army. This was to be carried out over a depth of a mile and for a period of 90 to 120 minutes. With between 150 and 204 guns and between 12 and 20 tanks in a direct infantry-support role for every kilometer of attack frontage, the Soviets had a rough 10:1 advantage on their selected axes of advance and a tactical doctrine that enabled them to make the most of their material superiority.

A third novel feature of this operation involved an air force which was assigned roles and adopted practices that were important in the development of Soviet offensive concepts. Thus far in the war Soviet aviation had not been very effective. Its crippling early losses, a high rate of attrition resulting from having to commit inadequately trained pilots into the fight, and the generally low quality of Soviet aircraft, ensured that at least for the first two years of the war in the east, the *Luftwaffe* was able to give battle on a minimum basis of equality. But by June 1944 this situation had changed, mainly due to the destruction of German air power in the west. The eclipse of the *Luftwaffe* over the *Reich* resulted in a catastrophic decline of its effectiveness over every front, and in the east this came at the time when the Soviet air force was becoming an efficient entity.

Bagration saw three significant advances in Soviet air force practice. First, though the Soviets lacked bombers with the range, payload and sophistication of those of the Americans or British, in support of Bagration they made an intense effort to strike deeply behind the enemy front in an interdiction role and against enemy airfields. This they had been doing throughout the war, but in June 1944 they were to do so on a scale and with tactical formations (recognizably similar to those of the Americans) that made this particular operation a notable stepping stone for the air force. Second, in the course of the offensive the air force provided immediate tactical air support for the ground forces. This was new. It had previously been tasked to secure air supremacy over the battlefield and to operate against preselected targets. It had not had the means to provide the type of close air support that was so readily available to the Allied armies in Normandy with such aircraft as the Typhoon.

By 1944, however, the Soviets were beginning to acquire the communications and technique that enabled them to carry out the close support role, and herein was the third development. By mid-1944 the Soviet air force was in some small way beginning to decentralize and adopt command arrangements that provided it with previously unknown flexibility and effectiveness. At army level commanders were under orders to issue only the broadest of instructions to subordinate commands and to dispense with the close scrutiny of operational detail that had always been a characteristic of Soviet command procedure. For armed forces that used a language that had no equivalent for 'initiative', because the concept itself was alien to a society that had always been rigidly hierarchical, the inauguration of such arrangements was a major development of operational procedure.

While the final arrangements of the Fronts neared completion, Bagration opened with air force attacks on enemy rear areas and a deliberately orchestrated attempt by the partisan groups in the Minsk salient to destroy German communications. Most of the air effort was concentrated into the 1,472 sorties that were flown on four night attacks between 13 and 18 June against German airfields near Bobruysk, Minsk, Baranovichi, Pinsk, Bialystok, Brest and Luminets, the Soviets claiming that in these operations they attacked bases that housed some 60 per cent of the strength of *Luftflotte 6*.

More significant were the activities of the partisans. An estimated 143,000 people served with the 199 brigades and independent detachments in Belorussia at the time of Bagration, and one of the features of the war in the east was that the effectiveness of such formations was at its greatest when the Soviet ground forces least needed it. In the dark days of 1941 and 1942 partisan activity had been fitful, but in 1944, with the tide of war clearly turned against the occupier and the Soviet army on the offensive, the partisans were in positions to conduct reconnaissance, carry out attacks on German lines of communication, mark and protect river crossing sites, and generally engage in activities intended to draw German strength away from the front line.

It was the partisans who informed Soviet planners of German defensive preparations in many sectors and who, in the three days immediately before the offensive, carried out a series of attacks throughout the Minsk salient. An estimated 5,000 mines were laid on roads and railroads behind the *Second* and *Fourth Armies* alone, and while the planned 40,000 operations in enemy rear areas proved far too ambitious a program, an estimated 10,500 attacks were made against various types of targets throughout the salient. Little direct loss was inflicted upon the Germans, but by concentrating much of their attention against land lines, the partisans brought the rail system to the verge of chaos even before Bagration began. Because the railroad had no means of communication other than by telephone, German troop movements slowed and in some areas stopped in the days immediately before the start of the Soviet offensive.

THE FIRST SOVIET ONSLAUGHT

As this slow paralysis began to affect *Army Group Center*, Bagration opened on 22 June with preliminary reconnaissance by the 1st Baltic and the 3rd and 2nd Belorussian Fronts. In accordance with normal Soviet practice, 'reconnaissance by battle' involved an approach to contact by fighting groups, anything up to unit-sized and with armor in support. Their objective was to draw enemy fire and thereby reveal enemy positions to the artillery. In some places reconnaissance was pushed forward to depths of four miles before being brought to a halt, but the obvious indication of an offensive against *Third Panzer Army* led the German high command to commit one of its reserve divisions around Polotsk to *Army Group Center* and the latter in turn to support *Third Panzer Army* with a single infantry division from its reserve.

Thus the Germans fell into the error of weakening an already inadequate reserve even before the Soviet air force opened its account with bombing raids during the night of 22-23 June by more than 400 bombers in the sectors opposite the 3rd and 2nd Belorussian Fronts. On the following morning the main attacks began, the 1st Baltic and 3rd Belorussian Fronts starting with a series of heavy air and artillery attacks, the 2nd Belorussian Front having . to forego significant air support. On the Polotsk-Vitebsk sector the 1st Baltic Front, attacking with the 6th Guards and Forty Third Armies, registered an advance of ten miles on a 20-mile front on 23 June, and on its left flank the 3rd Belorussian Front, attacking on the other side of Vitebsk with the Thirty Ninth and Fifth Armies, secured a bridgehead eight miles deep over some 20 miles of the Luchesa.

On the Orsha sector, where the Soviets knew the Germans to be strongly positioned, the 3rd Belorussian Front's 11th Guards and Thirty First Armies made little headway, and on their left the 2nd Belorussian Front fared little better. Its Forty Ninth Army was able to record an advance of about five miles on an eight-mile front in the general direction of Mogilev, but other than that Lieutenant-General Kurt von Tippelskirch's *Fourth Army* was able to hold on to most of its positions during the day.

Its relative success on 23 June could not disguise three facts, however; that Soviet pressure in the two most important sectors of its front increased during the day and showed no signs of slackening; that it became all but separated from the *Third Panzer Army* during the day as the latter reeled back on either side of Vitebsk; and that the full weight of the enemy offensive remained to be developed. The last point was one which *OKH* and Hitler refused to accept on 23 June.

The German high command still believed that an attack on *Army Group Center* would be a diversion intended to support an offensive led by the 3rd Ukrainian Front into Romania, and not even the 1st Belorussian Front's preliminary reconnaissance on 23 June alerted the high command to the reality of the situation. No immediate action was taken to deal with Busch's warning that the *Third Panzer Army* would not be able to restore its front unless it gave up Vitebsk and thereby release the corps in the town for mobile operations.

Unwilling to weaken the *Second Army* in the one quiet sector of the front on the upper Pripet, *Army Group Center* had problems of over-commitment that only increased on 24 June when Rokossovsky's Third and Forty Eighth Armies attacked in the direction of Bobruysk on a 20-mile front from the Rogachev-Zhiobin sector. During 24 June these armies recorded an advance of about 12 miles, but their success was upstaged by that of the armies around Vitebsk. The 1st Baltic Front, attacking along the operational boundary of *Army Groups Center* and *North*, reached the Dvina and then set about detaching the *Third Panzer Army* from its northern neighbor, the *Sixteenth Army*. On the *Third Panzer Army*'s other flank Senno had to be abandoned, and the 3rd Belorussian Front, freed from any concern about Vitebsk, prepared to advance along the Minsk highway and thereby turn the left flank of the *Fourth Army*. This formation was already under pressure both around Mogilev and on its right flank because of the 1st Belorussian Front's drive against the *Ninth Army*. With the front already beginning to look like a sieve, General Kurt Zeitzler, the chief of the general staff, paid a lightning visit to Minsk before flying to Berchtesgaden with a report that suggested that *Army Group Center* could withdraw or be shattered in the positions it presently occupied.

On 24 June *Army Group Center* itself chose to order the *Fourth Army* to maintain its position despite the pressure it was under, but the real issue that faced the German high command was whether or not to evacuate Vitebsk. The *Third Panzer Army* had one-third of its strength, the *4th* and *6th Luftwaffe Field* and *206th* and *246th Infantry Divisions*, in Vitebsk, and it had no means of stabilizing its front unless these could break out of the town and rejoin. It was not until the early evening that Hitler gave permission for *LIII Corps* to break out, and then he stipulated that one division should be left behind to continue to deny the town to the Soviets.

This decision was nonsense because one division could not succeed where four had failed, but the real error was in the lateness of this ruling. By the time *LIII Corps* was able to attempt the break out, the Thirty Ninth Army had thrown a ring around the town that was too strong to be broken. On 26 and 27 June the complete corps was annihilated, the town of Vitebsk itself being liberated on 26 June. Thus between the second and fourth days of the enemy offensive the Germans lost their strongest single position in the Fatherland Line.

THE WRITING ON THE WALL FOR
ARMY GROUP CENTER

Even before the final battle of annihilation around Vitebsk began there was clear evidence that the whole of *Army Group Center* was in desperate trouble. By 25 June it had committed its reserve without having stopped or even slowed the Soviets on any single axis of advance. With little possibility of substantial reinforcement for about one week, *Army Group Center*'s reaction to the situation in which it found itself was a display of what was either *sang froid* or *rigor mortis*. On 25 June, when Berlin acknowledged Soviet success before Mogilev, on the Minsk-Smolensk highway and around Vitebsk and admitted that its forces were involved in a 'heavy defensive struggle,' Busch countermanded von Tippelskirch's order to his *Fourth Army* to pull back and at the same time refused Lieutenant-General Hans Jordan's *Ninth Army* permission to withdraw from its positions east of the Berezina.

Faced with disaster on all points, *Army Group Center*'s initial response to events was to order an unyielding resistance on every front and to concur with Jordan's dismissal. This decision to maintain present positions came just at the time when the Soviets increased the tempo of their operations by feeding armor on a large scale into the battle. In their initial efforts the Soviets had relied on their two traditional mainstays, the infantry and artillery, to smash a way through the enemy defensive system. In June 1944 the Soviets had not yet discarded their practice of using divisions until total annihilation.

This practice was becoming less common as the high command generally preferred to rotate formations and top them up with replacements before their effectiveness was irrevocably impaired. But in June 1944 it was not uncommon for a badly depleted division, down to regimental strength, to be assigned first a full division's worth of artillery and second – the bad news – a shock role on an attack frontage of half a mile or less. The expectation was that such a formation would be destroyed in making a break-in, if it made one at all, but that the second echelon would be able to pass through the debris, open a breach, consolidate and then allow the armor to exploit through the gap.

In preparing for Bagration the Soviets had concentrated their attention on the organization, training and indoctrination not of the first-echelon formations, but those of the second-echelon and units likely to be at point in assault river crossings. By 25 June these specially-prepared formations had more or less completed their tasks and the Soviets were beginning to pass their armor through the many breaches in the German front. The 1st Belorussian Front had the 1st Guards and 9th Tank Corps, plus one mobile group, under command in the immediate theater of operations, while the 1st Baltic Front had only the 1st Tank Corps in support. Zakharov's 2nd Belorussian Front was afforded no specific armored formation. In view of the amount of armor the Soviets had on hand and were beginning to push into the battle on and after 25 June, it was somewhat ironic that Moscow chose this day to announce that thus far in the war the Soviet armed forces had lost 49,000 tanks – plus 48,000 guns, 30,000 aircraft and 5,300,000 killed, wounded and missing.

A TIDAL WAVE OF SOVIET ARMOR

The quickening pace of operations after 25 June as ever more Soviet armor was committed to the offensive had two immediate effects. The Germans found that successive attempts to reorganize and withdraw were superseded by Soviet advances. And, the Soviets moved into positions from which to complete the destruction of the various garrisons on the Fatherland Line. Between them, these two developments ensured that by 28 June, when Busch was relieved of his command, *Army Group Center* was beyond recall. Orsha had been lost the previous day, Polotsk came under mounting pressure and Mogilev was lost on 28 June itself, and Bobruysk and most of its garrison were lost to the German high command within the next 24 hours. Moreover, all semblance of order and command within the area of operations was breaking down under the sheer weight and fury of Soviet attacks.

General Georg-Hans Reinhardt's *Third Panzer Army* by this stage was in the process of being divided into three very separate parts as its center lost contact with both flanks while its right, shattered by the close encirclement of Orsha by the 2nd Tank Corps and the deep penetration beyond Tolochin by the Fifth Guards Tank Army, was driven into the *Fourth Army*'s area of responsibility. At the same time the *Fourth Army* found that on its right the left flank of the *Ninth Army* was similarly forced to intrude into its sector after Jordan's army was split in front of Bobruysk on 27 June, the town itself being surrounded when the pincer formed by the 9th and 1st Guards Tank Corps closed just short of Osipovichi.

In fact, by this time both the *Fourth* and *Ninth Armies* were caught in a pattern of defeat strikingly similar to the one that had overwhelmed the *Third Panzer Army* around Vitebsk. On 25 June the *Fourth Army* was ordered to hold its present positions, but on 27 June it was first given discretion to pull back to the Drut and then ordered to withdraw to the river while still holding Orsha (which fell that day) and Mogilev. Finally, on 28 June, the *Fourth Army* was given the right to withdraw behind the Berezina and to cede Mogilev. By that time Mogilev had been lost and the 2nd Belorussian Front's Forty Ninth Army, having crossed the Dnieper on 26 June, had managed to reach Berezino (and the only bridge over the Berezina between Mogilev and Minsk) in advance of much of the *Fourth Army*.

The *Ninth Army*, as we have seen, attempted to pull back from the

Berezina and Bobruysk as early as 25 June, only to be told to stand where it was. On 27 June, when Bobruysk was encircled, the *Ninth Army* was ordered first to withdraw, then to maintain its positions, and finally to pull back but to leave a garrison in Bobruysk. Hitler ordered *Army Group Center* on 28 June to hold a line either side of Berezino despite the fact that the *Third Panzer Army* had been pushed well to the west of it and that the greater part of the 1st Belorussian Front had never been to the east of such a line at any time during the offensive. The least that could be said about the German conduct of operations was that its quality appears to have deteriorated rapidly after a poor start.

On 28 June, as the scale of the Soviet offensive and the disaster facing *Army Group Center* impressed itself on the German high command for the first time and it was realized that Minsk was under real threat, Hitler reorganized his commands in the east. Busch was dismissed and Field Marshal Walter Model was appointed in his place while still retaining command of *Army Group North Ukraine*. So unusual a combination of two commands in a single person was justified on the basis that command of both *Army Group Center* and *Army Group North Ukraine* would allow Model to switch formations between the two. The German high command by this time had realized that an enemy offensive against *Army Group North Ukraine* in the near future was more than a distinct possibility, but that this command alone had the armor that might yet stabilize *Army Group Center*'s front and still be in a position to counter any enemy move against the Lvov-Lublin sector. The policy of robbing Peter to pay Paul was one that carried with it very obvious risks, but given German overcommitment and lack of reserve, there was no real alternative. The only other possibility for Hitler was to pull back *Army Group North* from Estonia and Latvia and thereby free divisions – but little armor – into the reserve. It has been suggested that a contributory factor in Model's appointment was Hitler's determination to avoid this very course of action.

Command over forces that extended across more than half the Eastern Front could not disguise the fact that Model had been dealt a losing hand on 28 June. On that date *Army Group Center* at last parted company with *Army Group North*, and by 1 July a gap of more than 50 miles separated their closest formations. On 28 June the Soviet advance lapped around Polotsk and reached Berezino, and on the following day the 3rd Belorussian Front reached Borisov while to the south the 1st Belorussian Front, in completing the destruction of *XXXXI Panzer* and *XXXV Corps* at Bobruysk, advanced as far as Slutsk. By 1 July Chernyakhovsky's forces were through Borisov and heading both for and past Minsk, the Fifth Guards Tank Army carrying out the close investment of the city while the Eleventh Guards Army on its right aimed for Molodechno.

Rokossovsky's formations, on the other side of Minsk, had cleared Slutsk and were heading for Bobovnya on the road to Baranovichi, and even by dawn on the next day (2 July), when the Soviet Forty Eighth Army reached and secured Stolbtsy in front of the Germans, the *Fourth Army*'s rearguard had yet to recross the Berezina and its advance units had still to reach Minsk. Minsk itself fell on 3 July, Baranovichi the following day, and with the fall of these two towns the German defense had to face up to one disconcerting fact: the Soviet offensive showed no signs of slackening as it neared Minsk. By normal Soviet criteria the impetus of the offensive should have been slackening by this time since by 3 July, Soviet forces would have been in action for anything up to 11 days and had advanced between 125 and 160 miles. Equally serious for the defense was the fact that surrounded German forces showed little ability either to tie down disproportionately large enemy forces or to break out.

On all too many occasions in the past both sides had been unable to prevent at least part of an encircled enemy force from slipping away because of a lack of infantry, but in June and July 1944 the Soviets showed a disconcerting ability to move their infantry into position very quickly. At Bobruysk the Germans did manage to fight their way into an encircled position and bring out a part of their garrison, but this was very much the exception and there was no such reprieve for the five corps of the *Fourth* and *Ninth Armies* trapped between Minsk and the Svisloch and Berezina rivers. The annihilation of these formations occupied the Soviets between 5 and 11 July, but even in that time the front-line moved much further to the west. By 6 July the 3rd Belorussian Front was through Molodechno, and within another two days the Fifth Guards Tank Army was setting up yet another encirclement of enemy forces, this time at Vilna. (That particular engagement, resulting in the destruction of the equivalent of two German divisions, was concluded on 13 July.)

In the center the Thirty First Army secured Lida and in the south the Sixty Fifth and Twenty Eighth Armies combined to take Baranovichi, both towns falling on 8 July. What made the fall of Vilna, Lida and Baranovichi so significant was the fact that these were places Model selected as the centers of resistance on the second of two lines that he intended to defend. His initial intention had been to hold the Dvinsk-Molodechno-Stolbtsy- Baranovichi line, but this purpose had been thwarted by the speed with which the first three places fell. In any event Model's attempt to seal the front by assembling one light, one infantry and three panzer divisions along the Dvinsk-Baranovichi line by 4 July was totally inadequate. The

German front had been destroyed over 250 miles of its length, and five divisions, however strong, were insignificant compared to Germany's needs.

In this situation von Schwappenberg's observation made about the Normandy front at the end of June to the effect that the time for trying to improvize a continuous rigid front was over, was even more appropriate; and its poignancy was only increased by the fact that even before the fighting around Vilna died away the Soviets had widened their offensive with disastrous results for *Army Group Center*'s neighbors. On 12 July the 3rd and 2nd Baltic Fronts joined an attack that was to result in the 1st Baltic Front briefly establishing itself on the Gulf of Riga at the end of the month. On 13 July the reorganized left wing of the 1st Belorussian Front and the 1st Ukrainian Front opened an offensive that was to carry the front to the Carpathians, the borders of Slovakia and Hungary, and to the Vistula and Narew, but those events are another story.

WORSE THAN STALINGRAD

The contemporary German record assessed its losses in the Belorussian campaign at 300,000 killed, wounded and missing, and Guderian subsequently stated that in this single offensive 25 German divisions were destroyed. Some acounts have suggested that German losses were slightly higher. The fact that 31 of the 47 corps and divisional commanders involved in this battle on the German side were taken prisoner or missing at the end of the offensive was indication enough of the completeness of the Soviet victory in Belorussia.

Bagration stands out as one of the most comprehensive Allied victories of the war, and on the Germans' own account the defeat was worse than Stalingrad. What made the Belorussian defeat so much worse than that on the Volga was not just the heavier losses that *Army Group Center* incurred but the fact that there could be no recovery from them. After the loss of the *Sixth Army* in February 1943 there had been the recovery in front of Kharkov in the spring. Now, in the summer of 1944, the Germans were fast running out of space in which they could let enemy offensives exhaust themselves, and they were even more quickly running out of men with which to replace their losses.

In June and July the *Wehrmacht* suffered more than 620,000 casualties, half of which were incurred by *Army Group Center* in the course of the Belorussian campaign. The missing accounted for almost half the German losses of these two months, and herein lies a small and thoroughly vicious postscript to the campaign in Belorussia. Upwards of 10,000 German soldiers are thought to have evaded immediate capture by the Soviets in the Minsk salient and to have set out westwards in an attempt to get back to friendly lines. About 800 are believed to have made home-runs as they, stay-behind parties, local nationalist groups, bandits, and agents of the London-based Polish government-in-exile were hunted down with equal impartiality and extreme ruthlessness over the weeks, months and even years to come by tracker teams organized by the secret police, the NKVD.

This counter-intelligence effort in recently-cleared and foreign territory was organized by a little-known branch of the service called Smersh. It is one of the more surprising features of Soviet historiography and literature that rather than keeping this whole episode very quiet, the occasional publication lionizes this organization as guardians of the revolution, true friends of the people. Such works invariably gloss over what Smersh and NKVD teams in general did to Poles and others who were unconvinced by the promises of the Soviet liberations. In Poland and in certain parts of the Ukraine where nationalists remained active even as late as 1947, the NKVD was distinguishable from the *Gestapo* and *SS* only by the differences of uniform. A little book entitled *August 1944* gives a factional account of Smersh activity in the Belorussian and Polish rear areas after the battle had moved westward and its dedication to Smersh makes interesting if not quite original reading: 'To the few to whom so much is owed by so many'. With, it is estimated, Smersh firing squads and the Gulags accounting for one third of all Soviet wartime losses, the validity of at least some of this dedication cannot be denied.

PART THREE

THE WAR IN ASIA
AND
THE PACIFIC

CHAPTER 1

STRATEGIC BACKGROUND

In January 1943 the Japanese prime minister, General Hideki Tojo, warned the Imperial Diet that the next 12 months would be 'the year of decisive battles'. At the end of the year, just after the loss of the Gilberts, Tojo warned the same assembly that 'the real war is only just beginning'. For the 'real war' to begin after the 'decisive battles' had been fought seems a contradiction of terms, but the 'real war' was about to start only because by the beginning of 1944 the 'decisive battles' had been lost.

There is one historical view which suggests that Japan was doomed to defeat from the time she went to war with the United States in 1941. But at least until the beginning of 1943 the Japanese high command could delude itself into thinking that even if things were not working exactly to plan it might yet be successful in realizing its basic war aim. Japan had never intended to defeat the United States, an aim that she knew to be beyond her. She sought to wear down the Americans and her other enemies until they were ready to accept a compromise that would leave her with control of her conquests in east and southeast Asia. In the first 20 months of the war situation maps could convey the impression that such an aim might indeed be within Japan's grasp.

For example, on 7 August 1942 American forces invaded Guadalcanal in the southern Solomons but it was not until 30 June 1943 that they were able to land on Rendova in the New Georgia group, in the Trobriand Islands and near Salamaua. If such a rate of advance was maintained, decades rather than years would pass before the Allies neared the Japanese homeland but appearances were deceptive. Japan had conquered easily, and then in a series of ferocious exchanges that were costly to the navies of both sides she maintained herself along a defensive perimeter that when established in 1942 had marked the extent of her conquests. It was along this perimeter that her initiative had died amid the drag of the miles and the strength of her enemies. This perimeter testified for a time to the mutual exhaustion of the combatants.

By December 1943, however, exhaustion was no longer mutual. In the course of 1943 the Americans added a growing qualitative advantage to their rapidly expanding quantitative superiority over Japan, and at the end of the year they were poised to carry the war into the western Pacific, through the various Japanese defensive positions in the central and southwest Pacific. Unlike the Japanese, in 1942 and 1943 the Americans were able to more than make good

149

their losses, and by 1944 they were in a position to exert increasing pressure not just on Japan but on her allies.

Such was the simplicity and totality of the final American victory over Japan that it is very easy to lose sight of two important facts. First, that the war between Japan and her enemies was in fact a two-part conflict fought both on the continent of Asia and in the vastness of the Pacific. And second, that for most of the war the American high command believed that even without allies it could beat Japan (though any contribution others might make to the common cause was more than welcome). These two matters were obviously related as inter-Allied relations unfolded in the course of the war, none more evidently than in 1943 when the Allies made a number of decisions setting in train events that came to a head in June 1944.

CHINA'S ROLE

The critical element in this situation was less the reality of growing American power as China and the part she was to play in the prosecution of the war. For many years the United States had cast herself in the self-appointed and allegedly disinterested role of guardian and friend of China, and war had convinced her to regard the latter as potentially *the* military power of the anti-Japanese alliance. Properly supported and equipped, China could provide the manpower for a major land force that would tie down the Japanese army in Asia and thereby ease American problems in the Pacific.

Ideally, American and Chinese efforts directed along exterior lines of communication would be mutually supporting, but things never worked out in so neat and simple a manner. China was never able to play the part Washington selected for her, and in trying to provide her with the very substantial aid that alone would have been the basis of a major Chinese contribution to victory, the Americans ran into bewildering problems whose complexity and intractability increased with the passing of time.

At least part of the American difficulty was self-inflicted because there was no basic agreement within the US high command on what should be attempted in China. In the first year of the Pacific war the American priority had been to strengthen first China's army and then her air force, since neither could hope to meet the enemy with any hope of success. At that stage the American efforts were complementary, but (mainly as a result of an increasingly vociferous air lobby in China and Washington) priorities became disputed and confused as the military and air programs emerged as competitors for increasingly scarce resources. With time the emphasis of American policy shifted from trying to strengthen the Chinese army so that China became a major combat theater, to the attempt to develop China as the main base from which American air power could strike at the Japanese homeland. Certain members of the American military hierarchy believed that such an effort was certain to be self-defeating, since it was guaranteed to provoke the Japanese into an offensive against American bases that the Chinese army would be unable to resist.

Another American difficulty lay in the fact that only very belatedly did Washington realize that Chiang Kai-shek was unwilling and perhaps unable to make a serious and sustained effort against the Japanese. The ineffectiveness of his government; his seeming unwillingness to fight the Japanese when he could conserve his strength in order to deal with domestic rivals; and finally, his 'generosity' to his generals, family and officials with American aid progressively eroded American confidence. By late 1943 his evident determination to exact the greatest possible financial benefit from the American war effort while doing little or nothing to justify the aid given to him was beginning to rouse American resentment. But long before such matters began to cloud American calculations Washington had become familiar with a third problem – Burma.

BURMA – THE FOCUS OF ALLIED PROBLEMS

Burma had been a British colony until most of it was overrun by the Japanese in early 1942. Thereafter it remained in the British area of responsibility and the only point where British forces could engage the enemy, and herein lay the rub. Once Burma was lost it ceased to have any real value to the British. It was important only to the Americans and Chinese because it was a natural land link between the Chinese interior and the outside world, and both wanted to see Burma freed from Japanese control in order that American aid might once more flow into China via Rangoon, the railroad to Lashio and the Burma Road to Kunming and Chungking.

The American-Chinese problem with Burma arose on three counts. First, in both 1942 and 1943 the British lacked the means to clear Burma. At best they might be able to clear northern Burma, but Allied lines of communication into Burma from India could not support an attempt to reconquer the whole country or sustain the construction of a road from Assam via the malarial morass that formed the Hukawng valley to the Burma Road. Even if the lines of supply could have maintained such efforts, it was unlikely that the Allies could develop an overland route to Yunnan before the Americans fought their way across the Pacific to the Chinese coast.

Second, there was very little the Chinese could do in this theater to help their own cause. Any attempt to support a British effort in northern Burma would have to be made from the wastes of Yunnan, and such an effort was not possible unless the route into China was open in the first place. The only solution would be a reconquest of

Burma from the south with an offensive against Rangoon and thence up the river valleys to Mandalay, Lashio and Myitkyina. Because communications within Burma via the valleys were superior to those leading overland into the country, this was indeed the only sensible course of action.

But if the British acquired the means to carry out such an offensive there was no doubting that they would have little inclination to do so. Possession of an amphibious capability in the Indian Ocean could only encourage Britain to bypass Burma entirely, to seek targets anywhere between the Andamans and Timor rather than in a backwater. The British hoped to develop an offensive against the Andamans and northern Sumatra, but without the amphibious vessels needed to transform the dreams of 1943 and 1944 into reality, they were forced to refocus their attention on Burma.

Herein lay the third part of the Allied problem of Burma. The British realized that in spite of Chinese difficulties in Yunnan the best hope of success in northern Burma would come as a result of converging Anglo-Chinese offensives against the Mandalay-Myitkyina position. But the British had little enthusiasm for the Chinese connection. They had reservations about Chiang, his security and Chinese military effectiveness, and they were aware of the danger of fighting in a British colony in such dubious company as that of the Chinese and Americans. The former were distrusted because of their territorial claims on Burma and the latter because of their well known anti-imperialism.

Britain's weakness in this theater and her dependence on the United States meant, however, that she had little choice in the matter, and the Americans had made the realities of power very clear even before Burma was lost. After the start of the war, the Americans sought some measure of administrative and operational control over Burma, and after the colony was lost Washington insisted on imposing an American command on the British command structure in this theater of operations.

THE REALITY OF AMERICAN POWER

This was the CBI (China-Burma-India) Theater with headquarters in Delhi, and as its commander Washington appointed the legendary and vitriolic Lieutenant-General Joseph W Stilwell. In this role Vinegar Joe (as he was nicknamed) was to be commander of all American troops in China, Burma and India, and in charge of all American aid programs. He was *ex officio* the American representative on any Allied war council that might exist in this theater, and he was also Chiang Kai-shek's chief of staff and field commander of any Chinese forces Chiang might assign him. Stilwell was not accountable to the British authorities in India, and he did not come under British operational or administrative control. He reported to and took orders from his national command. By these extraordinary arrangements the American high command sought to ensure that its wishes with regard to Burma and China were carried out, if necessary in spite of British objections.

In fact the American high command had a much more powerful means of having its way in Burma than reliance on administrative devices and expedients that always threatened to be a source of confusion rather than clarity. The imbalance of British and American resources, and the transformation of the Anglo-American relationship from one between equals to one of dependent and benefactor, ensured a declining British freedom of action regarding Burma. This was naturally part of the process whereby Britain was prepared to make concessions over what were relatively minor interests in order to try to safeguard the more important ones. The British sought to preserve their present options in the Mediterranean and future options in the Pacific, but they could not really hope to encroach upon the US Navy's preserve if Burma remained under unchallenged Japanese control. A British role in the Pacific had to be in addition to and not instead of a campaign for Burma.

Such was the background to the various Allied decisions that resulted in the denouement of June 1944, but which unfolded in a manner very different from that envisaged by the Allies.

On the Asian mainland there were three theaters – China, Indo-China and Burma – where the Japanese were engaged in garrison and defensive duties and where the Allies were as yet unable to mount a major challenge. But in both 1942 and in 1943 the British realized that in the coming 12 months they could not stand on the defensive in their own theater of operations in the Far East while the Americans mounted a series of offensive operations in the Pacific.

The politics of the situation ensured that in 1943 the British had to commit themselves to offensive operations in Burma in 1944, and similarly the Americans found themselves with an inescapable commitment to an expansion of the air war in China in the course of 1944. Their first raids within China were carried out in March 1943, and after May heavy and medium bombers struck at a growing number of targets at sea, in Indo-China, on Hainan, in southern China and (in November) on Formosa. This spread of activity foreshadowed the Americans carrying the war to the Japanese homeland from bases in China, but the first such attack was in fact delayed until 15 June 1944, when their bombers struck at the steelworks at Yawata on Kyushu.

In both sets of Allied calculations involving operations in Burma and China there was an assumption that the power of decision and choice in the conduct of operations rested with the Allies. This was not the case. In both Burma and China the Japanese were on the defensive, but not because they had been forced to conform to Allied moves. In both theaters the Japanese were on the defensive *from choice*, because they believed that they already occupied the parts of these countries that were worth having and that their enemies were welcome to the rest. In Burma only the mountains along the borders with India and China remained beyond their control, and in China they had long held the richest parts of the country north of the Yangtze and in the coastal areas to the south. The Japanese had little interest in the mountains of the interior.

A CHANGE OF ATTITUDE

But in the course of 1943 Japanese attitudes began to change as earlier victories lost their attraction and the significance of the drift of events began to impress itself on various commands. Burma, it was realized, led nowhere and produced little. It provided a forward base for the defense of the Gulf of Siam, Thailand, Malaya and the Indies, but the Japanese knew that they could never match an Allied buildup in this theater and that in time they would be subjected to attack by much superior enemy forces.

The first such attack was one that the Japanese weathered with surprising and almost embarrassing ease. In the first dry season campaign after the Japanese conquest of Burma the British put together two separate efforts. In the first, in Arakan, greatly outnumbered Japanese forces outmaneuvered and then outfought the British, destroying much of the latter's credibility with the Americans in the process. In the second results were less clear cut.

What amounted to a reconnaissance in force by the equivalent of an infantry regiment in the Myitkyina-Mandalay-Bongyaung-Kyaikthin area imposed little serious or permanent loss on the Japanese but incurred heavy losses amongst the units committed to the operation: these facts were however overlooked because of two considerations. First, the British columns spent four months behind Japanese lines without suffering the pulverizing defeat that had always been the British lot thus far in the war with Japan. Second, this operation suggested that the Japanese calculation that large numbers of men could not invade Burma from India was false.

Lack of cross-border communications had appeared to guard Japanese conquests as effectively as any defense line or field force, but what was to become known as the first Chindit operation served to discredit this view as the local Japanese command was forced to the conclusion that what had been done once could be repeated in greater strength – in either direction. Given a hardening conviction that the British would repeat their effort in northern Burma at a time of their own choosing, Japanese thoughts began to turn to the possibility of a spoiling operation of their own. In China, too, a similar type of logic was beginning to impose itself on the theater command.

The Japanese were aware that their difficulties could only increase unless they secured the final victory over Chiang Kai-shek's regime that had eluded them since 1937. By 1943 the Japanese were no nearer resolving 'the China incident' in their favor than they had been six years earlier, and they had good cause for concern as the American presence in China began to assume significant proportions. In April and May, and again in August, the Japanese army air force mounted a series of attacks on American air bases in southern China with scant and declining success. In the course of American offensive operations the Japanese found their fighters were outclassed by those of the enemy and quite unable to deal with heavy bombers.

The corollary of this situation was exactly as those Americans who had doubted the wisdom of an air policy in China had feared: a growing Japanese determination to overrun the bases from which the bombers operated and thereby drive the Americans beyond the range of the Japanese homeland. With the Japanese disinclined to wait meekly for the Americans to mount a sustained air offensive, their attention in the last quarter of 1943 turned to the possibility of a major ground offensive south of the Yangtze for the first time in five years. In this way they could keep the Americans at arm's length from the home islands, forestalling any offensive that Chiang Kai-shek might be preparing and perhaps even securing a victory that would discredit Chiang's regime and force China from the war. As always, the prospect of a 'decisive battle' and 'final victory' would be the spur to Japanese endeavors.

An earlier desire to end the interminable war in China by extending it to southeast Asia had been partially responsible for a march of events that led to the outbreak of the Pacific war, a process whereby the Japanese exchanged one war for another while one fact remained constant: they lacked the means to win either of them. Without ending one war the Japanese embarked upon a second, assuming in 1941 and 1942 a primarily defensive stance in Asia while they undertook offensive operations in southeast Asia and the Pacific. But in 1943, with the Japanese high command determined to cut its commitments in the Pacific as her forces there came under mounting pressure, and with the war effort showing unmistakable signs of strain, Japanese thoughts turned to the possibility of offensive action in Burma and China as the means of resolving her growing difficulties on the mainland. With the war clearly about to enter a new and more critical phase in the Pacific since it was obvious that some American move in the central Pacific was at hand, there was evidently something very wrong with the direction of the Japanese war effort.

This, however, was not the only weakness within Japanese command arrangements and decisions. The attempt to instill some belated realism into strategic policy in the Pacific theater was hopelessly overdue. In theory, the inauguration of a new operational policy in September 1943 should have given the Japanese the flexibility which had been so conspicuously absent from their conduct of operations over the previous 12 months. In reality, the change was merely a meaningless shift of emphasis.

JAPANESE STRATEGIC OVERSIGHTS

During the previous year, Japanese policy had been to fight to a finish at the point of contact. Obsessed with the importance of space and depth, the Japanese had denied themselves any chance to exploit either by adopting a policy of forward linear defense in an attempt to fight their enemies to a standstill at the furthest extent of their conquests. Now, in September 1943, Japan adopted a plan that envisaged her establishing 'an absolute national defense sphere'within an inner defensive perimeter that was to include the Kuriles, the Bonins, the Marianas and Carolines, western New Guinea, the Malay Barrier and Burma. The areas beyond this inner perimeter – the most distant parts of the southwest Pacific where the Eighth Area Army and the Southeast Area Fleet were in position – were where the Japanese would fight 'strong delaying actions' to buy time in which to prepare positions along the Saipan-Truk-Timor line.

But the idea of fighting on shorter lines of communication across a restricted front was doomed for three reasons. First, the whole idea of flexible defense had little meaning to armed forces whose concept of war drew no distinction between a defense that would end either in suicide or death at the enemy's hands. The distinction between 'strong delaying action' and 'all-out defense' was meaningless since standard operational procedure envisaged any form of defense as a battle to the last man and last round. Moreover, even if the Japanese military establishment had possessed the mental flexibility that would have enabled it to absorb a fresh *tactical* approach, it lacked the *strategic* insight needed to abandon its forward formations to their sacrificial role.

In November 1943, after the new operational policy had been instituted, the Japanese navy's continuing concern for Rabaul led it to reinforce the base with a heavy cruiser squadron and, more critically, air squadrons from the fleet carriers. This piecemeal deployment led to the destruction of the air units to no useful purpose and also resulted in the strike power of Japanese carrier forces being compromised. They navy's decision ensured that it could not present any threat to or check on the Americans either in the southwest or the central Pacific. The Combined Fleet's inability to meet the American challenge at Tarawa later in the month stemmed largely from this division of Japanese air strength after a series of decisions that should have ensured its concentration for the trials ahead.

Second, compounding this crucial error of deployment was the simple fact that the Japanese lacked the resources and time to secure their new defense zone. Japan did not have the industrial base and the manpower needed to prepare a series of defenses in depth in the central Pacific. She had no means to prepare a continuous position or one sited in depth in the Marianas and Carolines. Since August 1942, the emphasis of Japanese preparations had been the provision of defenses in the Marshalls and Gilberts. Even after the inauguration of the new defense policy in September 1943, however, the fortification of the central Pacific islands was not made an urgent priority. Indeed, with the Americans thousands of miles from the main bases at Truk, Kwajalein and Saipan, and with Rabaul still unreduced, there was no apparent need to speed construction.

This proved a major error of judgement on the part of the Japanese. By the end of 1943 the Americans were in possession of a plan of campaign and the means to put it into effect that invalidated the Japanese concept of defense in the Pacific. Herein was the third reason for Japanese failure. The whole idea of defense in depth through the use of concentrated land-based aircraft against a carrier force was not an effective substitute for an adequate number of carriers with trained and experienced air groups. In short, the Japanese had a static concept of war that incorporated dispersal and weakness, in contrast to the American determination to sidestep main centers of resistance in order to bring an overwhelming concentration of mobile firepower against an exposed, inferior part of the Japanese defense system. At the end of 1943, the clash between these two concepts – offensive and mobile versus a defensive and static concept of warfare – was at hand. By a decision to stand on the Saipan-Truk-Timor line, the Japanese marked out the place where the clash would take place in June 1944.

American planning for a war in the Pacific had been geared to an offensive into and through the maze of Japanese bases wrongly assumed to be in the Marshalls, Carolines and Marianas. The Americans had realized that their own possessions in the western Pacific would be untenable in the event of war with Japan, but they planned to redress any early losses with a progressive and systematic clearing of the central Pacific. This had two aims. First, to force their way through to either the Philippines or the China coast. Second, to

157

provoke and win a cataclysmic battle against the Japanese navy in the enemy's home waters.

The US Navy knew that the only way it could ensure the defeat of Japan was if it advanced into the western Pacific and crushed the Imperial Navy in a fight in waters that the latter regarded as its own. Yet in the first 20 or so months of the war, the US Navy found that it had to fight where it was rather than where it wanted to be. The disastrous opening months of the war and the subsequent realities of military geography directed American efforts mainly to the Solomons and New Guinea. Even though the Chief of Naval Operations and Commander-in-Chief US Fleet, Admiral Ernest J King, had been the crucial influence in the American decisions in March 1942 to pick up the enemy's challenge in these areas, as American thoughts turned to the possibility of a future offensive the prospect of an advance in the southwest Pacific became increasingly unsatisfactory to King for two reasons.

In the first place, most of the Solomons were in an 'enemy' theater of operations and King and the US Navy were never prepared to contemplate a naval war being fought under the direction of any American general, and certainly not General Douglas MacArthur. In the second place, King was virtually alone inside the American and naval high commands in seeing the Marianas as the key to the Pacific war. King believed that naval warfare was about control of lines of communications, and that the loss of the Marianas would doom Japan. In King's view, the island empire of Japan could only survive and wage war if she was able to keep open her lines of communication with southeast Asia from where she drew her raw materials.

An American conquest of the Marianas would leave the US Navy in a position to sever these lines of communication, ensuring Japan's ultimate defeat. Others regarded the Marianas as important since an attack on them could force the Imperial Navy into giving battle in their defense. The Army Air Force could appreciate the prospects opened up by a conquest of the Marianas since the Japanese home islands would thereafter be within range of heavy bombers based in the southern islands. But for King such matters were side issues. The critical point was the strategic location of the Marianas between Japan and the Carolines and all points to the south, hence his determination to mount an offensive in the central Pacific that would include rather than bypass these islands.

ALLIED COMMAND STRUCTURE
IN THE FAR EAST

The first step on the road leading the Americans to the Marianas in June 1944 was taken at the Trident conference. With the British firmly instructed that, when it came to Pacific matters, they were to listen and approve and King's colleagues on the Joint Chiefs of Staff undecided on what they wanted to do in the Pacific, King secured acceptance of a basic framework for the defeat of Japan. This involved the clearing of the Aleutians and Burma; the start of a bombing offensive against Japan from bases in China; the intensification of the submarine campaign against enemy shipping; and offensives across the southwest and the central Pacific.

After Trident, King sought to guard against any adverse revision by devising a timetable for central Pacific operations and by securing the role of coordinator of the southwest and central Pacific theaters. This rather transparent attempt to place MacArthur and his command under naval direction was not accepted by King's colleagues on the Joint Chiefs of Staff, but King nevertheless secured most of what he wanted in two fields. MacArthur's protests at what was in effect a downgrading of his command were set aside by the JCS who also ordered MacArthur not to undertake a frontal attack on Rabaul but to bypass it.

This decision was based on the need to take forces away from MacArthur in order to provide for a central Pacific offensive, choice and necessity coming together as far as King was concerned. Without the forces needed for a direct assault, MacArthur had no option but to neutralize and then isolate by engaging in the most intelligent form of warfare, namely attacking and advancing in areas where the enemy was not. Although he had to make certain concessions about certain targets and timing, King won acceptance for an amphibious and carrier drive to secure the Gilberts, Marshalls, Carolines, Palaus and Marianas. This programme was endorsed at Quadrant and then finalized at the Sextant and Eureka conferences.

The last of these conferences, at which the Soviets were present, in Teheran, proved crucial in the unfolding of Allied strategy in the war against Japan. On this occasion the Soviets promised to join the Pacific war when the struggle in Europe was brought to an end. This undertaking had the obvious effect of lessening any British and Chinese land contribution to the war and two Allies hitherto regarded as important to the waging of the Pacific war now lost considerable status and significance. Such a situation was ironic, for the various Anglo-American conferences of 1943 had seen much metaphorical blood spilling on the subject of Burma and the part that the British were to play in an American-arranged order of things. At Quadrant the Americans and British concluded what should have been one of the more unworkable arrangements of the war but which turned out to be one of the better compromises, though it was never tested by defeat.

This agreement at Quadrant involved the creation of an inter-

Allied command with an operational area that included Ceylon, Burma, Thailand, Malaya and Sumatra. With all but Ceylon held by the enemy, this command was charged with recovering Burma. Dearly though the Americans would have wished to have their own man in the post of supreme Allied commander, they accepted that this post had to go to the British. After the first three nominees were rejected, a junior British vice admiral, Mountbatten, was accepted as supreme commander with an American deputy.

The American concerned turned out to be the ubiquitous Stilwell, who outranked his superior. Stilwell, moreover, still retained all his other posts, including that of commander of Chinese forces in India. In the latter capacity Stilwell was subordinate to the Allied land commander-in-chief in this new theater. This was an unacceptable situation as far as Stilwell was concerned, but he proved amenable to the suggestion that he accept orders from the land commander's deputy, who was discreet enough never to issue Stilwell with orders that he knew would not be obeyed.

To complete this tangled command organization reporting to the Combined Chiefs of Staff via London, the Allied land, sea and air commanders-in-chief were all British and all outranked Mountbatten and Stilwell. Moreover, the naval commander also commanded the British Eastern Fleet and was responsible for the whole of the Indian Ocean, in which capacities he was under the direct control of the Admiralty. The air commander similarly had responsibilities outside this theater that directly linked him to the Air Ministry in London. With Stilwell able to circumvent anyone according to which hat he chose to wear at any given moment, the British side of this command establishment completed what in any theater other than Burma would probably have been called a fair-weather arrangement.

ALLIED AND JAPANESE STRATEGIES — A SUMMARY

Such were the main considerations shaping the strategic deliberations of the Allies and Japanese alike and the framework of the policies that the two sides intended to put into effect in the course of 1944. Because of the demands of time and space in theaters as vast as the Pacific and the Asian mainland, decisions taken in the third and fourth quarters of 1943 could not be carried out much before mid-1944, and this was a factor behind the one major policy change adopted by the Allies after Quadrant and Sextant.

Whereas the Japanese intended to stand on the defensive in the Pacific while undertaking major offensives on the mainland, the Americans and British planned to carry the fight to the enemy in the Pacific and Burma respectively while the Chinese remained on the defensive. By the end of 1943 the basic outline of an offensive Allied strategy in Burma had been drawn. The resultant plan of campaign envisaged a main British effort into the Kabaw valley and then into the Chindwin valley with the aim of linking up with infiltrated Chindit forces on the upper Irrawaddy.

At the same time, Stilwell's Chinese forces were to advance into Burma from Ledo via the Hukawng valley, while other Chinese formations from Yunnan advanced into northeast Burma. These operations, backed by a diversionary attack in Arakan, were ambitious, but like so many other intentions with regard to Burma they had to be set aside. On this occasion, however, discarding the plans was not the result of previous failure or present weakness but realization about the enemy's intentions. As the British prepared for their invasion of Burma, they became aware of the Japanese determination to invade India, and under the circumstances the British decided to let the Japanese come to them and be destroyed. It made more sense to fight a defensive battle that would be won rather than to run the hazards of an advance into Burma to attack an intact, prepared and well-supplied enemy.

This was the only major departure from the various decisions taken in 1943. The first six months of 1944, therefore, saw three quite separate developments as the finalized arrangements were put into effect. In Burma, the Japanese began offensive operations that carried them into India in March and to what was until that time the greatest defeat in the history of the Imperial Army around Imphal and Kohima between April and July. In China, the Japanese began a series of offensives, codenamed Operation Ichigo, in the south: these offensives were in full spate in June 1944. In the Pacific, the Americans unleashed offensives in the central and southwest areas and both efforts reached a climax in June 1944 with landings on Saipan in the Marianas, with an invasion that provoked one of the greatest naval battles of this or any war – the battle of the Philippine Sea.

CHAPTER 2

CAMPAIGNS ON THE MAINLAND

In planning their offensive on the mainland, the Japanese made no effort to coordinate their efforts in northwest Burma and southern China. With so much distance between the two theaters there was apparently no reason to try to run the two campaigns in tandem. In the event, however, a very considerable overlap occurred as both Japanese offensives miscarried. The operation in southern China proved more deliberate and protracted than anticipated while the drive into India, planned as a short, intense effort, developed into a disaster from which the Japanese could not extricate themselves.

The latter operation began to take shape in August 1943 when the local commands, *Burma Area Army* and the *Fifteenth Army*, issued orders for a two-division operation on the Salween in October and in the Tiddim-Kalemyo area in November and December. Both operations were intended to prepare for a major offensive in India, the first by securing the right flank against possible Chinese interference and the second by securing bases in and around the Kabaw valley from which such an offensive could start. These preliminary moves did not automatically commit the Japanese to an offensive in India but Lieutenant-General Renya Mutaguchi, commander of the *Fifteenth Army*, hoped that such an operation would follow the initial undertakings. Conscious of but not alarmed by Chinese concentrations in Yunnan and more concerned by the growth of Allied strength in northeast India, Mutaguchi firmly believed in preemptive action to wreck British preparations and hopefully bring down the crumbling facade of the Raj behind the front.

Such views did not command enthusiastic support at any level within the Imperial Army. The dangers of awaiting attack were obvious but hardly sufficient reason for an offensive certain to be something of a lottery because of the lack of overland communications into India from Burma, the paucity of supporting services for an attack, and the marked numerical superiority the enemy was sure to enjoy in Manipur. Moreover, the higher echelons of the Japanese armed services could not but be aware of the danger of undertaking an overland offensive into India at a time when Rangoon's vulnerability to a seaborne landing was growing. Nevertheless, after a series of staff conferences at ever exalted levels at the turn of the year, *Imperial General Headquarters* on 7 January 1944 sanctioned *Operation U-GO*, and *Burma Area Army* was issued with instructions eight days later.

The plan of campaign for this offensive was not finalized until 11 February, by which time the offensive itself had been underway for a week. Such a strange state of affairs was the result of the offensive opening with a feint that was put into effect before planning was completed and as extra formations were moved up to the front in readiness for the offensive.

In the end the Japanese assembled nine divisions for a series of operations intended to break Allied power in northeast India. These nine divisions were organized into three armies, the *Fifteenth*, *Twenty Eighth* and *Thirty Third*, the latter two being raised specifically for or during this offensive and assigned defensive tasks intended to secure the flanks and rear of the *Fifteenth Army* as it undertook the main offensive effort.

Initially, the *Thirty Third Army* consisted of the two divisions that should have eliminated the Chinese bridgeheads over the Salween in October, but because this had never been a practical proposition the *18th* and *56th Infantry Divisions* had settled to guard the approaches into Burma. But with the *18th Division* stationed in the Hukawng valley and the *56th* between Wanting and the Salween, the *Thirty Third Army* was assigned the *53rd Infantry Division* for lines of communication duties. In western Burma the *Twenty Eighth Army*, charged with the defense of the coast, had the *2nd Infantry Division* in position south of Taungup and the *54th* to the north as far as Akyab. In Arakan the *Twenty Eighth Army*'s remaining formation, the veteran 55th Infantry Division, was under instructions to carry out *Operation HA-GO*. This was the diversionary effort planned to begin three weeks before *U-GO*, the Japanese intention being for the *55th* to slash at XV British Corps, known to be in northern Arakan, and thereby force the British to commit their reserves to the aid of this formation. The Japanese objective was to ensure that these reserves, once committed, could not break contact and redeploy when the main action unfolded in Manipur.

The main effort was to be undertaken by Mutaguchi's *Fifteenth Army* which had the *15th*, *31st* and *33rd Infantry Divisions* under command and the regimental-sized *1st Indian National Army Division* making its operational debut in a supporting role. The task of the *Fifteenth Army* was nothing less than the destruction of enemy positions and forces in and around Imphal. Because of the peculiarities of geography, any British concentration for an offensive into Burma had to take place at Imphal, and the only major overland route to Imphal other than the track from Silchar made its way south from the vital railhead at Dimapur via Kohima. This road ran parallel and uncomfortably close to the Chindwin. With this river line already in Japanese hands, it was Mutaguchi's intention to launch an offensive that would erupt from the valley, cut the road about Imphal and thereby isolate the Allied forces there. Then the Japanese would follow up with a battle of encirclement and annihilation.

THE STRUGGLE FOR IMPHAL

Mutaguchi intended to open his attack with a feint by the *33rd Infantry Division*. Operating with armored support, the *33rd* was to mount a two-pronged offensive, one thrust directed along the main route that ran via Tiddim and Bishenpur and the other up the Kabaw valley to strike at Imphal via Tamu and Palel. These drives were to begin in the second week of March, and with British attention and forces held by this emerging threat, the *15th* and *31st Infantry Divisions* would be unleashed one week later. Working in conjunction, the *31st* was to sweep down on Kohima via Jessami and Ukhrul while the *15th*, pivoting on Ukhrul, was to envelop Imphal from the north and northeast and to sever the Silchar track as the *33rd* fought its way into the Imphal plain from the south and southeast. With the *31st Infantry Division* in position to block any relieving attempt from Dimapur, the *15th Army* was to brush aside British resistance and complete the destruction of the enemy's Imphal position within a month.

Indeed, when the Japanese offensive began, Radio Tokyo announced a three-week timetable for the capture of Imphal. The Japanese had no option but to try to take Imphal within a month – and thereby leave the British with less than a month in which to mount a major counteroffensive before the monsoon – because they lacked the means to sustain an offensive for a longer period. With a minimum of supporting units, *U-GO* had to be carried out with only the equipment and supplies that the attacking troops themselves could carry over the mountains. These amounted to 20 days' supplies and ammunition with an extra five days in reserve. Thousands of draught animals were rounded up for moving supplies and for slaughter, but even with these the guns had no more than 300 rounds each. Other needs would have to be met from captured enemy stocks at Imphal.

Before *U-GO* the British had worried about the proximity of the Dimapur-Imphal road to the upper Chindwin. It was clearly vulnerable to any enemy raiding party moving out of the valley, but because any move from the Chindwin to the road across the grain of the land had to be very difficult, the British calculated that the largest force that the enemy could infiltrate across their line of communication was a battalion group, perhaps a regiment. This was a reassuring calculation because if the Japanese moved in unit strength they would be crushed and if they attacked with a formation they would starve. This assessment was correct and borne out by subsequent events, but only by the narrowest margin. The Japanese, by dispensing with a normal line of supply, brought a whole division against the Dimapur-Imphal road. Most of the British difficulties in and after the second half of March stemmed from this very natural failure to anticipate the speed and size of the Japanese advance into Manipur.

Even before *U-GO* began, there were indications that the more serious planning errors had been made by the Japanese, not the British. In drawing up their plan of campaign the Japanese relied on the formula that had served them so well to date in both Burma and Malaya. On every occasion when they had met the British, they had outmaneuvered and outfought their roadbound enemy with outflanking attacks through the jungle against the rear. British reaction to any Japanese move against the flanks or rear was always to withdraw and to fight out of any encirclement that they could not evade.

Such encounters ran a predictable course. Masses of equipment and all semblance of order were abandoned by the British as the Japanese invariably harrassed their formations if not to disaster then to severe defeats. Such was the ease and frequency with which the Japanese out-thought and outfought the British between 1941 and 1943 that it is fair to say that withdrawal became as much a British standard operational procedure as British rations and supplies became the natural expectation of attacking Japanese forces. This latter feature was even incorporated into the planning for *U-GO*. Japanese plans for the offensive into India assumed that the British would collapse as readily as they had in the past, but ominously for the Japanese, in view of the fact that *HA-GO* and *U-GO* were remarkably similar in concept, the initial results obtained during *HA-GO* by the *Thirty Third Army* were hardly encouraging. When *HA-GO* was put into effect it was not the British but the offensive itself that collapsed, and it did so with remarkable swiftness.

HA-GO began to get underway on 4 February when the *55th Infantry Division*'s holding force gripped the 5th Indian Division in and around Maungdaw while the rest of the formation tried to sweep around and through the 7th Indian Division's open flank at Buthidaung. These initial attacks, as successful as any made in the previous two years, provided the Japanese with positional advantages that in any earlier offensive would have ensured decisive success. On this occasion, however, they found themselves opposed by an enemy who stood and fought. At Maungdaw and Buthidaung the British countered Japanese infiltration tactics by forming themselves into irreducible 'boxes' that were to be supplied by air. The British intended to turn these 'boxes' into anvils on which attacking Japanese units would be pounded to destruction by

165

relieving columns, and the effectiveness of such a tactic was admitted by the *Thirty Third Army* on 24 February when it acknowledged failure in *HA-GO*.

The *55th Infantry Division*'s attempt to overrun the opposition was thwarted by its failure to carry the Sinzewa position, and as its attack faltered the slenderness of its logistical support ceased to be an asset and became a liability. Speed was not an effective substitute for assured supply. Everything about the *HA-GO* plan had rested upon the effective exploitation of the initiative, but in the face of unyielding resistance by the 5th and 7th Indian Divisions, a move south from Daletme against the Japanese flank by the 81st West African Division, and an advance by the 25th, 26th and 36th Indian Divisions, the *55th Infantry Division* was helpless. It lost about 5,500 men from its original strength of 12,000 as its offensive stalled around Sinzewa and it was counterattacked by the British reserve, the 26th and 36th fighting their way forward to relieve the 5th and 7th respectively. British casualties numbered about 3,500, half of which were incurred by the 7th before it had chance to settle its defenses.

Both sides drew the lessons they wanted to draw from this action. The Japanese could claim that it took four or so Indian divisions to deal with one of their own, and in this there was success because the British were obliged to commit formations that should have been saved for Manipur. The British, on the other hand, had no qualms about portraying these events as a major victory. In reality, it was no more than a moderate military success, the real value of which was psychological as it was the first occasion on which the British clearly outfought the Japanese. The British had no need to manufacture or exaggerate this success in the Arakan because real victory was at hand – though the initial exchanges in the battle of Imphal-Kohima hardly suggested a great British victory in the making.

A CHANGE OF PLAN, AND THE CHINDITS ATTACK

The British had not expected a Japanese offensive before mid-March, and having planned an advance into northern Burma in the wake of a Chindit operation in the Indaw area, they had the 17th Indian Division in and around Tiddim and on the road back to Tiddim; the 20th Indian Division similarly deployed with respect to Tamu; and the 23rd Indian Division in reserve at Imphal.

As the indications of an impending Japanese offensive appeared, the Allied high command had no difficulty in recasting its plans. Because the process of overland infiltration had already begun, the Chindit operation was allowed to proceed. The 17th and 20th Divisions, in positions from which they could advance into Burma but by the same token in danger of being outflanked and encircled by the *Fifteenth Army*, were to be pulled back to the edge of the Imphal plain. The British had no intention of fighting in exposed forward positions that would be difficult if not impossible to sustain when the comparatively open country of the plain would allow their armor, air power and superiority of numbers, firepower and tactical mobility to be utilized to the full in a battle of attrition.

By holding naturally strong positions on relatively narrow frontages that the Japanese could neither take nor bypass, the British hoped to draw the Japanese into a battle that the latter could not win but in which their well-known proclivity for all-out attack would prove their undoing. If the Japanese pressed their attack, they risked adding to the size of their final defeat, the possibility for the British being that the battle of attrition might prove to be a battle of annihilation, without the encirclement that is normally an essential part of such a battle.

Maneuver and guile were at a discount in a British plan of campaign that was realistic if unsubtle. But delicacy was needed in at least one part of the conduct of operations: the withdrawal of the 17th and 20th Indian Divisions before an advancing enemy. These formations had to observe a careful balance between determination and caution in standing firmly enough to delay and cause disproportionately heavy losses to the Japanese, but at the same time they had to ensure that they were not trapped by enemy outflanking movements. The obvious danger to the defense was the Japanese beginning their offensive and getting into position to encircle these forward formations before they had time to withdraw, and this was precisely what happened on the Tiddim front. The *33rd Infantry Division* began a three-pronged advance – up the Kabaw valley, along the Tiddim road, and over the mountains to come around the back of the Tiddim position – on 4 March.

Despite Radio Tokyo's announcement that Imphal was to fall by 27 March, these advances remained undetected until the 12 March, and by then it proved almost too late to extricate the 17th Division as the Japanese, after coming over the mountains, established a scries of roadblocks that ultimately stretched over 60 miles of the Hengtam-Tongzang road. The most formidable Japanese position was established just to the north of Sakawng, but the 17th was able to mount a series of very deliberate attacks along the road and nearby ridges that carried it through successive Japanese positions and enabled it to link up with the sortie to relief by the 23rd Division. The significance of the 17th's breaking clear of the Japanese positions was not lost upon Lieutenant-General Motozo Yanagida, commander of the *33rd Infantry Division*. Never an enthusiast for *U-GO*, Yanagida noted that an absence of prisoners and booty indicated an enemy withdrawal in good order. His conclusion was that his formation was faced by a resolute, able and (crucially) undefeated enemy, and his pessimism about the whole venture was so great that Mutaguchi decided upon his being replaced.

On the Tamu road, the 20th Indian Division did not encounter serious problems until the first half of April when the Japanese advance reached Shenam on the most direct route between the Chindwin and Imphal. It was further to the north, where the Japanese advance was at its fastest and most spectacular, that the main threat to the British position developed. By 21 March the *15th Infantry Division* had bundled the British out of Ukhrul and Sheldon's Corner, and was preparing to advance down the valley into the Imphal plain. At the same time the *31st Infantry Division*, using Ukhrul as its hard shoulder, moved against Kohima and cut the road from Imphal at Mao Songsang on 3 April. On the following day one of its columns entered the sprawling hill town of Kohima after an advance along the track from Jessami.

At this stage the battle appeared to be moving the Japanese way, notwithstanding Yanagida's failure to catch the 17th Indian Division before it could scamper back to the temporary safety of the plain. By 4 April, with the *31st Infantry Division* ahead of schedule, the Japanese deployment was complete with all three divisions committed along the length of the front. The *31st* had reached Kohima while the *15th* and *33rd* had between them closed the ring around Imphal from the north, east and south. The Japanese advance had reached Kanglatongbi on the Kohima road; Nungshigum and Kameng on the approach from Ukhrul; Shenam on the Tamu road; and Shunganu and Torbung on the approaches to Imphal from Tiddim.

By then the British had completed the first stage of a strategic redeployment. With transport aircraft making their way to Assam from as far away as the Mediterranean in order to airlift troops to threatened sectors and then to sustain them once in battle, forces from the Arakan were withdrawn from the line and moved to Imphal and Dimapur, and other formations converged on eastern India from various parts of the subcontinent. Some 758 sorties saw the 5th Indian Division moved to Imphal and Dimapur, its leading brigade arriving at the former as early as 22 March. After having trained for amphibious landings, the 2nd British Division arrived at Dimapur on 1 April.

Given this Allied ability to redeploy transports and divisions across hundreds of miles, the logic of *U-GO* was becoming clear by 4 April. However impressive the speed of the Japanese advance thus far, if the *Fifteenth Army* was not in Imphal by 4 April it was never going to get there. The Japanese tragedy was that it would take another three months and the destruction of the *Fifteenth Army* before their commanders admitted this fact.

Events in Manipur after 4 April proceeded with an inevitable military logic flowing from the fact that the Japanese, having failed to force a favorable decision when they held advantages of surprise, initiative and superiority at various points of contact, tried to maintain their offensive in the face of the enemy's superior strategic and tactical mobility. The Japanese had begun their offensive with a strength only marginal to requirements and a line of communication unable to sustain the demands of a major battle and a heavy flow of casualties. They lacked the numbers and logistics that might have enabled them to adopt a fresh tactical approach once their initial onrush was checked, and they also lacked the lateral roads that could have allowed their forces to reconcentrate and thereby secure an advantage on one particular part of the front. By starting with dispersed forces that could not support one another, the Japanese found that when their offensive stalled British air supremacy and internal lines of communication within the Imphal plain presented insuperable obstacles to Japanese success.

KOHIMA AND ITS EFFECT ON THE
JAPANESE ARMY

In this situation the only sensible course of action open to the Japanese was to break off the battle, but this was not their way. The various 'front lines' established in and around Kohima and Imphal in the first week of April had barely shifted by June. The Japanese made their first effort at Kohima on 6 April when they mounted a frontal attack and came around the flank to cut the road to Dimapur at Zubza. It took the British until 18 April to break into Kohima and relieve the town's exhausted garrison, and then needed another seven weeks to clear the surrounding ridges and break through the various Japanese positions on the road to the south. It was only on the 65th day of the battle that the Japanese were blasted from the village of Phesema, five miles to the south of Kohima, and even after the *31st Infantry Division* was forced to abandon this position it continued to resist with such ferocity that the British were denied Viswerna until 15 June and Mao Songsang until 18 June. The siege of Imphal itself was not lifted until 22 June when units from XXXIII and IV British Corps linked up near Kangpokpi.

It was this capacity for prolonged and bitter resistance that made the Japanese army so formidable, but on this occasion its efforts produced a condition that was terminal. With their supply arrangements disintegrating during the campaign as the jungle tracks turned to mud with the onset of the monsoon, the Japanese had no means of treating their sick and wounded and thereby ensure that they returned to the front. The result was that Japanese casualties mounted until they accounted for 53,000 of the 85,000 with which the *Fifteenth Army* had started the campaign, and of these 30,000 were missing or fatalities. Such was the evidence of total defeat that the XXXIII Corps encountered as it came south from Kohima that it deemed the further pursuit of the *31st Infantry Division* beyond Ukhrul as unnecessary.

It was this situation and the responsibility of the *Fifteenth Army* in bringing it about by insisting upon a continuation of the offensive long after it had clearly failed that provided the background to the famous exchange between Mutaguchi and the commander of the *31st Division* when the latter told his superior that 'the tactical ability of the *Fifteenth Army* staff lies below that of cadets,' and that Mutaguchi's incompetence absolved the *31st* from any obligation to obey any more of his fatuous orders. Such a breakdown of command and discipline within the Japanese army, plus the subsequent failure to call Lieutenant-General Sato to account for such insubordination, was a reflection of the much wider collapse of the *Burma Area Army*'s attack formations.

What made the losses incurred at Imphal and Kohima so intolerable and the persistence with *U-GO* so unrealistic was the fact that this offensive left the *Burma Area Army* too weak to counter the other threats developing elsewhere in the theater. In March 1944 the Japanese had some 200,000 men in Burma, the best of them with the *Fifteenth Army*, but on 7 March, the very day when the *33rd Infantry Division* moved out to attack Imphal, Stilwell's Northern Combat Area Command cleared the Maingkwan-Walawbum area, securing undisputed control of the Hukawng valley. With five Chinese divisions and Anglo-American special forces to oppose the solitary *18th Infantry Division*, Stilwell planned to advance into the Mogaung and Irrawaddy valleys with three objectives: Kamaing, Mogaung and Myitkyina.

NORTHERN BURMA AND THE SALWEEN

Stilwell's plan was to attack along the fair-weather road via Shaduzup into the Mogaung valley and to mount outflanking attacks on enemy positions via Nprawa and the upper Tamai. The Japanese, reacting swiftly to attempts to get around their positions between Shaduzup and Inkangahtawng, countered with an outflanking attack of their own that led to the two sides fighting one another to a standstill between 28 March and 8 April in a battle for control of Nhpum Ga. Because of the imbalance of strength, the Japanese were more severely depleted by their efforts at Nhpum Ga than the Allies, and with Stilwell taking full advantage of this and urging his formations over the Kumon Range in spite of the monsoon, the American special forces – Merrill's Marauders – took Myitkyina airfield on 17 May. With the Chinese 22nd and 38th Infantry Divisions securing Kamaing on 16 June and Chindit and Chinese forces occupying Mogaung ten days later, Myitkyina city fell on 3 August.

The fall of Kamaing and Mogaung were of major significance because this offensive showed what well-trained and properly commanded Chinese troops could achieve. Stilwell had trained three of his Chinese divisions himself, and these proved as tough and effective as any to be found on the Allied side. This was not the case with regard to the 12 Chinese divisions committed to the Salween offensive on 10 May.

This was an improvized offensive, put together to placate the Americans. On 3 April the Americans, tiring of Chinese procrastination and passivity, warned Chiang Kai-shek that the gravy train of aid would end unless Chinese forces began to take an active part in the war. The result was a Chinese offensive with some 72,000 troops from the Eleventh and Twentieth Army Groups on a 100-mile front that straddled the Burma Road west of the Salween. Opposing these formations but deployed across a 250-mile front between Lashio and the Hpimaw Pass were 11,000 troops from the *56th Infantry Division*, and over the next seven weeks this single formation proved a match for the Chinese. By a combination of judicious use of interior lines of communication, clever choice of ground, tactical professionalism, tenacity, and (in the Kaoli Kung mountains in general and the Ma-mein Pass in particular) a resort to cannibalism, the *56th Division* fought a series of highly successful rearguard actions that denied the Fifty Third and Fifty Fourth Armies routes through the mountains until 13 June and then prevented the fall of Ku-feng and Chiang-chu until 19 June and 20 June respectively.

Thereafter the Japanese in the northern sector concentrated in the walled city of Tengchung which lay across the tracks leading southwards to the all-important Burma Road. The defense of Tengchung was entrusted to a single regimental group, and it was not until September that five Chinese divisions, powerfully backed by American air power, broke into and secured the town. By then the Japanese had weathered the initial storm, and had even managed to counterattack in the south while carrying out their rearguard actions in the north.

In the first half of June the *56th Division* counterattacked in the Tengchung-Lameng-Lungling-Mangshih-Pingka area, and by the end of the month it had reasserted Japanese control over this part of the Burma Road. Subsequently the Japanese position began to crumble, as it had to do given the fact that the *56th Division* was denied substantial reinforcement. The position around Lameng, on the Sung Shan ridge, was one of the Japanese positions that came under increasing pressure, but possession of it was to cost the Chinese 7,000 dead and many weeks of fighting. By the end of 1944 the whole of this area resecured by the Japanese in late-June had been recovered by the Chinese, but this was something of a hollow victory.

The Japanese pulled back from the northeast in order to conform to the contraction of the front elsewhere rather than as a result of Chinese success on the Salween. The significance of events was not lost on Washington. Liaison teams reported Chinese ineffectiveness, and while the quality of performance improved substantially during the fighting no American could fail to note the discrepancy between promise and performance. A Salween offensive had been promised for October 1943, and began seven months late. The intention was to reach Myitkyina before Stilwell's forces, and after a month the Shweli had yet to be reached and the Salween had been crossed only because the Japanese made no attempt to defend the river line.

Washington could not ignore the fact that after years of generous aid and Chinese passivity that went under the name of preparation, 12 of Chiang's divisions were outfought by one depleted Japanese formation at the very time when three American trained Chinese divisions under Stilwell met and defeated the *18th Infantry Division* in northern Burma. The implication of events was obvious, but in case it was missed, the Salween fiasco coincided with a much larger and far more serious Chinese defeat in Honan, Hunan and Kwangsi as the Japanese launched their offensive to clear southern China of American air bases. The irony of this, however, was not that the military defeat discredited Chiang Kai-shek but that it provided him with a major diplomatic victory over an American administration that overestimated its ability to shape the course of events on the mainland.

A LITTLE KNOWN OFFENSIVE

Because of its coincidence with Imphal-Kohima and the landings on Saipan and the battle of the Philippine Sea, the Japanese offensive in southern China in the summer of 1944 is one of the many neglected operations of the war, yet it proved to be a singularly important campaign. It was the exception in that at a time when the tide of war ran fiercely against the Axis, the Japanese put together a very successful offensive that produced not a Chinese failure, which might have been excused, but a collapse which could not be dismissed with a casual lack of concern that had accompanied previous Chinese setbacks.

Defeat at Japanese hands had been China's lot since 1931, her worst failures having been in 1937 and 1938 when her northern provinces and the Yangtse valley as far upriver as the Wuhan cities had been lost. These defeats could be explained away; China without allies could not avoid defeat by an undistracted Japan. But by 1944 the situation had changed, and the old excuses no longer sufficed. Now it was Japan, not China, that was alone and forced to divide her attention between various defeats. Now China had great allies who, by the Moscow Declaration of October 1943, had placed her on an equal footing with themselves. A great power of 1944 could not rest content with further defeats or more years of under achievement: past quiesence had to be justified by effective future resistance.

ICHI-GO brought home to Chinese and foreigner alike that Chiang Kai-shek's armies of 1944 were no more effective than they had been in 1937, and if there were mitigating circumstances for the failure on the Salween there was no explaining away the defeats in southwest China. Here the Kuomintang regime had lived off the backs of the people for years, and its exploitative rule, its corruption and merciless treatment of its domestic opponents could only be justified by successful resistance to any future Japanese move. In the spring of 1944 the Japanese *Twelfth Army* overran Honan at a cost of 869 dead and 2,281 wounded, and it was small wonder that enraged peasants massacred Kuomintang troops whose only thought was flight in the face of an advancing enemy.

An augury for the future, this was the first large-scale repudiation of the Kuomintang on the part of the ordinary people. A regime and army that claimed to be nationalist, revolutionary and popular were revealed to be none of these things, merely tyrannical and incompetent. An American source in 1944 dubbed the Honan Kuomintang as a combination of Tammany Hall and the Spanish Inquisition, and the events of 1944 in the province proved to be a foretaste of what was to happen after 1946 when the Kuomintang and the communists renewed their civil war with all its former fury.

The Japanese army planned *ICHI-GO* as a multiphase affair, the first stage, *KO-GO*, beginning on 17 April when the *37th Infantry Division* crossed the Hwang-ho into Honan. Signs of a Japanese buildup north of the river had been treated by the Chinese and Americans as indication of an enemy offensive in May, and at first the *37th Division*'s incursion into Honan was thought to be yet another of the rice raids that had been common since 1938. On this occasion, however, the *62nd* and *110th Infantry Divisions* crossed the Hwang-ho two days after the *37th*, thereby ending any possibility of this being a small-scale or local affair.

The three Japanese divisions pushed along the Peking-Hankow railroad, their advance supported on the right by the *26th Infantry Division* and complemented by a single brigade from the *Eleventh Army* which advanced from Hankow. The latter cleared the

Washengkwan Pass, the Chengchow-Peking line was secured on 9 May, and the *26th Division* took Loyang on 26 May. These successes provided the Japanese with a direct line of supply to Hankow, enabled them to straighten their front and give depth to what had been the Wuhan salient, and left the *Eleventh Army* free to develop *TOGO 1*, the drive via Changsha to Hengyang.

The general Japanese intention was then to develop *TO-GO 2*, the advance by the *Eleventh Army* on Kweilin while the *Twenty Third Army* fought its way from Canton to secure Liuchow, the hub of Kwangsi's rail system. Later, in *TO-GO 3*, the *Twenty Third Army* was again to advance from Canton, this time towards Kukong with the aim of linking up with the *Eleventh Army* coming south from Hengyang. Japanese planning envisaged rounding off operations with an offensive in the first months of 1945 from the Liuchow area to Nanning and thence into Japanese-occupied French Indo-China.

CHINA AT WAR

TO-GO 1 began on 27 May when five of the *Eleventh Army*'s eight divisions crossed the length of the middle Yangtse between Ichang and Wuhan. The Japanese committed 100,000 troops in the first echelon of an attack on a front whose width was intended to disguise the main axis of advance for as long as possible. Such an attempt could never be more than partially successful, because in the area of operations only Changsha and Hengyang possessed importance sufficient to justify so large a Japanese effort. The main Japanese thrust was along the Yoyang-Changsha axis, the Japanese making their major effort to the east of the Siang and only a supporting operation to the west of the river. It was this latter effort that ran into problems presented by the Ninety Ninth Army, but these difficulties were overcome and in any event they were overshadowed by the extent of Japanese success east of the river.

The sheer scale of the Japanese attack seemingly had a paralyzing effect on the Chinese as the *3rd* and *13th Infantry Divisions* breached the Changsha-Liuyang line and secured the latter on 14 June. Changsha was attacked that same day and was occupied on 16 June when the *40th*, *68th* and *116th Infantry Divisions* pressed an attack that was not resisted. The Fourth Army abandoned Changsha without a fight, claiming as justification for its withdrawal that the enemy had used poison gas during his attack. With Changsha secured, the *Eleventh Army* committed the *68th* and *116th Divisions* to the drive on Hengyang. The city's airfield was secured on 26 June and Hengyang itself attacked for the first time two days later. The city, however, was garrisoned by Major-General Fong Hsien-chueh's Tenth Army, and formation, commander, and area commander, General Hsueh Yueh, knew their business. But neither general was a member of Chiang's circle, and in the maze of personal and regional infighting that characterized the warlord politics of Chiang's court, Changsha suffered from the handicap of having formations and generals who were competent, willing to fight and hence considered unreliable. Competence threatened independence, and Chiang's only interest was to sustain shadows of himself.

Chiang's subsequent attempt to prevent the local Kwangsi command from reinforcing Hengyang provoked open talk of secession within the province that was only stilled by the realization that the United States would not support such a move and that Kwangsi could not 'go it alone'. With the Japanese pressing into the province, the Kwangsi command could not afford an open breach with Chiang, even though it continued to ignore his claim that the communists alone stood to gain if the Tenth Army was defeated and Hengyang lost. In the end, of course, Hengyang was lost, as it had to be from the time Chiang refused to provide any means for its defense. It is quite possible that Hengyang would have been lost even if Chiang had made an effort to support the Tenth Army, but that was not the point at issue. The point was that Chiang deliberately withheld support from Kwangsi and the Tenth Army, Hengyang being lost on 8 August after a month-long siege.

The fall of Hengyang enabled the Japanese to press ahead with *TO-GO* 2 and *3*, but though they continued to advance until the following March with a number of offensives throughout the south, they were obliged to relinquish their newly acquired gains during the spring in order to reinforce their depleted garrisons in Manchuria. Such a development was comment enough on *ICHI-GO*'s relevance. Japan's last offensive and last success had no value at a time of increasing enfeeblement and defeat on every other front. No amount of success in China could shape the course of the war to Japan's advantage, because victory on the mainland was irrelevant if she could not command the seas that washed her own coasts and those of northern China. The railroad south from Yoyang led the Japanese nowhere except to defeat, and this the Americans were beginning to realize.

In mid-1944 the American leadership for the first time glimpsed the possibility of a Japanese defeat without the need for a major land campaign in Asia. Such a conclusion ran contrary to all previous American strategic thinking that had always accorded China an important role in the prosecution of the war against Japan. But by June 1944 doubts about this article of faith, plus the view that if an effort on the mainland was needed then the Soviets rather than the Chinese were better placed to carry it out, naturally raised doubts about the wisdom and practicality of American policy in China. The American problem was that reexamination of the Chinese connection came at the very time when Japanese success in southern China provoked a series of major crises within China, within the American high command, and in Sino-American relations.

STILWELL'S ISOLATION

These various crises came to center upon Stilwell even though by mid-1944 his involvement in Chinese affairs, the formation of American policy, and the conduct of Sino-American relations was relatively small. This situation was partly the result of Stilwell's doing since he had deliberately maintained a low profile.

He did this for two reasons. First, he had given up hope of results from Chiang's regime. Whatever little respect he had ever had for Chiang had long since evaporated, and Stilwell was convinced that Chiang lacked the ability and will to reform and regenerate China. He believed that the generalissimo's intention was to sit out the war and that he would do all in his power to frustrate Stilwell's effective employment of the Chinese forces nominally placed under his command. Tiring of the corruption and incompetence of Chiang and the Kuomintang, Stilwell spent much of his time in northeast India with the Northern Combat Area Command where Chiang's writ did not run.

Stilwell's second reason for adopting a low profile was that he really had no wish to be associated with an American policy in China with which he strongly disagreed. His views on the need to strengthen Chinese field formations had been set aside in favor of those of his air commander, Major-General Claire L Chennault. Washington and Chiang had accepted the increasingly strident claims of Chennault and the air lobby that a strategic bombing campaign against Japan from bases in China could achieve significant results; that the Japanese would be unable to mount an offensive against American bases in southern China without withdrawing substantial forces from the Pacific; and that any offensive that the enemy did put together would be countered effectively by the combination of American bombers and Chinese troops.

All three claims were wildly wrong. The results achieved by the 14th Air Force in China never justified and never could justify the vast effort that went into base construction and the creation of a line of supply that reached halfway around the world. Far from being forced to withdraw formations from the Pacific to deal with American bases in southern China, the Japanese continued to reinforce the Pacific theater from Manchuria and northern China even as they completed their arrangements for *ICHI-GO*. Moreover, as *KO-GO* and *TO-GO* showed only too well, American bombers could slow but not halt a Japanese offensive while Chinese forces –

with certain honorable exceptions – could do neither. Stilwell had foreseen the possibility of an air offensive against Japan from bases in China provoking an attack that could not be resisted, but having been overruled on this matter of policy, his subsequent low profile represented a double invitation to Chiang, Chennault and Washington – to implement their chosen course of action, and to accept the consequences. Only in the last weeks before the Japanese attack did Chiang and Chennault have second thoughts about the policy to which they were committed, and by then there was nothing that could be done to forestall disaster. The only course of action available to them was to try to fix responsibility for their failures on Stilwell.

STILWELL'S DISMISSAL

In the wake of *TO-GO 1*, Washington turned to Stilwell as the only person who might still be able to remedy the situation in China, and during July Roosevelt sought to have him appointed field commander of all Chinese forces in China. In formulating this demand, the exchanges between Roosevelt and Chiang became increasingly acrimonious for one very obvious reason. Such an appointment could not be seen as anything but an open admission of incompetence on Chiang's part. With so many enemies within China and an unbroken run of failures behind him, Chiang could never have given way to demands that were forwarded to him by Stilwell himself.

This was the final element in the problem of command within China, for by this time there was an irreconcilable breach between Chiang and Stilwell. Stilwell had a rasping contempt for Chiang, and indeed the latter's historical reputation has never recovered from the withering scorn to which it was subjected by Stilwell. Chiang knew of Stilwell's loathing of him. Mutual antagonism was heightened by the fact that 1944 sharply contrasted their ability to command. Chiang achieved nothing to compensate for the failure in southern China and Stilwell did nothing to mitigate the success at Myitkyina. These events therefore served to underline rather than reconcile the differences between Chiang and Stilwell.

Amid this web of personal and political calculations, the Roosevelt demands were doomed to disappointment because Washington failed to think through its policy. Its attempt to raise Stilwell to the *de facto* position of supreme commander in China was not accompanied by a willingness to have or see Chiang removed from power as the means of realizing that aim, and it was not prepared to use aid as the means of beating concessions from Chiang and the Kuomintang. In the final analysis, the Americans were frightened to end aid or discard Chiang in case either resulted in the one thing they were trying to avoid; the collapse of China. Thus the Americans foreswore use of the only means that might have enabled them to achieve their objectives, and in so doing they failed to realize the limits of American power when it came to dealing with Chiang and shaping events on the Asian mainland.

In so doing, Washington overplayed its hand and pushed Stilwell too far into the center of the stage for him to escape unscathed when Roosevelt's initiative collapsed. Chiang had no intention of actively assisting his own political demise, and with all the obstinacy of the ineffectual fool that he was, he knew that he had the beating of Washington because he knew the weakness of the American demands. The Americans could not have their way unless Chiang allowed himself to be shunted into the political and personal sidings, and Chiang knew that if the Americans threatened to choke him to death he had only to threaten to die to have their measure. Roosevelt's charm and occasional fervor could not compete with such realism, and when Chiang rejected Roosevelt's demands, castigated Stilwell as the cause of all China's problems, and demanded the recall of his chief of staff, Washington found that it had no option but to comply and to try to gloss over what was clearly a very serious reverse for American diplomacy.

Stilwell had compensation of a kind for this treatment and the shabby homecoming he was afforded. One of only five four-star generals in the American army in 1944, he assumed command of the Tenth Army on Okinawa after its commander was killed in action, and he would have commanded it during Operation Coronet, the invasion of Honshu planned for March 1946, had it not been for the Japanese surrender of September 1945. As it was, Stilwell was present at the surrender ceremony aboard the *Missouri* in Tokyo Bay on 2 September, though this was an indication of the weakness and drift of American policy towards China at this time.

For all his vituperation, Stilwell's place was in China where he proved irreplaceable – a fact that Washington acknowledged when it appointed *three* generals to fill the various posts that he had held during his time in Asia. But far more important than any question of personalities was the fact that Stilwell's departure heralded a steady purging of those American military and civilian personnel who shared Stilwell's low opinion of Chiang and the Kuomintang. With key American posts in China held by individuals increasingly uncritical of a worthless, doomed regime, American policy towards China became ever more erratic.

Deep down, Washington knew that the Kuomintang regime was politically, morally, socially and economically bankrupt, but the United States, in social and industrial terms the most radical state in the world, emerged as a conservative superpower that would not accept the radical alternative of a break with Chiang. In the third quarter of 1944, American policy towards China was confronted by its acid test, and it was resolved in favor of a regime devoid of competence and integrity. With the American government recommitted to an increasingly discredited regime, Stilwell's removal from the scene marked the start of irrationalism in American policy towards China. This lasted for nearly three decades.

CHIANG'S PYRRHIC VICTORY

But as many observers have noted, Chiang's diplomatic victory over the Americans regarding the Stilwell affair was the last victory of any kind that the generalissimo was to win for many years. In any event, it was a triumph that could never offset the impact of *ICHI-GO* in the eyes of the Chinese population. The recall of an American general from Chungking was not a *quid pro quo* for the loss of half a dozen provinces. The significance of the Kuomintang's defeats in central and southern China in the course of 1944 is hard to understate because the events that took place in Honan clearly showed the direction in which opinion within China was moving.

Years of Kuomintang rule slowly but remorselessly led to general social collapse as every section of society was progressively alienated from a regime that combined indulgence and repression with ineffectiveness. Since the fall of the Manchu dynasty had ended a period of imperial instability in favor of a republican variety, the Kuomintang had been the dominant political force within China. In name and (at certain times and in certain areas) in fact, the Kuomintang had been the legal and sole government of China, but by 1944 it had outstayed its welcome.

In three decades it had exhausted any fund of goodwill it had once enjoyed. The peasants, loaded down with debts and taxes, expected nothing from a regime that refused to tackle the problem of land reform and which was identified with the monied interests that kept the peasantry in its state of thralldom. Unless they were corrupt, the administrative and professional classes were crushed to the status of coolies by staggering inflation, and they had little reason to support a political party that was devoid of ideological commitment and was little more than a vehicle of personal ambitions. The Kuomintang could not exercise power radically, and its inability to use power positively was matched by its refusal to share it with others.

Public opinion was slowly moving in favor of the communists, who alone seemed willing and able to carry the war to the Japanese. For many years the communists had claimed to be actively prosecuting the war against the invader while the Kuomintang sanctioned Japanese occupation by its inaction. In prosecuting a guerrilla struggle against the Japanese – though with nothing like the singleness of purpose that they claimed for their actions – the communists had begun to tap the reservoirs of Chinese nationalism and xenophobia that the Kuomintang fondly imagined to be its own exclusive preserves. The Kuomintang could not see that its nationalism had been rendered threadbare by 1944 because of its passivity in the face of Japanese occupation.

By 1944, the various political and military forces within China had achieved an uneasy balance. For most Chinese their country's great power status counted for little when part of it was occupied by the Japanese and the remainder was misgoverned by a regime that was, in the words of one observer, too weak to rule but too strong to be overthrown. Although by 1944 the communists had emerged as the only possible alternative to the Kuomintang, they had yet to secure the initiative.

The Kuomintang's corruption and violence towards its opponents left it with no moral advantage over the communists, and it could not claim to be a bastion against communist tyranny when it had long since adopted the form and ethics of the police state as the soft option to a policy of reform and honest government. The communists were pressing the Kuomintang harder with every passing year, but their piecemeal nation building within the areas they controlled had not yet brought them to a position to challenge Chungking. Two more years passed before the communists were able to emerge from the shadows, and then their moment came only after Kuomintang licentiousness and rapine in the liberated areas of Manchuria and northern China completed the process of alienating the one part of society that was hitherto uncommitted to either side. The peoples of these provinces greeted the returning Kuomintang as liberators and saviors, until painful experience revealed otherwise and drove them into the arms of the communists.

FINALE

Given these events, the significance of June 1944 is obvious. *ICHI-GO* was probably not quite the point of no return for the Kuomintang, but it would hardly be an exaggeration to suggest that this offensive was the swansong of one empire and the death warrant of another – a kind of collective Japanese-Kuomintang death rattle while both were still alive. Neither really recovered from the campaign, and herein was one very important difference between the events in China and those in Burma. By the time that the British had fought and won the battle of Imphal-Kohima there was no disguising the fact that India, Burma and China were backwaters that had lost their immediate significance for the waging of war against Japan. Moreover, neither India nor Burma retained any long-term significance for Britain, which had divided the two in 1937 because of the strength of Burmese separatist opinion and which in 1942 had conceded the principle of post-war Indian independence.

Except in the narrowest of senses, Britain was not fighting in India and Burma in order to retain one imperial possession and to recover another. Nevertheless, the battles for Imphal and Kohima and the subsequent campaign in Burma, possessed a very real importance for Britain and her empire.

Manipur and northern Burma were where the Indian Army – soon to be divided between India and Pakistan – recovered its self-respect after the disastrous middle years of the war. Burma was where East and West African formations assumed a maturity and status that would have been unthinkable even a few years before, with all that that entailed for the future. Burma was where the British did much to wipe away the disgrace of 1941 and 1942, the clearing of Burma between June 1944 and May 1945 being the basis of the post-war British return to southeast Asia. After September 1945, the British restored their authority over Malaya and Singapore, Hong Kong and their old possessions on Borneo. At the same time, they occupied the Indies and southern Indo-China in order to disarm and repatriate the Japanese. While none of these operations could have been carried out had it not been for the American victory in the Pacific, the British reearned their right to be regarded as a major power in Asia at Imphal-Kohima and in the course of the reconquest of Burma.

The battles for Imphal and Kohima, the greatest defeats suffered by the Japanese army before Luzon and Manchuria, were the title deeds of the British return to their lost possessions, though these same deeds were to be surrendered a second and final time within two decades. Yet these second 'surrenders' were orderly affairs. When the British ceded independence to their various possessions they did so from a position of strength, with good will on both sides. For the British, their final retreat from Asia was not marked with the defeat and bitterness that stained the departure of the Dutch, the French and finally the Americans in southeast Asia. Clearly many factors were at work in deciding the fates of the various powers in their particular areas of interest, but in the case of Britain the events in eastern India in 1944 played their part in allowing her to return to her possessions in 1945 and then to rule with a large measure of popular support and success. Such a development would have been impossible had the defeats of 1942 remained unexpurgated and had the British been seen to be returning, not in their own right, but as an American appendage.

Such, then, were some of the events, and their consequences, on the mainland in June 1944. Imphal-Kohima marked the end of a successful recuperation of the British after their humbling of 1942, while *ICHI-GO* in a sense proved the ruination of the three parties involved in it. The Japanese achieved nothing but their own overextension and exhaustion, the story of their whole war effort since 1937. The Kuomintang lost credibility, stature and authority. The Americans lost their way in trying to save something from the debris.

What the future would bring was far from clear in June 1944, but in retrospect it can be seen that this month marked the end of Japanese ambitions on the mainland, despite their success in southern China. June 1944 saw Kuomintang power compromised, another step on the road to ultimate defeat. It witnessed a British recovery, and a surprising American irresolution even in their finest moment. As we have seen, on 15 June B-29 Superfortresses struck at Japan from their bases in China, and on the same day 20,000 marines landed on the island of Saipan, thereby sparking off perhaps the most important naval battle to be fought in the course of the Pacific war.

CHAPTER 3

STRUGGLE FOR THE PACIFIC

Until November 1943, the Japanese were able to delude themselves with the thought that their policy of wearing down the enemy at the forward point of contact throughout the Pacific was working successfully. The defense line laid down in January – through Wewak, New Britain, New Ireland, the northern Solomons and New Georgia group, and around the Gilberts and Marshalls – remained intact, and even if Japanese problems during the year increased to the extent that the 'new operational policy' of September called for withdrawal and a contraction of the 'front,' such difficulties did not seem insurmountable to armed forces whose 'unquenchable military optimism' precluded the thought of failure and defeat. The American carrier raids on Marcus (1 September), Tarawa and Makin (18-19 September), and Wake (5-6 October) clearly augured ill, but the overall lack of American progress since the landing on Guadalcanal (more than a year earlier) could not be anything but a source of reassurance to the Japanese.

Illusions began to end in November. Slowly at first, and then with terrifying suddenness and in overwhelming, irresistible force, the Americans shattered the outer ring of Japanese defenses in the western Pacific, neutralized Truk and bared Japan's proposed new defense line long before it was ready to meet attack. Because of the piecemeal commitment of the air groups from the 1st Carrier Division to Rabaul, the Imperial Navy was unable to counter any of the American strikes in November against the Marshalls, Bougainville, the northern Solomons and even Rabaul itself. Nor was it able to meet the landings on Bougainville (1 November), the concentration of American forces on Goodenough Island in readiness for landings in the Cape Gloucester area, and the American descent on the Gilberts.

With six fleet and five fleet carriers in support, the Americans took six atolls in the Gilberts between 20 and 29 November, five of them without undue difficulty and loss. Makin was taken between 20 and 24 November, Apamamu between 21 November and 24 November. Abaiang, Maiana and Marake were secured on 29 November. Where things went wrong for the Americans was on Tarawa where they incurred 3,301 casualties. With the garrison suffering 4,690 of its number killed, this was one of the few actions in the Pacific war when there was a rough equality of losses between an attacking American force and a defending Japanese garrison, but the appropriate comparison was not numerical but relative loss. On

Tarawa the American marines lost one in six of their number; the Japanese, with seventeen soldiers surviving to be taken prisoner, lost their entire garrison.

The losses of Tarawa shook the United States and American high command, who were becoming accustomed to the low-casualty returns of the Pacific war. Losses during the six-month campaign on Guadalcanal, for example, were just twice as heavy as those incurred in six days on Tarawa, and if the casualty lists from Papua were rather long this was of small account, since most of the losses were non-American. Yet the *real* point of Tarawa was not the heaviness but the relative lightness of American losses, particularly when the strategic results that flowed from the capture of the Gilberts are considered. Two carriers, the *Lexington* and *Independence*, were both torpedoed, and the escort carrier *Liscome Bay* was sunk with heavy loss of life by the submarine *I-175*. But even when these are added to the losses incurred ashore, the United States did not pay an orbitant price for securing the base for a triple offensive: the isolation of Rabaul, the move into the Marshalls, and the raid through the central Pacific as far to the west as the Palaus.

In December 1943 and then in January and February, the Japanese were powerless to prevent the encirclement and neutralization of Rabaul. The Cape Gloucester area was lost, then Saidor on New Guinea, and finally Green Island in the lesser Admiralties. On 31 January, the undefended atoll of Majuro in the Ratak group of the Marshalls was taken, and on the following day American forces came ashore on the largest atoll in the Pacific, Kwajalein in the Marshall's Ralik group. With Kwajalein secured on 4 February, the Americans then moved to secure Eniwetok (17-22 February) even as their carrier forces struck at Truk in an attempt to neutralize the bastion of Japanese naval power in the central Pacific.

On 17 and 18 February, aircraft from nine carriers, supported by six battleships, ten cruisers and 28 destroyers, landed a series of attacks and sweeps on and around Truk that accounted for 15 warships and auxiliaries, 24 merchantmen of 137,000 tons, and perhaps as many as 200 Japanese aircraft. Then, with the remaining Japanese positions in the Marshalls bypassed and Truk shorn of its power, the Americans moved to destroy enemy air power in the southern Marianas. Operating some 1,200 miles from Japan and 3,300 miles from Pearl Harbor, the Americans lost five aircraft in destroying 168 of the enemy on and over Saipan, Guam, Tinian and Rota. Thereafter, the carrier force bypassed the western Carolines to strike at enemy positions in the Palaus on 30 and 31 March, on Yap on the last day of the month and on Woleai on 1 April during the withdrawal to Majuro.

FRUSTRATION AND IMPOTENCE IN THE
JAPANESE CAMP

These operations drew no response from the Combined Fleet. Even before the American move against Truk, the Imperial Navy had concluded that Truk was untenable and could no longer function as a fleet base. It had pulled back most of its units when it became aware of the imminent American strike on the atoll, and in exactly the same way it was to pull back the Combined Fleet from the Palaus before the Americans arrived off the islands in March. During this latter withdrawal, the battleship *Musashi* was torpedoed by the submarine *Tunny*, but while she was able to shrug off her damage as being of little account, the Japanese high command could not do the same with regard to these events. The basis of earlier Japanese plans – the preservation of 'a fleet in being' at Truk to check and inhibit any enemy move in the central or southwest Pacific – had been swept aside, and the Combined Fleet had been forced to conduct a series of withdrawals across the whole of the western Pacific and even to fall back behind the line regarded as the one that had to be held inviolate at all costs.

The Imperial Navy could not retreat forever across the Pacific as if its own preservation was more important than the defense of Japanese possessions. At some time or another the Imperial Navy had to stand and fight, and such was its intention – though only when it had made good the error of putting its air groups ashore in Rabaul. With a minimum of six months needed to reconstitute the carrier air groups, the Imperial Navy had little option but to cede the initiative in the central Pacific and to accept the damage that the American rampage of February-April caused to its plans and installations. Given the weakened state of the Combined Fleet, the Imperial Navy knew that it could not meet an American challenge before the middle of 1944.

The Japanese planned to fight, yet the problem confronting their intention was not simply that present enemy moves had to go unchallenged but that future enemy moves could well prove unchallengeable. Off the Marianas and Palaus not a single American ship was attacked, still less sunk or damaged, and this singular ineffectiveness threatened to grow rather than diminish in the future for one very obvious reason.

These American raids, plus those against the Hollandia area (21-24 April) and Truk, Satawan and Ponape (29 April-1 May), marked the coming of age of the carrier – or, at least, the *American* carrier.

In February, March and even in April, individual American carriers attacked single targets in the western Pacific, but the fact of the matter was that such operations were becoming dated. By mid-1944 American carrier groups, backed by escort carriers that could ferry replacement aircraft and oilers that could keep them at sea for weeks at a time, had a strength and flexibility that allowed them to conduct not single raids but sustained operations in massive strength. A whole new generation of fleet carriers built for 16 days' high-speed steaming and ten days' operations were joining the fleet, and with their arrival the Americans acquired the means to move into sea areas previously barred to them, with every intention and hope of fighting for and securing command of the air. In the six months when the Japanese pulled back across the Pacific to rebuild air groups that when reconstituted would still not be able to do anything more than raid, two fleet and four light fleet carriers joined the various American task groups, thereby adding some 300 combat aircraft to the Pacific Fleet's order of battle. In the same period a further three fleet carriers were commissioned into service, but in June 1944 they remained to be deployed operationally.

Given this massive buildup of American power at a time when the Japanese were unable to cover their relatively light losses, it was clear than even as the latter made their plans to stem the tide of defeat, the means of doing so was being denied them. Between the outbreak of war and 31 March 1944, they commissioned three fleet carriers to pit against eight of the Americans, and four light fleet carriers compared to the American nine. Of their new additions only one, the fleet carrier *Taiho*, was purpose-built. Indeed, the *Taiho* was arguably the best carrier the Imperial Navy ever built, and she was certainly fit to take her place alongside the last surviving veterans of the Pearl Harbor raid, the *Shokaku* and *Zuikaku*.

Apart from these three exceptions, all the other carriers available to the Combined Fleet were very definitely 'second-team' material. All were conversions that were too slow, too weak in size of air group, or too poorly provided for defensively to be considered proper front-line units. These various conversions would have been useful complements to purpose-built fleet carriers, but they were not effective substitutes for the ones that had been lost or remained uncompleted. For example, the *Chitose*, *Chiyoda* and *Zuiho*, the members of the 3rd Carrier Division, were too small to operate the latest aircraft coming into service in 1943 and 1944 and were therefore obliged to embark obsolescent aircraft unfit to meet those of the enemy.

Even the *Taiho* was handicapped because of the shortcomings of the navy's procurement branch. Because the latter failed to insist upon the minimum possible unfolded span for its carrier aircraft and in the case of the Judy divebomber accepted an aircraft with wings that did not fold at all, the *Taiho* was limited to a 63-strong air group instead of the 84 for which she had been designed. Such inadequacies and errors littered the Japanese procurement effort, with obvious effects on battle efficiency and survivability of units. Thus while it was clear in the spring of 1944 that the next American moves would be the Saipan-Truk-Timor line, it was equally obvious to the Japanese that the Combined Fleet would have to do battle on the basis of a marked numerical inferiority of carriers and escorts, with inexperienced air groups, and with aircraft that were grossly inferior in quality to and heavily outnumbered by those in American service.

MISMATCHED COMBATANTS

Given these considerations it is hard to resist the conclusion that such was the disparity between American and Japanese carrier strengths and the sheer scale of American power that the Japanese could never hope to be able to strike decisively against even a part of the Pacific Fleet's main strength.

That, of course, was not the perspective of early 1944. The Americans began the year rightly wary of Japanese power even while they were confident in their own growing strength. But there was no real agreement within the American high command on the question of how that growing strength was to be used. As we have seen, King's was the dominant influence in devising Pacific strategy, partly because he was virtually alone in the American and Allied high commands with a clear idea of the policy that should be adopted, partly because he was head of the service that played the key role in the conduct of this war.

King's view was that in 1944 the Americans had to secure the Marianas and thereby get their thumb on the Japanese windpipe. But King's view regarding the paramount importance of these islands to Japan did not command widespread acceptance within his service, and in one crucial respect King failed to think through the logic of his assertion that in taking the Marianas the American forces would secure what amounted to a war winning position. If this was the case, the Japanese would have no option but to give battle in defense of these islands with their fleet, but having made so perceptive (and accurate) an analysis of the military geography of the western Pacific, King failed to realize how little choice his course of action would leave the Japanese.

In a manner similar to the events of late 1941 when the Americans only belatedly realized that their policies left Japan with little option but to go to war, King woke up late to the fact that a descent on the Marianas would force the Combined Fleet to come out and give battle. His subordinates, because they did not share King's absolute certainty regarding the importance of the islands, were even less convinced of the idea that the Japanese would have to commit their fleet to the defense of the Marianas.

Herein lay the basis of an ambiguity that surfaced during operations off the Marianas in June. In moving against Saipan, the fast carrier force had to discharge two tasks, the protection of the assault forces committed to the Marianas operation and the destruction of the enemy fleet in battle should the latter attempt to intervene. It was only on the very eve of battle that the American high command began to realize that these objectives were not necessarily one and the same thing.

But the various arguments within the US Navy about Pacific strategy did not take place in isolation. The service was fortunate in that the main theater of operations in the Pacific was both a service and national command, functioning under King as agent of the JCS, rather than as an Allied inter-service command directed by the CCS. The US Navy did enjoy a large degree of autonomy in its devising and implementation of policy, but it nevertheless only *shared* the Pacific with MacArthur's Southwest Pacific Command and because these two authorities could not agree on long-term objectives, the JCS was unable to settle policy a long time in advance. This was in complete contrast to the situation in Europe where the JCS always tried to commit the British to firm dates, be they ever so distant. In the Pacific the Americans adopted an opportunistic policy of the kind they would have condemned had it been British-sponsored, and as a result policy arose as much from reaction to events as from decisions that shaped circumstances.

This element of improvization could not last. By early 1944 the Pacific situation demanded firm decisions, schedules and an end to the disjointed manner in which policy was settled within the American high command. Two considerations prompted this incentive to review command arrangements and decisions. First, at the beginning of 1944 the Southwest Pacific Command made a concerted effort to abrogate for itself direction of the war effort in the Pacific. Second, the time scale involved in Pacific operations was such that casual improvization was no longer possible. A single assault landing could tie up assault and battle forces for anything up to three months, and for the invasion of Saipan assault shipping came from as far afield as Guadalcanal and Pearl Harbor and some of the support shipping from the New Hebrides. Clearly such demands of time and distance insisted upon a settled order of priorities.

THE DOUBLE OFFENSIVE

The Pacific arrangements that emerged from the Trident and Quadrant conferences represented a compromise between the demands of the Southwest Pacific Command and Admiral Chester W Nimitz's Pacific Ocean Areas command, in effect the rising level of

American production being judged sufficient to give both what they wanted. Each was to develop an offensive across the western Pacific, but in the aftermath of Tarawa, MacArthur sought to subordinate the navy and the central Pacific option to his own requirements. Lack of an overall commander in the Pacific irked MacArthur because he believed himself uniquely qualified for such a post. In trying to alter the balance between the two Pacific commands to his own very considerable advantage MacArthur used three arguments: the dangers inherent in divided command; the danger of a twin offensive being defeated in detail for want of overwhelming concentration at the point of contact; and the assertion that his own losses, being much smaller than those incurred in the Pacific Ocean Areas, were reason enough to concentrate future efforts on a single axis of advance in the Southwest Pacific Area.

These views were expounded for the first time at a liaison conference of the two Pacific commands held in Pearl Harbor on 26-27 January 1944, and quite amazingly they were accepted by Nimitz and his subordinates. Senior officers of the Pacific Fleet showed little enthusiasm for a drive against the Marianas, and there was little support for any move into the central Pacific other than one directed against Truk. This reluctance to embrace the central Pacific option stemmed from the combination of the Tarawa experience, skepticism about the alleged importance of the Marianas, and justified concern at the prospect of mounting operations in the Marianas without the support of shore-based aircraft.

But while this liaison conference was held before the Majuro-Kwajalein landings and the carrier rampage of February and March revealed the opportunities that presented themselves to the Pacific Fleet on the central axis, it came after King had very deliberately set out for Nimitz the strategy to be employed in the central Pacific in 1944 during one of their routine conferences at San Francisco on 3-4 January. The subsequent MacArthur-Nimitz accord therefore provoked King's fury, not least because he obviously felt badly let down by Nimitz.

King had no intention of allowing any subordinate, however illustrious, to assume powers of decision properly reserved to the JCS and CCS, and it formed no part of his plans to create the most powerful fleet in history in order to see it become the vehicle of MacArthur's ambitions. King refused to defer to MacArthur's strategic opinions, and in his view the idea of a drive along the northern coast of New Guinea to the Philippines could never get around the awkward fact that at some stage the central Pacific would have to be cleared in order to free communications to the west.

To King the proposed *schwerpunkt* inside the line of the Marshalls, Carolines and Marianas was nonsense. The danger of converging enemy counterattacks, the presence of strong enemy forces in rear areas that could be reinforced, and the obvious advantages to be gained by mounting a two-pronged offensive that would keep the enemy's forces divided and on the wrong foot were to King sufficient reason to dismiss the 27-28 January out of hand. The upshot was the Joint Chiefs of Staff directive of 12 March 1944.

This direction was the master plan for the coming year. Under its terms and those of its various codicils, MacArthur and Nimitz were instructed to abandon any thought of directing their respective forces against Rabaul and Truk. The two great Japanese bases of the southwest and central Pacific were not to be subjected to direct assault but bypassed and isolated. MacArthur was to advance beyond Rabaul and then, after bypassing enemy concentrations along the northern coast of New Guinea, was to aim to land on Mindanao on 15 November. Because sigsint had identified the *Seventeenth Army* in eastern New Guinea and the *Second Army* around Manokwari on the Vogelkop, but few enemy combat troops in the Hollandia area, MacArthur was instructed to sidestep Wewak, seize Hollandia in April, and thereafter advance westwards into positions from which the offensive into the southern Philippines could be developed. Because Hollandia was 500 miles from the nearest Allied air base at Nadzab, MacArthur's effort at Hollandia was to be supported by the fast carrier force, not, as MacArthur wanted, for an indefinite period but for three days.

This refusal by King and Nimitz to be more generous in their support subsequently prompted the decision to secure Aitape in order to obtain a covering position for the main effort at Hollandia. Nimitz's own orders were to secure the southern Marianas on 15 June, and thereafter move into the western Pacific in order to secure the Palaus in mid-September. In this way the Pacific Fleet would obtain a position from which to support MacArthur's drive into the southern Philippines in November. Subsequent objectives remained undefined.

Landings on either Luzon or Formosa and Amoy were scheduled provisionally February 1945, the thinking being that the Chinese islands were to be targets if it was felt that Luzon could be bypassed. Luzon would be attacked if it was believed that the northern Philippines had to be secured as an essential requirement for the move towards China. On this matter the Americans were prepared to wait upon events before coming to a decision, but after July 1944 the thoughts of the navy increasingly turned to the possibility of bypassing the Philippines, Formosa and China entirely and to aim for Iwo Jima and Okinawa. Such imaginative flexibility was diluted for several reasons, the Americans ultimately settling for the Luzon option in conjunction with Iwo Jima and Okinawa.

But if the 12 March directive failed to settle all arguments about strategic policy, there was no avoiding the fact that it provided the basis of a plan of campaign designed to carry the war into the western Pacific in the course of the next 12 months. In doing so the JCS directive set down a program and timetable that would involve American forces breaching the positions that the Japanese considered their *ne plus ultra* line in the second half of 1944, by which time the Japanese reconstitution of their air groups would have been completed. Clearly, therefore, a fleet action was more than a mere possibility. As it was, months of planning and preparation by both sides were even then coming together at roughly the same time. Four days before the JCS directive was promulgated, Admiral Mineichi Koga, commander-in-chief of the Combined Fleet, issued the plan which he intended to put into effect to prevent the Americans breaking into the western Pacific basin and which would allow the Imperial Navy to fight and win 'the decisive battle' that would shatter American power.

INTRODUCING PLAN Z

Koga's plan of campaign, known as Plan Z, was based upon and elaborated the main features of the 'new operational policy' of September 1943 that had defined the Saipan-Truk-Timor line as the one on which the Japanese would stand. Downgrading the Palaus to the status of staging post for formations in forward positions on New Guinea because he discounted the group providing a fleet base in the future, Koga reconfirmed the policy of strengthening positions on the Vogelkop and in the Carolines and Marianas, and reaffirmed instructions to forces in eastern New Guinea, the Bismarcks, the northern Solomons and the Marshalls to continue to resist to the limit of their strength in order to buy time for the preparation of defenses to the west.

Even so modest a framework for plans presented the Japanese with problems because even before Plan Z was issued the attempt to reinforce the various garrisons was not carried out without loss. An increasingly effective American submarine campaign against Japanese shipping exacted a heavy toll amongst reinforcements, and continued to do so even after Koga's directive was issued. Indeed, the seriousness of Japanese losses increased in the second quarter of 1944 as the pace of war quickened, the losses incurred by the *32nd* and *35th Infantry Divisions* in May when *en route* to western New Guinea being particularly grievous. Even more serious, however, was the fact that by the time Koga completed his plans this same submarine campaign had exacted such a toll of the tanker fleet that Japan no longer had the means to continue the war on the basis of the amounts of oil reaching the home islands.

The fleet could no longer stay in home waters, close to the yards where its units could refit and be repaired, because it no longer had the oil it needed to exercise in the relatively safe waters that washed Japan. The Combined Fleet had to go south to be near its sources of oil, and in effect this meant its using Tawi Tawi in the southern Philippines as its advance base. There the fleet would be within whatever cover the Philippines-Halmahera line provided, and it would still be within easy reach of the oil fields of northern Borneo. In an emergency, the Japanese units could use the almost pure oil of these fields without its being refined, but in its crude state this oil was dangerously volatile and contained impurities that gutted ships' boilers.

The forced interest in Tawi Tawi explains why the Palaus were discounted as a fleet base, but that did not mean that the Japanese relinquished their interest in these islands. It was their hope and expectation that the next American move would be against the group. If the Americans proved so obliging, the Combined Fleet at Tawi Tawi would be ideally placed to counterattack – though very clearly there was a strong element of wishful thinking about this particular scenario. The Combined Fleet had little option but to hope that the Americans would move against the Palaus with the result that battle was joined west of the Eauripik-New Guinea rise. It did not have the means to conduct sustained operations further to the east. Any action in defense of the Marianas would represent a supreme effort (in more ways than one) at the very limit of the Combined Fleet's endurance.

Other elements of optimism, indeed self-delusion, pervaded Plan Z, but it has to be admitted that any Japanese plan drawn up at this time with the aim of doing battle with American carrier forces would have needed a fair measure of both ingredients. The fact of the matter was that Vice Admiral Asaburo Ozawa's 1st Mobile Fleet, with its nine carriers and 450 aircraft, was of such uncertain quality and inadequate quantity that it needed a miracle to have any possible chance of success in an action with enemies who had given clear indication of what they could do if given the chance.

Plan Z tried to provide this miracle by utilizing the network of bases in the western Pacific to concentrate shore-based air power and the aircraft from Ozawa's fleet against an enemy carrier force trespassing in the western Pacific. The Japanese idea was to use their carrier aircraft to 'shuttle bomb' the enemy by landing on airfields, their shore-based and carrier-borne aircraft thereby complementing one another and making up for individual lack of strength while the carriers themselves stayed outside the range of American carrier aircraft.

There was a neatness, an almost geographical and mathematical precision, in this plan and intention, especially in its provisions for the ideal battle in defense of the Palaus. Nothing the Americans could do would be more calculated to destroy every existing American advantage than their moving into positions in which they could be attacked from the Marianas, Carolines, Philippines, Palaus and New Guinea, and by the carriers. Herein was a weakness obvious to the plan's author. There could be no guarantee that the enemy would contribute to his own embarrassment by moving into a position from which he could be attacked from three sides. The Japanese must have been aware of the possibility of an American move against the southern Marianas or western New Guinea – ignoring the open door and choosing instead to smash down the door frame.

Plan Z made two further false assumptions about a battle in the western Pacific. First, it assumed that the defense would be able to concentrate before the arrival of the enemy as the American carriers were detected at ranges beyond their strike capability. In this way the Japanese would be able to use their feeder routes to bring up forces before the enemy had chance to overwhelm a local formation or group of formations. The Japanese failed to realize that the Americans had the means to neutralize not an island base or a number of bases within a single island group but *several island groups* at one and the same time. Second, Plan Z assumed, as indeed it had to assume, a reasonable level of effectiveness on the part of Japanese air formations. This, unfortunately for the Japanese, was not the case.

KOGA'S IMPOSSIBLE TASK

Plan Z was probably as good a plan as the Japanese could put together in early 1944, but Koga himself had no illusions about the nature. When appointed to the command of the Combined Fleet, he remarked that his predecessor had been killed at the right time, before the unavoidable defeats began. Koga had been dealt a losing hand from the time of his appointment, and in his year as commander-in-chief he was obliged to conduct a series of withdrawals as a bewildering multitude of threats began to develop across the whole of the Pacific.

After nearly a year of retreat, Koga knew that the time for withdrawals would have to end. His best chance of ever making Plan Z work came just three weeks after the plan itself was issued and two months before the fleet was ready to fight. The American operation against the Palaus in March was exactly the type of operation the Japanese wanted the enemy to carry out when the Combined Fleet was ready to give battle, but because his forces were unready when the Americans moved to attack the Palaus in late March, Koga ordered them back to the southern Philippines. He himself set out for Davao on Mindanao – designated as command headquarters in the event of a naval battle in southern waters by flying boat on 31 March.

This flight proved Koga's last, and provided the Americans with their most distinguished victim of their Palaus raid, because Koga's flying boat was lost without trace. His chief of staff, Vice Admiral Shigero Fukudome, travelling separately, was also caught in the same storm and his aircraft was forced to ditch in the sea just to the south of Cebu City. Fukudome and eight subordinates were taken prisoner by Filippino guerrillas who also recovered certain documents that Fukudome had in his possession when captured. These documents included Plan Z and a special cipher.

This turn of events left the Japanese with a compromised plan of campaign and the enemy with full details of Japanese intentions. Equally important, the disappearance of fleet commander, chief of staff, and most of the fleet staff came at the very time when the enemy was moving against Japanese positions in central New Guinea.

On the same day as American carriers raided the Palaus, Liberators from the 5th Air Force struck Hollandia and repeated their raids on 3, 5, 12 and 16 April. In the course of these attacks the Americans accounted for a minimum of 340 aircraft at a cost of four combat losses. The ease of this victory reflected American strength and effectiveness plus the fact that two years of constant attrition had destroyed the effectiveness of the *6th Air Division* to the point where its physical annihilation was completed in just six raids. Such was the extent of American success in this episode that the Hollandia operation lost the overwhelming need for carrier support, but all the same the fast carrier forces came south to cover the landings at Hollandia and Aitape on 22 April. Their operations between 21 and 24 April were unchallenged by Japanese aircraft remaining at Hollandia and were all but unopposed even by aircraft from other bases to the west.

The ease with which Japanese power in central New Guinea was broken naturally encouraged the idea of an immediate offensive into western New Guinea. The capture of Hollandia provided the Americans with bases from which they could subject every Japanese garrison and base east of the Moluccas to attack, but it was obviously those bases nearest to Hollandia – in the Geelvink Bay area – that attracted the 5th Air Force's attention. Indeed, even before the landings at Hollandia and Aitape American thoughts had turned to the possibility of securing Sarmi because in Japanese hands this base could pose a constant threat to any attempt to build up air power in central New Guinea. But after the Hollandia landing Sarmi began to fade from American calculations.

Reconnaissance suggested that its air strips could not be used by heavy bombers, and as a result American interest began to focus on nearby Wakde Island which had airfields that suffered from no such disability. With the Americans determined to secure a base from which to strike at the southern Philippines and the Palaus and Carolines, a plan of campaign for landings on Wakde and in the Arare-Toem area on 17 May was drawn up and approved by MacArthur. The same plan also envisaged a further development of the offensive with landings on Biak Island on 27 May. The American calculation was that Biak was lightly held and could be secured quickly if obvious Japanese weakness could be exploited immediately.

The crucial point about the Hollandia-Aitape operation for the Japanese was that it took place in an interregnum. It took time to decide upon Koga's replacement and to gather a new staff to replace the one lost on 31 March, and the lack of any Japanese response to American moves in central New Guinea was in part the result of the new fleet commander, Admiral Soemu Toyoda, having yet to complete the process of gathering all the threads of battle into his hand. By the time he had done so the possibility of countering enemy moves at Hollandia and Aitape had passed, Sarmi had been rendered untenable, and the means of preventing further enemy moves in this area had been destroyed.

On 2 May the Imperial Navy took the decision to abandon the center and to make Biak Island and Manokwari the twin centers of resistance in western New Guinea, but the success of the submarine *Harder* on 6 May in accounting for the equivalent of a division from the combined strength of the *32nd* and *35th Infantry Divisions* ensured that neither could be held in strength. The navy, now aware that the losses of previous weeks had robbed it of the troops and transports needed to reconstitute a defense line anywhere between Manokwari and Sarmi, on 9 May designated Sorong and Halmahera as the new centers of resistance in the Indies.

Thus within a single month the Japanese, who had begun April locked in battle in the Madang area, were obliged to write off Hollandia-Aitape plus the Biak-Manokwari line in favor of a policy of holding the toehold of Sorong and the Halmahera group. This involved drawing back the front over a distance of a thousand miles in the 17 days from the time that American forces came ashore at Hollandia. But this did not mean an end to the campaign on New Guinea. The Japanese high command might decide to pull back, but its forces left behind knew what was expected of them.

In the Hollandia and Aitape areas the *Eighteenth Army* tried desperately to concentrate against the Aitape beachhead in the sure knowledge that any attempt to withdraw through the jungle to western New Guinea could only have one outcome. The *Eighteenth Army* lacked the strength, equipment, supplies and command organization to have any chance of throwing the Americans back into the sea. Its attempt to do so only resulted in its own ruination at the battle of Driniumor, but it was not until 27 November that the Americans handed over the sector to the 6th Australian Division, and it was not until 10 May 1945 that this veteran formation was able to secure Wewak. Even then, Lieutenant-General Hatazo Adachi and the remnants of his army remained in the field, and they were the last Japanese in southeast Asia to surrender in the following September.

WAKDE AND BIAK: THE TRAGIC TOLL

The situation that was to develop on Wakde and Biak was not dissimilar. On Wakde, the Americans quickly overcame Japanese resistance. Within four days of landing on the island, and at a cost of 40 dead compared to the 800 of the enemy, the Americans had the air strips back in service. On the mainland, however, the story was rather different. The initial landings in the Arare-Toem area were almost unopposed, but thereafter American problems mounted as the Japanese in the region reacted, and as always the violence of the Japanese reaction was in inverse proportion to their chances of success. It was not until 30 June, after ten days of heavy fighting, that Japanese resistance on the Lone Tree Hill position was broken, and the Woske river line, designated the immediate American objective on 25 May, was not secured until mid-July. It was only at this time that the Americans were able to secure Maffin Bay and its air strip; and it was not until 1 September that the beachhead opposite Wakde could be declared secure. By then it was time for the position to be abandoned because the flow of battle had reduced Wakde and Maffin Bay to backwaters. By February 1945, all the positions on the mainland opposite Wakde, which had taken four months to secure, had been abandoned.

On Biak the Americans came close to severe embarrassment because their assessment that the island was lightly held was mistaken. The Japanese had about 11,500 troops on Biak in May, and of these some 4,000 were front-line combat troops. Moreover, geology had conspired to produce terrace-effects on the island, the Japanese therefore being provided with naturally strong positions and good fields of fire. The defense, therefore, could be expected to give a good account of itself, and it took the American forces almost a month to secure the island's airfields and to bring them back into service. Such was the slowness of their progress on Biak that the American forces were obliged to use air strips on nearby Owi Island for emergency purposes. It was not until 22 July that the back of

Japanese resistance on Biak was broken, and even then sporadic resistance ensured that the American forces were not able to consider Biak secure until 20 August. Once more, Japanese resistance had been fierce but decreasingly effective, and as on the Salween front, it was marked by a recourse to cannibalism.

The fact that the Imperial Navy had written off Biak some two weeks before the 41st Infantry Division landed on the island should have ensured that this campaign ran to an end which both sides could clearly foresee. Isolated and cut off from reinforcement and supply, the Biak garrison could only fight on to destruction and annihilation because Japanese military doctrine made no distinction between the two. But when the Americans showed their hand at Biak, the Imperial Navy threw over its 9 May provisions in an effort to secure the type of battle Koga had envisaged under the terms of Plan Z. Biak was not the Palaus and hence not the ideal location for 'the decisive battle,' but it was not an unreasonable alternative and a counterattack could lead the enemy to commit his carrier forces to the defense of his beachhead just as he had done at Hollandia five weeks earlier.

However reasonable this decision might appear, it was an impulsive and incomprehensible reversal of policy. The Japanese had just one air formation – the *23rd Air Flotilla* – with only 18 fighters and bombers within range of Biak on 27 May, and the lack of air power in this general area precluded this decision to force battle being part of a reasoned long-term strategy backed by an appropriate deployment. Moreover, with so little air power in this area the Japanese obviously ran the risk of committing their forces piecemeal against an enemy with the initial advantages of timing, position and concentration that they themselves needed to have any chance of success.

It appears that the decision to fight for Biak was shaped by a number of considerations of which two were of major significance. First, Biak had long been a major base, and its three airfields testified to the importance the island held in Japanese thinking before 9 May. Its loss would threaten to make the task of defending the Moluccas and Timor an impossible one and would undermine the whole of the Japanese position in the Palaus and western Carolines. The whole idea of an inviolate defense line that ran through western New Guinea but left Biak beyond its forward edge did not make sense, and the logic of the situation was that the initial decision to pull back from Biak was an error, the speed of the Imperial Navy's reaction to the American invasion of the island perhaps being a belated realization of this mistake.

The second consideration lay in the fact that on 3 May the navy high command in Tokyo ordered major units to Tawi Tawi in readiness for fleet action. This concentration of the carrier task groups was completed by 16 May. Thus when the American forces landed on Biak the Japanese had completed the concentration of their strength within striking distance of the island. Having concentrated to meet an emerging threat, the Japanese could hardly remain passive when the threat they were to counter began to materialize. And by 27 May these threats had begun to multiply with a vengeance. On 17 May American forces had come ashore on Wakde and at Toem; American bombers from Nadzab, took Biak under attack for the first time while compatriots from Darwin began an offensive against air bases on the Vogelkop. Further to the west, the multi-national TF 70 (26 ships from six navies) struck the city and naval base of Soerabaja on Java. Then on 20 May, Marcus was taken under attack by an American carrier task group that doubled back to strike against Wake four days later. Surface units also struck at Japanese garrisons in the Marshalls on 17, 22 and 26 May while in the same period the Imperial Navy had to contend with increasingly effective submarine activity around Davao, Halmahera and the northern exit of the Makassar Strait, and after 13 May even around the Tawi Tawi anchorage itself.

Clearly, therefore, necessity and opportunity were coming together for the Japanese with a desperate urgency. They could not remain passive in the face of all these threats, and given the danger posed by American submarines they could not remain in Tawi Tawi at all. Even before the Biak landings the Combined Fleet was under growing pressure to counter any further westwards encroachment by the Americans, and with the Biak invasion the Fleet was given its first chance to strike against an enemy who appeared to be moving into a position in which he might be counterattacked effectively.

REASONS FOR BIAK'S IMPORTANCE

While these considerations undoubtedly shaped Japanese calculations, two other matters arose from the timing of American operations that helped mould the decision to move to the support of Biak. First, the very fact that Biak represented the first chance to counterattack was itself important, not least for a new fleet command. Biak was the first test of Toyoda, and it was a test Toyoda was prepared to meet perhaps for that very reason. Second, on the matter of timing alone the Americans could not have been more provocative than picking 27 May as the date for their landings on Biak. This was 'Navy Day', the 39th anniversary of the Japanese victory over Russia at Tsu-shima.

The initial impetus for a countermove at Biak came from Tokyo, but as events unfolded the main drive was provided by Ozawa and the Combined Fleet's new chief of staff, Vice Admiral Ryunosuke

Kusaka. The latter suspected that Biak represented the enemy's main effort or could be made thus if a counterattack provoked the Americans into a setpiece battle. His own intelligence officer, Commander Chikataka Nakajima, disputed this interpretation and set out the view that the enemy's main effort would be made not in the south but in the Marianas. Inevitably the views of Kusaka rather than those of Nakajima prevailed, with the result that at the very time when the American strategists were applying the final touches to their plan of campaign in the Marianas, the Combined Fleet sought to put together a counterattack at Biak.

Nothing could have better illustrated the advantages that stemmed from the American ability to mount two complementary offensives across the western Pacific. By the time the Japanese were able to respond to the Biak episode, the American forces had shifted the point of attack back into the central Pacific. As events were to show, the Japanese proved unable to counterattack effectively at Biak, while their attempt to do so had some part to play in ensuring that they failed to meet the subsequent challenge at Saipan.

The initial Japanese reaction to the invasion of Biak was to attempt to reinforce the island's ground forces and the area's air formations. Thus in the last three days of May some 118 fighters, 40 bombers and eight reconnaissance aircraft came south from Japan, the Marianas and the western Carolines to the Vogelkop in order to revitalize the *23rd Air Flotilla*. This represented roughly one-third of the land-based air strength that the Imperial Navy had horded in readiness for 'the decisive battle.' Unfortunately for the Japanese, much of whatever effectiveness this formation had was to be lost as malaria and other tropical diseases accounted for many of the newly arrived aircrew even before combat had a chance to make inroads into their numbers.

At the same time as air reinforcements made their way to New Guinea, the fleet staff drew up an operational plan, codenamed *KON*, to reinforce Biak with troops from the *2nd Marine Brigade*. Between 31 May and 2 June some 1,700 marines were assembled first at Zamboanga and then at Davao for the move to Biak, while another 800 were gathered at Zamboanga for the run to Sorong. Both formations sailed on 2 June, the day when the Japanese made their first major air effort against American forces off Biak. The American inability to secure the airfields on Biak meant that the Japanese were unopposed in the air, but neither on this occasion nor on the following day were the Japanese able to record more than superficial damage on any units off Biak yet they lost a quarter of their number in this demonstration of ineffectiveness. The Japanese air formations fought with none of the skill of their predecessors.

The troops bound for Sorong reached their destination, but those *en route* for Biak were recalled at midday on 3 June when their presence was discovered by the enemy. With this setback went the opportunity to call off an operation that was clearly going to be an extremely hazardous affair. The smallness of the military force available as reinforcement for Biak was comment enough on Japanese hopes of success and the realism of the navy's planning. The Japanese had just one transport in the southern Philippines for the reinforcement of New Guinea, and even if the navy managed to put forces ashore on Biak it had no means to sustain or further reinforce its garrison over a prolonged period of time.

The Japanese lacked the troops, transports, logistics, escort and air power to maintain Biak, and even if an initial effort was successful then each succeeding effort would inevitably erode their remaining strength more rapidly than losses could be replaced. As it was, the effort on behalf of Biak was ill-prepared and conducted on a scale that condemned it to failure: one marine formation to Biak was irrelevant when set against Japanese needs in the theater. When they recalled their forces on 3 June the Japanese would have been well advised to have abandoned any hope of reinforcing Biak, but despite increasing enemy air activity to the west of the island and mounting Japanese destroyer losses in the Celebes Sea, the Combined Fleet decided to persist in its attempt to maintain Biak and its garrison.

FAILURE

A second reinforcement attempt began from Sorong on 7 June, the Japanese on this occasion using six destroyers, three of which towed barges in an attempt to increase the number of troops to be set ashore on Biak. On the following day, Mitchell bombers sunk the *Harusame*, but the Japanese reformed their convoy and resumed course despite reports than an enemy heavy force lay between them and their objective. Little credence was given to these reports since similar reports on 3 June had proved erroneous.

An Australian-American task force of one heavy and three light cruisers, plus 14 destroyers, was on patrol to the west of Biak, and contact between the two forces was made in the hour before midnight on 8-9 June. The Japanese showed no inclination to stand and fight such a vastly superior force, and with the three towing destroyers cutting their charges adrift the Japanese turned about and trusted to their speed to take them out of danger. Though the Allied force gave chase it could not catch or destroy the enemy, and in the course of a two-hour stern chase conducted at high speed American destroyers fired 2,005 rounds but recorded just a single hit on their elusive opponents.

The Japanese units made good their escape to Sorong, but in their turn they had failed to damage any enemy unit and had once more failed to bring succor to the Biak garrison. It would appear that a handful of troops from the barges did manage to struggle ashore on Biak, but the vast majority of their colleagues were drowned or killed by gunfire from the Allied destroyers as the latter raked the barges, speeding past them in pursuit of the fleeing Japanese units. To all intents and purposes, this second attempt to reinforce Biak proved no more successful than the first.

But the failure of 7-9 June only stiffened Japanese resolve to see things through to the bitter end. Because he was determined to force the enemy into a general fleet action in defense of their beachhead, and because he was convinced that the retention of Biak was essential to Japanese hopes of success in such a battle, Ozawa determined to make a third attempt to reinforce Biak on 15 June, but this time with such strength that success would be assured. To this end he detached a task group from his carrier fleet in order to support the units that thus far had twice failed to get through to Biak. In order to secure the initiative and an assured margin of superiority over any enemy force known to be in the area, the formation Ozawa detached for this operation consisted of the *Yamato* and *Musashi*, one heavy and two light cruisers, and eight destroyers.

This formation left Tawi Tawi on 10 June under the command of Vice Admiral Matome Ugaki, but by the time it reached Batjan on the following day the irrelevance of Biak and the futility of the effort that the Combined Fleet was making in its defense had been brought home to the Japanese. On the very day that Ugaki led his force into Batjan, American carrier forces struck at Guam, Tinian and Saipan, and thereafter continued to operate against airfields on the Marianas and shipping off the islands. On 13 June the fast battleships of Vice Admiral Willis A Lee took up the attack, and on the following day two fire support task groups, consisting of seven old battleships with cruisers and destroyer support, took up the task of leveling the beach defenses of Saipan.

The Japanese did not need these veterans of Pearl Harbor to tell them where the enemy's next blow would fall. From the time that American carriers appeared off the southern Marianas on 11 June the Japanese naval command knew that the American forces would not make any effort around Biak, and they now knew where the long anticipated 'decisive battle' would have to be fought. Accordingly, on 12 June Toyoda suspended the Biak operation and ordered Ugaki to join Ozawa in the Philippine Sea.

THE BEGINNING OF THE END FOR JAPAN

But by the time Toyoda ordered the 1st Mobile Fleet to reconcentrate, the last chance of its fighting a successful action in defense of the Marianas had gone, though Japanese commanders had no inkling of the extent of their helplessness. The situation had turned decisively against the Japanese on three counts.

First, Japanese carrier and battle forces could not advance to contact without being discovered by enemy submarines. By 12 June, 11 were covering the various exits from Tawi Tawi, 17 were off the Bonins and the Japanese home islands, and another 15 were in the Philippines, the Philippine Sea or the western Carolines. Thus the initial movement of Ozawa's forces on the morning of 13 June was immediately discovered and reported back to Pearl Harbor by the *Redfin*, and two days later the *Flying Fish* found Ozawa as he came through the St Bernardino Strait into the Philippine Sea. At almost the same time the *Seahorse* found Ugaki coming north from Batjan. From the outset there was no chance of the 1st Mobile Fleet securing either strategic or tactical surprise.

Second, because American intelligence was in possession of the documents that had been recovered from Fukudome off Cebu and were able to read most of the Imperial Navy's high-grade signals because they had broken various codes, the American high command had a very fair idea of how the Japanese might try to fight the forthcoming battle.

Third, and perhaps the most important single factor, the American carrier strikes against the southern Marianas from now onwards hit weakness. Japanese hopes of success in 'the decisive battle' rested in large part on the ability of their land-based aviation to concentrate and remain intact in order to cooperate with carrier aviation in massed attacks on the enemy. But in trying to reinforce Biak the Japanese had either lost or misdirected a third of their strength in New Guinea, and only a third remained in position to meet the American forces when the offensive against the Marianas opened. In order to break a set pattern and in the hope of securing tactical surprise, the American forces began their attack on 11 June in late afternoon, and thereafter struck at Iwo Jima and Chichi Jima on 15 and 16 June and at Guam and Rota on 16 and 17 June. Perhaps as many as 150 Japanese aircraft were destroyed in the course of these operations, and with the American forces continuing to batter the staging posts from Japan to the southern Marianas the effectiveness of Japanese land-based aviation was broken some four days before battle was joined by the two carrier fleets.

Japanese air power in the Marianas was broken even before the first American troops came ashore on Saipan on 15 June, and thereafter Ozawa's attempt to fight 'the decisive battle' could only result in a battle that was indeed 'decisive' but not in the manner that the Japanese had intended.

CHAPTER 4

SAIPAN AND THE PHILIPPINE SEA

Few shafts of humor illuminate William Manchester's grim and sombre memoir *Goodbye, Darkness*. One that does break up the account's often frightening intensity is a story, certainly apocryphal, that relates to Saipan. On board a transport bound for the island a sergeant tells his men:

'Saipan is covered with dense jungle, quicksand, steep hills and cliffs hiding batteries of huge coastal guns, and strongholds of reinforced concrete. Insects bear lethal poisons. Crocodiles and snakes infest the streams. The waters around it are thick with sharks. The population will be hostile towards us. There was a long silence. Then a corporal said, "Sarge, why don't we just let the Japs keep it?"'

As we have seen, the answer to this perceptive question was that Admiral King in Washington had decided otherwise, and with the support of his colleagues of the Joint Chiefs of Staff, he was prepared to deploy 127,571 amphibious assault troops and more than 600 ships of all types to take this and certain other islands in the southern Marianas.

Operation Forager identified Saipan as the initial American objective, and the island was to be invaded on 15 June after preliminary bombardment by carrier aircraft and battleships and cruisers from 12 June onwards. If the battle on Saipan developed favorably Guam was to be invaded on 18 June. But the main American objective was neither Saipan nor Guam but Tinian. Notwithstanding Aslito airfield in southern Saipan, Tinian offered the Americans the better airfields from which to bomb Japan, but given the fact that Japanese artillery in southern Saipan could cover the intended landing beaches in northern Tinian whereas their artillery in northern Tinian could not reach the beaches over which the Americans were to cross in assaulting southern Saipan, the American forces had to reduce Saipan before moving on to secure Tinian.

The American belief was that Tinian would fall easily enough once Saipan had been captured, but in moving against Saipan the United States inaugurated a new phase of the Pacific war. With the exception of Guadalcanal, all American offensives in the Pacific had been directed against small islands, atolls or single small places on an extended coastline. The resultant battles had been thoroughly vicious but short, and the outcome was always the same; the Japanese fought well and died to a man. But Saipan was not a small island, and the campaign for it promised to be anything but short. Saipan covered some 72 miles of difficult terrain, and before the start of Forager American Intelligence had credited it with a garrison of 17,600 troops, of whom perhaps as many as 11,000 were combat soldiers.

Even ignoring the fact that Japanese strength on Saipan was almost *double* these estimates, the taking of the island was not going to be a four- or five-day affair as had been the case at Tarawa, Kwajalein and Eniwetok. Saipan was certain to be more protracted, and it was certain to be a campaign fought over a sizeable civilian population. Moreover, there was one other difference between Forager and all the other landings that had taken place since the Guadalcanal campaign. The relative smallness and remoteness of previous American targets had in effect precluded their becoming the site of a fleet action: in the final analysis the Japanese could lose some of their outlying garrisons without suffering any real ill-effects. Saipan was different. The Marianas formed a vital link in the Japanese defensive system in the western Pacific. Their loss was not something that the Japanese would be able to shrug off with apparent lack of concern. With the Japanese having declined to fight a fleet action since the Battle of Santa Cruz Islands in October 1942, the United States had to face the possibility that the Japanese might try to use their carrier forces to contest their landings in the Marianas.

This combination of amphibious landings and the need to organize the fleet to fight a set-piece battle dictated the nature of American command arrangements for Forager. The overall venture was entrusted to Spruance, commander of the Vth Fleet, in his operational capacity of Commander TF 50. He had under command Vice Admiral Marc A Mitscher's Fast Carrier Force. This, TF 58, consisted of one battle and four carrier task groups. The former was made up of seven fast battleships, four heavy cruisers and 13 destroyers: the latter between them totalled 53 destroyers, 17 cruisers of all types and 15 fleet and light fleet carriers with a total of 904 aircraft. TF 58 was to eliminate Japanese air power in the Marianas and then to protect the amphibious forces against any attack on them that might be mounted by the enemy's carrier forces.

Because of its knowledge of Koga's Plan Z the American command was aware of two things: that the Japanese might attempt to contest the landings in the Marianas with their own fleet, and the tactics that the Japanese might employ in such an attempt. But it was not sure whether or not the Japanese would rise to the bait of an American landing in the Marianas because they could not fathom the enemy's intentions. Spruance's own view was that the Japanese were unlikely to commit their carrier forces to the defense of the Marianas. This was a view based on the belief that since the Japanese had failed to move against Biak when they had their full strength concentrated and had a clear superiority over their opponent, they were unlikely to move in the Marianas when they were certain to be clearly outnumbered.

Command of the amphibious forces assigned to Forager was entrusted to Vice Admiral Richmond K Turner. His command, the Joint Expeditionary Force or TF 51, was in charge of all amphibious operations in the Marianas, but given the distance between the various objectives in the southern Marianas command was divided between TF 52, the Northern Attack Force, and TF 53, the Southern Attack Force. The former was to direct its attentions against Saipan and Tinian, and operated under the command of Turner himself. When it came to the invasion of Tinian, Turner turned over command to his deputy, Rear Admiral Harry W Hill. Rear Admiral Richard L Conolly commanded TF 53 which was charged with securing Guam.

As commanders of their respective task forces, Turner and Conolly were to exercise operational control of the amphibious assault troops until the time when the latter were firmly established ashore. Thereafter command would devolve upon Lieutenant-General Holland M Smith, USMC, who was commander of all ground troops (Expeditionary Troops or TF 56), garrison troops and (duplicating the naval chain of command) the ground forces committed to the Northern Attack Force. These consisted of the reinforced 2nd and 4th Marine Divisions, constituted as V Amphibious Corps. The ground element of the Southern Attack Force comprised 111 Amphibious Corps with the 3rd Marine Division and the 1st Provisional Marine Brigade under the command of Major General Roy S Geiger, USMC. The decision to begin the Guam invasion would be Turner's, and he similarly exercised the power of decision with regard to any commitment of the floating reserve, Major General Ralph C Smith's 27th Infantry Division. A second Army formation, Major General Andrew D Bruce's 77th Infantry Division, was constituted as the theater reserve, but was stationed at Hawaii. Because of shipping shortages it could not be committed in the Marianas until the twentieth day after landings on Saipan.

KING'S UNIQUE INSIGHT

The American plan of campaign and command arrangements were complicated, perhaps unnecessarily so given the fact that it was the American intention to use two of their carrier task groups to hit the Bonin and Volcano Islands at the very time that the landings on Saipan took place.

The division of strength during what was certain to be the crucial phase of the whole operation was a matter that vexed King. He could see the obvious danger to American forces if the Japanese were really quick off the mark, but more importantly, King seems to have been alone in realizing that there was a basic confusion about American priorities. The role of TF 58 was ambiguous. It was expected to deal with any enemy fleet that put in an appearance: it was to protect the amphibious forces. If it managed to sink the enemy then it would automatically and simultaneously protect TF 51, but, of course, what King foresaw was the unlikelihood of events unfolding in such a convenient manner as to allow the American forces to realize two quite divergent aims at one and the same time. The plan of campaign called upon TF 58 to carry out both offensive and defensive missions, and the assumption that it would be able to do both simultaneously was too neat, too glib. It might be able to do so, but this was not something on which reliance could be placed. In identifying this weakness, King actually put his finger on the most important single flaw within the American plan of campaign, and this flaw was at the root of the controversy surrounding Spruance's conduct of operations off Saipan.

In a sense, there was no way around this problem. In moving against the Marianas, the American forces had to be prepared to fight for air supremacy against Japanese land-based air power, and they had to be prepared to fight for air and sea supremacy against the enemy's fleet. Given the fact that neither could be accomplished before any landings in the Marianas took place, there was certain to be an element of ambiguity about priorities, but off Saipan Spruance, perhaps overly concerned about the safety of his amphibious forces, fought TF 58 defensively, with the result that Mitscher was able to mount only one attack on the enemy's carrier forces before they withdrew out of range. With only one enemy unit sunk in the course of this strike, and without the knowledge that their submarines had earlier despatched two enemy fleet carriers, the American forces at the time regarded the result of the battle of the Philippine Sea as a sore disappointment.

The contemporary American view was that a battle that should have ended with the annihilation of the enemy resulted in no more than a partial victory. Subsequent analysis of the battle revealed that the victory was far more substantial than was immediately apparent on the basis of a ship count. Ship losses represented one yardstick by which the results of the battle had to be assessed, but it was not the only criterion. In the course of the battle TF 58 devastated Japanese land-based air power in the western Pacific, and then it destroyed more than 90 per cent of the carrier aviation that the enemy committed to battle. At the battle of the Philippine Sea the Japanese deployed nine fleet and light fleet carriers: at the end of the engagement they retained enough aircraft to equip just one light fleet carrier.

In effect, in a little more than a week, Mitscher's carriers undid two years of effort on the part of the enemy's air service to reconstitute their air forces. TF 58 destroyed Japanese carrier aviation to the point where it could never be regenerated. Never again was the Imperial Navy able to offer battle with properly balanced carrier forces, and the extent of the victory at the Philippine Sea can be gauged by the fact that thereafter the Japanese had to turn to *kamikaze* tactics in a despairing effort to ward off defeat. Far from its being a partial victory, the Philippine Sea was an overwhelming American victory that opened up the whole of the western Pacific to further attacks and cost the Japanese position, time and their last hope of wresting the initiative away from the enemy's fast carrier force.

THE FIRST WAVE HITS SAIPAN

As we have seen already, Forager opened with the Americans moving with the full power of TF 58 into the Marianas in order to fight for and to secure air supremacy over the islands. In the course of the first two days of operations TF 58 secured so great an advantage over the enemy that thereafter it was more or less unchallengeable, at least by Japanese shore-based aviation, and on the basis of its success the landings on Saipan began at about 0843 on the morning of the 15 June. First to come ashore were troops from the 6th Marines, on the very left of the line, but within ten minutes landings had taken place along the entire length of a six-mile front on either side of Afetna Point. By the time another 20 minutes had elapsed more than 8,000 troops had been put ashore from an invasion fleet that deployed 34 LSTs with a total of 719 amphibian tanks and tractors. By nightfall on 15 June, a total of 20,000 troops had been put ashore. In addition to the units landed in the first wave the Americans had disembarked reserve units, seven artillery and pack howitzer battalions, and elements from two armored units.

By sunset on June 15, the assault troops had managed to fight their way off the beaches, but only in the extreme south, in the sector held by the 25th Marines, had the Americans been able to consolidate their line along the first-day objective. On other parts of the front the marines had reached their targets, but unable to consolidate their gains, they had been forced to withdraw into a shallow defensive perimeter. At the end of the day only about half of the designated beachhead had been secured. The two assault divisions remained to bind their flanks by reducing the Japanese positions on and around Afetna Point, and in the north the 2nd

Marine Division had managed to penetrate only 1,300 yards inland. Moreover, American forces had failed to push the Japanese off the ridge that overlooked the landing beaches. Nevertheless, as the American command appreciated only too clearly, the crucial part of the landings had been successfully concluded. The Japanese, despite their policy of trying to meet the enemy at the water's edge, had been unable to prevent or defeat the American landings.

The Americans lost about 2,000 dead and wounded on 15 June but given the enemy's relative weakness in armor and infantry, the American troops escaped a concentrated and balanced counterattack when they were at their most vulnerable. It was not until after dark, by which time the worst of the chaos on the beaches had subsided, that the Japanese were able to counterattack the 6th Marines. For their effort the Japanese used marines of their own along the coast and a reinforced armor battalion in the area of the ruins of the radio station. But the fact was that the Japanese had missed whatever chance they might have had of crushing the enemy. The Japanese counteroffensive was broken up by the marines with the aid of naval gunfire, including that of the battleship *California*.

The shallowness of the beachhead was a major concern to the various commanders ashore, but Turner and Holland Smith read the signs correctly on 15 June. Both were convinced that if their forces were able to fight their way off the beaches and establish themselves ashore then there was never any prospect of their being defeated. Accordingly, on 15 June Turner ordered the proposed landings on Guam to go ahead as planned on June 18.

This was a very confident decision, but by the following morning when Spruance came aboard Turner's flagship much of that confidence seems to have evaporated. Turner was concerned to get as much supply and as many troops ashore on Saipan as soon as possible, but Spruance knew from the report by the *Flying Fish* that the enemy was on the move. Given the fact that the American commanders dare not divide their forces and open up a second amphibious operation when a fleet action was clearly imminent, Spruance cancelled the landings on Guam and ordered a reconstitution of reserve forces. The 27th Infantry Division, only then approaching the Marianas, was to be committed ashore as and when its first two regiments arrived off Saipan, while III Amphibious Corps, which was to have gone to Guam, was to become reserve for Saipan. The various transports and supply ships were to continue to unload at Saipan, but after 17 June were to haul off to the east and to stay beyond the range of the enemy forces approaching from the west.

The forces ashore were to continue to enjoy the support of the escort carriers that operated off the island while the two task groups of old battleships, after having shed some of their escorts to Lee's TG 58.7, were to take station some 25 miles to the west of Saipan. There they would be in a position to counter any enemy attempt to work around the flank of TF 58. Mitscher's force, then split between the Bonins and Saipan, were to be reconcentrated and ready for a fleet action by 17 June. While this reconcentration (and refueling) took place Mitscher's carriers were to continue to strike at Guam and Rota, while patrol aircraft were to be flown up to Saipan in order to search to the west for the approaching Japanese fleet.

So far there appeared to be no real problem for Spruance and his forces. The timetable imposed upon Mitscher's TF 58 was a severe one, given the fact that two of its task groups were off the Bonins, but at the time of the conference it did not seem that Mitscher's carriers were being given a task that was beyond them. On the American side there was not a shadow of a doubt that any fleet action would be won and won decisively, and it did not need a signal from Nimitz to remind Spruance that nothing less than such a victory was expected of him. It was not until after this conference that the hitherto latent discrepancy between Mitscher's offensive and defensive missions began to become apparent, and this inconsistency became obvious because of the combination of two sets of circumstances. These involved a misreading of the enemy's intentions on the part of Spruance, and problems of position and meteorology that left TF 58 at a disadvantage to the Japanese.

SPRUANCE AND THE PACIFIC WAR

Spruance's original plan of campaign for a sustained offensive against the southern Marianas involved his forces taking up a position to the west of the islands. There the American forces would have the advantage of the weather because they would be able to launch and recover aircraft while steaming eastwards, into the prevailing trade winds. By standing to the west and operating into the wind they could constantly close the target and not move out of range of the objective.

Thus TF 58 enjoyed a very great advantage when operating against the enemy positions in the Marianas, but it was an advantage that was double-edged. First, the prevailing trade winds forced the Americans to plan all their landings in the Marianas on a lee shore, on those coasts nearest an enemy approaching from the Philippines, the islands themselves providing the amphibious forces with protection from the worst of the weather. Second, this matter of the positioning of the amphibious forces ensured that TF 58 would have to move between Saipan and the transports to the east and the enemy and his bases in the Philippines and Indies to the west. This meant that just as TF 58 held the advantageous position with respect to the

Marianas, so Japanese carriers operating out of the Philippines would hold an equal advantage over Mitscher's forces. Because TF 58 would have to steam eastwards to operate its aircraft, it could not simultaneously close the enemy and fly off and recover aircraft. The Japanese were in the position of being able to choose the range and decline a short-range action if they wanted to.

What in effect the Americans planned to do in the Marianas was to bring to success a plan of campaign remarkably similar to the one that the Japanese had implemented with such disastrous results for themselves in 1942 at Midway.

This was namely to take up a central position in order to strike in turn against a number of targets. The crucial weakness of both plans was that their authors did not know whether or not the enemy would risk a fleet action in defense of his island bases, but the difference between the Japanese effort in 1942 and the one that the Americans put into effect two years later was that with 15 carriers and 900 aircraft the latter possessed a clear superiority over the enemy that had been beyond the Japanese in 1942. The Americans retained a very healthy margin against failure, but that did not provide insight into the Japanese intentions.

It was in this area that Spruance blundered. After 16 June, he became increasingly convinced that the enemy's intention was to get amongst the amphibious forces. He believed that the transports would have been his target had the roles been reversed, and he calculated that the Japanese would think along similar lines. Thus Spruance settled upon the belief that his primary mission was the defense of TF 51.

As first the hours and then the days slipped by and it became clear that a number of enemy task groups were operating in the western Philippine Sea; Spruance became increasingly convinced that he should stay close to the Saipan beachhead as the defensive mission took priority over any inclination to seek out and destroy the enemy.

In this matter Spruance's reading of the situation was less than astute. He believed that the enemy's dispersal was out of choice, in keeping with the tactical doctrine that the Imperial Navy had used since the outbreak of war. On countless occasions the Imperial Navy had fought in separated and dispersed formations, and in June 1944 Spruance believed that the enemy was behaving in his normal manner. Thus he believed that in accord with the provisions of Koga's Plan Z the enemy main forces would feint in an effort to draw American main forces away from Saipan, leaving the flanks and rear vulnerable to marauding Japanese task forces that moved into the combat zone as the American strike forces were pulled out of position. What Spruance failed to realize was that by June 1944 dispersal was *forced* upon the Japanese and not adopted out of choice. What he also failed to realize was that Ozawa had not identified the American transports as his main target. Spruance also failed to appreciate that Ozawa intended to concentrate in order to do battle with TF 58.

On all matters, Spruance misread Japanese policy. It was not part of the Japanese plan of campaign to disperse forces in order to deal with enemy transports: it was the Japanese intention to concentrate as quickly as possible to strike at the enemy carrier forces.

Even after these errors of appreciation, the American forces would still have been left with an overwhelmingly powerful hand but for the wind. Having to steam to the east in order to conduct flying operations while the enemy lay to the west obviously lessened their chances of fighting and winning a battle of annihilation. Because of the prevailing wind, the Americans could not close the range unless the Japanese allowed them to do so. The only other way in which the range could be closed was if the Japanese intentionally threw caution aside with a death ride into the maw of defeat.

Ozawa was too capable to accommodate them on either score. He knew that he operated under too many handicaps to waste any advantages.

Ozawa knew that he held two advantages in particular. His first advantage was that of position, the weathergage. His second advantage was the superior range of his carrier aircraft compared to their opposite numbers. Japanese machines lacked the self-sealing tanks, extinguishers and armor of their American counterparts, and given a very rough equality of performance and weaponry, the only advantage that the Japanese held over the Americans was the superior operational range of their aircraft. Japanese scouts could search to a range of 560 miles compared to the 350 miles of American reconnaissance aircraft, and Japanese bombers could strike at ranges of up to 300 miles compared to the 200-mile range of American attack aircraft.

It was Ozawa's intention to try to capitalize upon these two advantages in order to win through against the odds. There was evidence enough of what American carrier forces could do to any enemy force sufficiently unwary to come within range of their strike aircraft, hence Ozawa's intention to keep the fight at long range. In fact it was his aim to keep his precious carriers beyond the range of enemy counterstrikes and to launch his aircraft on missions that would take them on to airfields in the Marianas after their attacks on the enemy fleet. There they could be refueled for the flight back to their carriers, perhaps after another crack at the enemy on their way. In such a manner the Japanese would be able to use their carrier aircraft to shuttle bomb the American forces while their own carriers remained invulnerable. Irrespective of the results that might be obtained by Japanese pilots (whether operating from carriers or from bases ashore), the one thing to emerge with certainty from this comparison of intentions was that the American forces lacked the means to force the Japanese to fight a battle of annihilation. For the forthcoming battle, Ozawa could take as much or as little of the action as he chose.

One other matter emerged from this comparison of intention and its combination with consideration of relative position and wind. If Ozawa had the advantage of position and range and stayed beyond the range of American strike aircraft then TF 58 could only fight defensively. Thus a combination of choice and circumstance had conspired to leave TF 58 in a curious situation. The most powerful force in the history of naval warfare was about to do battle with an enemy advancing to contact, *and it did not have the means to attack him*. All that it could hit were those airfields in the southern Marianas that had been neutralized over the previous few days. In effect, TF 58 could not deploy its offensive power effectively, and Spruance had no option other than to allow Ozawa the first strike of the battle.

OZAWA BIDES HIS TIME

But possession of the tactical initiative did not mean that Ozawa was prepared to use his first chance to strike at the enemy any more than it meant that the American forces were without any means of taking the battle to the Japanese carrier forces. The American forces still had their submarines with which to do battle, and on 17 June one of their number, the *Cavalla*, found the Japanese on two separate occasions, but it was not until 19 June that she was able to open the American account. In the meantime the two main Japanese formations – the three carrier divisions, plus escorts, that came through the San Bernardino Strait and the battle force that was diverted from Operation *KON* – effected a rendezvous some 300 miles east of southern Samar late on 16 June. They spent most of 17 June refueling before moving out to the northeast in order to try to locate TF 58 the following day. This attempt was successful.

In the afternoon, two contacts were obtained with the reconcentrated carrier forces some 200 miles west of Saipan. Japanese scouts reported the American forces to be further eastwards, but the error was not important. The Japanese had found the Americans with a reasonable degree of accuracy and had obtained the contact at a range of about 400 miles – an ideal range for Japanese strike aircraft at the very start of the battle. The initial contact reports led the Van Force, consisting of the light fleet carriers *Chiyoda*, *Zuiho* and *Chitose*, to launch strike aircraft immediately, but these had to be recalled when Ozawa made clear his intention to decline battle until the following day.

The gains that might be recorded by an attack at sunset in Ozawa's view were more than offset by the certain hazards that would be encountered by night landings either on carriers or in the southern Marianas. Any aircraft that put down on Guam, for example, would have to get back to its carrier on the following morning, and this would mean that it would not be able to take part in more than one strike mission on 19 June. Ozawa, unsuspecting that very few of his aircraft were to survive more than a single encounter with the enemy's combat air patrol, could not afford to limit himself to just one strike mission on 19 June, hence his decision to pass up the chance to strike at the Americans on 18 June. Thus he turned his forces away from the American ones in late afternoon before turning back towards TF 58 and Saipan under cover of dark. In the meantime he issued instructions for land-based air formations detailed to Operation *A-GO* to proceed to the southern Marianas in order to join the battle. At the same time Ozawa deployed his forces into battle formation.

At that point he left the three light carriers of Rear Admiral Sueo Obayashi which were destined to be sunk together on 25 October off Cape Engano in the course of the battle of Leyte Gulf. In company were the battleships *Yamato*, *Musashi*, *Haruna* and *Kongo*; six heavy cruisers; the seaplane-cruisers *Tone* and *Chikuma*, one light cruiser and eight destroyers. This task group, commanded by Vice Admiral Takeo Kurita, was divided into three with the carriers spaced at intervals of six miles across the line of advance. Each carrier had its own screen and each carried six Zeke fighters, 15 Zeke dive-bombers and nine torpedo-bombers.

Kurita's Van Force had a dual function. Its heavy concentration of battleships and cruisers left it well suited to act as a decoy in the event of any American counterattack. It was hoped that the heavily armored capital ships and cruisers would be able to soak up any punishment that the American forces might hand out, thereby sparing the more vulnerable fleet carriers to the rear. This same concentration of battleships and cruisers also produced a sizeable concentration of reconnaissance seaplanes whose task was to find and track the enemy, thereby delivering him up to the main strike forces coming up 100 miles in the rear. In this way Kurita's force was to operate as both scouting and picket line for the main task groups. Both of these groups were under Ozawa's command, but in keeping with normal Japanese practice Ozawa also exercised direct command of one of these groups while Rear Admiral Takaji Joshima commanded the other.

Joshima's was the smaller command. He had under command a task group consisting of the fleet carriers *Junyo* and *Hiyo*; the light fleet carrier *Ryuho*; the seaplane-cruiser *Mogami*; the battleship *Nagato* and ten destroyers. Between them the three carriers of the 2nd Carrier Division boasted a total of 54 Zeke fighters, 63 dive-bombers and 18 Jill torpedo-bombers. The cutting edge of Japanese naval power, however, was provided by Ozawa's *1st Carrier Division*. Half of the entire carrier strength that the Japanese put to sea for this battle was with the *Shokaku*, *Zuikaku* and *Taiho* which between them deployed 81 Zeke fighters, 90 dive-bombers and 54 Jills. Completing Ozawa's tactical command were two heavy cruisers, one light cruiser and nine destroyers.

The obvious weakness of the Japanese force, namely that it was outnumbered two-to-one in the air by Spruance's air groups, has served to disguise a second weakness that was to prove as important as this crippling numerical disadvantage. This related to the thinness of the destroyer screens afforded to the carriers. The Japanese had lost so many destroyers by mid-1944 that they no longer had the means to screen the fleet properly when it was at sea, and what exacerbated this crucial vulnerability was the fact that the concentration of more than Jake seaplanes with Kurita's vanguard for scouting duties could only be achieved by robbing Ozawa and Joshima's forces of seaplanes for antisubmarine patrols. The two main Japanese strike forces were desperately exposed to submarine attack, and this tactical weakness was exploited with ruthless efficiency by the *Cavalla* and *Albacore* on 19 June when battle was joined.

OZAWA'S FLAGSHIP DESTROYED

The battle seemed to begin well for Ozawa. Kurita's vanguard sent out two pre-dawn searches while Ozawa's own task group provided a third. The first search mission began at 0445 and involved 16 seaplanes. The second consisted of 13 Kates and a Jake, and these began launching 30 minutes after the first wave. The third search mission, carried out by 11 Judys from the *Shokaku* and two seaplanes from the *Mogami*, was launched at 0530.

The first and third missions made contact with the enemy. The first mission did so at about 0730 with TG 58.4 and TG 58.7 though it lost ten of its Jakes in the effort. The third mission had two contacts with American carrier forces, and even the second scouting effort secured a contact with destroyers. It was on the basis of the first contact, however, that the battle developed as first the vanguard and then Ozawa's task group committed their strike aircraft against the American carrier task groups. The first strike operation, mounted by the light carriers of the vanguard, consisted of eight Jills armed with torpedoes, 45 Zeke dive-bombers and 16 fighters. This strike force began to launch at about 0830 while the second mission began to launch at 0856 from Ozawa's *1st Carrier Division*. This consisted of 27 Jill torpedo-bombers, 53 Judy dive-bombers and 48 Zeke fighters, and it was in the course of the launching operations that the Japanese suffered their first serious reverse.

The *Albacore*, threading her way through the screen, managed to get sufficiently close to the *Taiho* to be certain of hitting her even when her firing computer failed her at the last minute. She fired six torpedoes by eye at Ozawa's flagship and would have secured two hits but for the fact that a Japanese pilot who had just taken off deliberately crash-dived one of the torpedoes. Only one torpedo hit the *Taiho*. More than six hours afterwards a spark in the upper hanger ignited volatile vapor in a monstrous explosion that was mostly directed downwards into the ship by the strength of the *Taiho*'s armored flight deck. The force of this detonation blew out the unarmored hanger walls, devastated the engine and boiler rooms and blasted its way through the bottom of the ship. The flight deck itself was torn upwards, and the carrier was set on fire throughout her length. Ozawa and his staff were tranferred to the cruiser *Haguro* by the destroyer *Wakatsuki* as the carrier settled very quickly. She capsized and sank soon after 1,700, taking with her most of her crew and 13 of her aircraft.

The *Taiho* was the first Japanese carrier to be damaged at the battle of the Philippine Sea, but she was not the first to be lost. That dubious distinction fell to the *Shokaku*, torpedoed by the *Cavalla* shortly after midday when she was some 60 miles southeast of the position of the *Taiho* when she had been hit. The *Cavalla* had been chasing the Japanese for more than two days when she finally caught up with the *Shokaku*, and she hit the carrier with four torpedoes of a salvo of six fired at a range of 1,200 yards. The torpedo hits set off a series of fires and explosions that became self-inducing. The result was that while the initial fires in the hangers were brought under control, they could not be extinguished before further vapor seepage led to an enormous explosion that blew the carrier to pieces shortly after 1500.

But the emasculation of Ozawa's task group by the infliction of fatal damage on two of its carriers proved to be just one aspect of the elimination of Japanese naval power on 19 June. At the very time when the *Taiho* and *Shokaku* were struggling to shake off the effects of the damage that they had incurred, their aircraft were making their contribution to a series of strikes on TF 58. These attacks proved disastrous as successive waves of attacking aircraft were annihilated for no return. In most instances Japanese aircraft were hacked from the skies by the American combat air patrol long before they came within range of their targets, such was the effectiveness of the American fighter direction and the pilots under its command.

American carrier immunity from damage and loss stemmed from Spruance's defensiveness and determination not to be lured away from Saipan. As Spruance saw matters, off Saipan the American forces were not so much on the brink of a very significant success as on the threshold of a long and arduous campaign intended to lead to the shores of Japan herself.

Spruance was not prepared to risk either his assault troops or his amphibious shipping, and hence his determination to use his carrier forces to keep the Japanese at arm's length from Turner's forces. In the run-up to the battle Spruance hardened in his view that the Japanese would try to lure him away from the Marianas in order to come around his open flank and then fall upon an exposed beachhead. This was what the Japanese had attempted at the battle of Santa Cruz in October 1942 and were to attempt again at Leyte Gulf in 1944. Various sighting reports by submarines and a radio fix on Ozawa's transmission of 18 June placed Ozawa to the southwest of TF 58 and served to convince Spruance that the outflanking move was not just a possibility but a certainty.

Thus Spruance passed up his last chance to close the advancing Japanese fleet when he ordered TF 58 late on 18 June to turn back towards the east and Saipan at midnight. In this way Spruance was certain of ending any possibility of his being outflanked from the south, but he also ensured controversy. The turnaway was to be instrumental in his subsequent inability to catch Ozawa's forces during their withdrawal on 20 June, and in any event there was more than a little evidence to suggest that Spruance's fears and defensiveness were exaggerated. By the 18 and 19 June the situation on Saipan had clearly begun to move in favor of the American forces, and the need for the transports to be off the beaches was nowhere near as acute as had been the case on 16 June.

Moreover, with the slow battleships and escort carriers off Saipan, and with long-range reconnaissance aircraft operating from the island on and after 18 June, there was little or no chance of the Japanese being able to outflank Spruance with a force small or fast enough to elude the carrier formations but large enough to overcome the support forces. Be that as it may, on 19 June Spruance's turn-away produced one other certainty: an overwhelming concentration of fighter strength for the defense of the fleet. By deciding to fight defensively and by declining to be drawn forward into the attack, Spruance was able to mass nearly 500 Hellcats for the fleet's combat air patrol. This assembled strength represented a crushing margin of superiority over any Japanese strike force that could come against TF 58. It was a superiority that was unchallengeable. The Japanese had no personnel, matériel or tactical advantage that could offset American superiority of numbers and technique.

AMERICAN TASK GROUP TACTICS

The course and shape of the battle on 19 June was largely fashioned by Spruance's turn-away and Mitscher's subsequent tactical deployment of the five task groups under his operational control. Mitscher placed each of his task groups on one of the cardinal points that together form a reversed F. This was an idealized arrangement that lost its text-book symmetry as the carrier task groups chased the wind at the expense of their station keeping, but even while the geometric precision was lost, one aspect of Mitscher's deployment was retained throughout the day. In unconscious imitation of Ozawa, Mitscher placed his battleships and the weakest of his four carrier groups on the engaged rather than the disengaged flank.

The seven fast battleships of Lee's TG 58.7 and the one fleet and two light fleet carriers of Rear Admiral William K Harrill's TG 58.4 were left in the position between the enemy and the other three carrier groups. It was the American intention to use TG 58.7 as bait, the battleships drawing upon themselves attacks intended for the carriers. With their massive armor and fire power, the battleships were deemed able to look after themselves. Moreover, their position as rearguard as American forces steamed eastwards would become pointless if and when the Americans came westwards in pursuit. Thus the battleships, two of which could make 33 knots, would be in the vanguard in the event of a chase. Harrill's TG 58.4 would provide Lee with close support, but the real backbone of the fleet's defensive effort was to be provided by the three carrier groups deployed behind Lee and Harrill. These were deployed in an ideal offensive-defensive position to continue operations over the southern Marianas even while they were involved in beating off the series of attacks mounted by Ozawa's carrier forces.

One of the surprising features of the battle on 19 June was that after flying off two unsuccessful search missions before and at dawn, the American effort opened with fighters from Task Groups 58.1 and 58.3 carrying out a series of sweeps over Guam and Rota. With the Japanese closing from the west, this initial commitment against Guam and Rota did not recommend itself to certain task group commanders and it was brought to an end when American radars detected the approach of Japanese aircraft from the west at about 1000 hours. This was the first wave of attacking aircraft that had been launched by the light carriers of Kurita's Van Force. When this contact was obtained, TF 58 recalled its Hellcats from the Marianas and thereafter concentrated all its fighter strength to deal with the attacks coming from the west.

Nevertheless, this recall did not spell an end to American air activity over the Marianas on 19 June. When contact with the incoming Japanese carrier aircraft was obtained, various American carriers flew off their strike aircraft simply to clear their flight and hanger decks and so facilitate the handling of the fighters. Many of these bombers chose to usefully employ themselves in attacking Japanese installations on Guam and Rota rather than circle aimlessly waiting for a lull or an end to the fighter battle. Moreover, certain of the Hellcats moved against the southern Marianas as they engaged in 'hot pursuit' of Japanese aircraft making their way to airfields ashore after their missions against the American task groups. In the course of these various actions that lasted throughout the hours of daylight, the Americans registered a very important *en passant* success.

In addition to those carrier aircraft that they destroyed on and over Guam and Rota, the American planes destroyed perhaps as many as 80 aircraft that were either on Guam or Rota or were in the process of being flown into the southern Marianas from either Truk or the Bonin and Volcano Islands. It was an extraordinary achievement to keep Guam and Rota neutralized even as TF 58 annihilated Japanese carrier air power on 19 June, but it was an achievement that partially obscured an even greater feat of arms. On 19 June the American forces accounted for perhaps 80 land-based aircraft in the southern Marianas, and their haul would have been even greater had they not destroyed or pulled into wrong positions the bulk of Japanese land-based air power that Ozawa needed for success. On 19 June, Ozawa needed his 500 shore-based aircraft to complement his equal number of carrier aircraft, but he had perhaps a peak strength of 50 aircraft at any time on Guam and Rota, and these were destroyed before they had any chance to make any impact on the battle.

JAPANESE AIR POWER ANNIHILATED

At sea, the battle developed along lines that the American command could never have foreseen even in its most optimistic assessments. The first attack force made the hoped-for mistake. It attacked the first target it came to, the radar picket line and the battleships. In doing so it lost two thirds of its strength in return for a single bomb hit on the battleship *South Dakota* that killed or wounded 50 men. One cruiser was shaken by a near miss, and one Hellcat was lost. For this attack the *3rd Carrier Division* committed every one of its 45 Zeke dive-bombers, and it lost 32 of them along with two of the torpedo-bombers. Such losses represented the annihilation of the offensive power of the Van Force, and with the enemy accounting for eight of the carriers' slim allocation of fighters, Kurita's defensive power had been badly compromised. To all intents and purposes, the air battle near and over TG 58.7 between 1039 and 1057 hours ended the active involvement of the *Zuiho*, *Chitose* and *Chiyoda*. Thereafter they lacked the means to operate offensively.

The second raid, flown off by the *1st Carrier Division* during which the *Taiho* was torpedoed by the *Albacore*, fared no better than the first. Even ignoring the damaging of Ozawa's flagship, this raid began inauspiciously with eight aircraft having to put back with engine trouble. Two more were lost and another eight were damaged and forced to return to their carriers when they were fired on by Kurita's ships as they overflew the Van Force. Thus with 19 of their number lost or forced to turn back even before contact with the enemy was obtained, the omens for the Japanese second raid were unpromising. Despite a successful diversionary move that drew off Hellcats from TG 58.1 by the use of 'window', 95 of the 109 aircraft that pushed home their attacks on Task Groups 58.3 and 58.7 were destroyed. The carriers *Wasp* and *Bunker Hill* suffered very minor damage while a Jill that suffered a collision with the armored belt of the battleship *Indiana* did less well.

Overall the Japanese lost 23 Jills, 32 Zekes and 42 Judys in the course of this mission, and the exchange that lasted between 1139 and 1202 hours had exactly the same effect on the *1st Carrier Division* as the earlier exchange had had upon the 3rd. As a result of a single strike that registered superficial damage on a handful of major units, the *1st Carrier Division* lost more than 40 per cent of its strength. Its losses were evenly distributed between fighters, dive-bombers and torpedo-bombers, thereby ensuring that offensive and defensive power alike was compromised, even without the misfortunes of the *Taiho* and *Shokaku*.

The breaking of the power of the *1st* and *3rd Carrier Divisions* remained for the future when Ozawa committed a relatively small part of the *2nd* to the fray. Between 1000 and 1015 hours 15 Zeke fighters, 25 Zeke dive-bombers and seven Jills were committed to battle, and between 1100 and 1130 Ozawa made his final move when he launched 30 fighters, 46 Judy, Val and Zeke dive-bombers and six Jills from Joshima's carriers and the *Zuikaku* in the fourth attack of the morning. With this attack, Ozawa committed his reserve.

Thus far 326 aircraft had been committed to offensive operations and another two dozen (plus the seaplanes) to scouting missions. This meant that Ozawa had used nearly all of his air strength on initial search missions and for four strikes, and he did so without being able to verify the results of his initial operations and without any knowledge of the state of the air battle as it involved his shore-based aviation. While in mitigation it should be pointed out that Ozawa could hardly have been expected to guess the ineffectiveness of his strikes and the high losses that they sustained, it is somewhat hard to resist the conclusion that in mounting four strikes on the morning of 19 June Ozawa overcommitted himself very badly. He left himself with barely enough fighters for a combat air patrol and without the means to mount any follow-up strike, yet at the same time the offensive had been weakened by dispersal and a failure to concentrate everything in a single effort.

By midday Ozawa's hopes for success had to be vested in his third and fourth strikes, but both proved to be misdirected. The third was sent too far to the north and as a result it had only a glancing encounter with Task Groups 58.4 and 58.7. Hellcats from TG 58.1 attempted an interception of the aircraft from the *2nd Carrier Division*, but contacts were too fleeting for serious loss to be inflicted to either side. No American ship was hit, and only seven of the 47 Japanese aircraft used in this operation were shot down. The fourth raid, on the other hand, fared disastrously. It was directed too far to the south with the result that most of its 82 aircraft failed to obtain any contact with the American task groups. One detachment found and attacked TG 58.2 with some flair but no luck, but the others, proceeding on to Guam, were detected by carrier radar. The American carriers – they had closed Guam during the day to such an extent that they were now operating in its lee and some had to dodge around the island – sent out Hellcats that shot down or severely damaged every Japanese aircraft trying to reach the safety of Orote airfield. All but nine of the aircraft committed to this attack were lost, and the extent of these losses meant that the *2nd Carrier Division* had been reduced to the same desperate straits as the Van Force.

Thus far during the day the Japanese had lost upwards of 300 aircraft, 80 in the southern Marianas and at least 260 from the carriers. By dawn on the following day the Japanese had just 100 fit for operations, and that total must imply that perhaps another 70 or 80 aircraft were lost operationally, damaged or rendered mechanically unserviceable as a result of their missions on 19 June. On the American side, 17 aircraft of which all but one were fighters were lost in combat over TF 58. Another eight were lost over Guam and five more were written off after operations over the island. Thus in the course of 19 June the American forces lost 18 Hellcats and 12 other aircraft in accounting for perhaps as many as 350 Japanese aircraft.

In the whole of military history there have been few such one-sided victories as the battle of the Philippine Sea on 19 June, and it was small wonder that the day's proceedings were to be dubbed 'the Great Marianas Turkey Shoot' by the victors.

JAPANESE LOSSES: HOW OZAWA WAS MISLED

By the middle of the afternoon of 19 June, as the fourth and last Japanese attack of the day staggered towards its bloody, futile finale over Guam, the American command knew that a great victory was in the making. Naturally its attention began to turn to the possibility of a turn back to the west and the enemy in order to try to close the range, and force upon the Japanese the type of battle that Spruance had earlier declined to fight.

Ozawa had no inkling of the enormity of his defeat. Very few aircraft had returned to their carriers, but the possibility of the missing aircraft having made their way to Guam served to hide the extent of Japanese losses at this crucial stage of the battle. As it was, two other confusing factors came into play.

First, Ozawa transferred his flag to a cruiser and it was not until shortly after noon on the following day, 20 June that he shifted his flag to the *1st Carrier Division*'s sole survivor, the *Zuikaku*. Ozawa's temporary flagship, the *Haguro*, lacked the communications needed to enable her to operate successfully as a flagship, still less a carrier flagship. Moreover, for much of the time that Ozawa was with the *Haguro* she was not in visual or radio contact with most of the fleet's carriers and junior commanders.

Second, what little information Ozawa received was extremely misleading. The first source of deception was unintentional. The aircraft that returned to the carriers reported staggering American losses, both of fighters and aircraft. The second source of deception was impossible to justify. Even before the Japanese carriers joined battle Vice Admiral Kakuji Kakuta, commander of shore-based aviation in the southern Marianas with his headquarters on Tinian, failed to inform Ozawa of the losses and ineffectiveness of his formations. Now, on 19 June, he continued to conceal the real situation. He informed Ozawa that carrier aircraft had been recovered on the airfields, failing to add that very few that were able to land were fit for further operations. He continued to claim that his forces were continuing to inflict heavy losses on the enemy. In a sense Kakuta's lack of honesty did not make much difference to the battle. Ozawa's strikes would have been defeated with or without support from Kakuta's aircraft, but candor on the part of Kakuta might well have prompted Ozawa to carry out the dusk attack on 18 June that Obayashi had wanted; and on 19 June it might have convinced Ozawa to get out of the combat zone as quickly as possible. As it was, Ozawa's intention was to refuel his ships on 20 June and then to resume the battle on 21 June. Spruance and Mitscher, however, never gave Ozawa this opportunity, not that the intention outlived Ozawa's realization of the extent of his losses once he resumed command of his fleet from the *Zuikaku*.

By the middle of the afternoon of 19 July American thoughts had turned to the possibility of offensive action against the Japanese fleet for two reasons. First, the enemy's offensive power, and with it any chance of a successful descent on the Saipan beachhead, had been broken in the course of the day's exchanges. For the Americans there was no longer any serious threat against which to guard: TF 58 was freed for offensive action. Second, the fleet had to turn back to the west because it was fast running out of searoom. By 1500 hours units of TF 58 were within visual or radar distance of Guam and Rota, and Spruance and Mitscher had no option but to bring their forces back to the west because there could never be any question of their voluntarily taking up positions behind the beachheads.

But while the intention to move west and seek out the enemy was there on the part of the American command, there was no blinking the fact that four very serious difficulties confronted TF 58 in any attempt to complete its victory. First, even as the Japanese turned away to refuel and TF 58 ran out of searoom, the American carriers could not turn to the west for a stern chase because of the need to recover its aircraft. With the approach of night landing operations had to slow down, and it was not until about 2000 that the last American aircraft were recovered and TF 58 was able to head west.

Second, even as it did so TF 58 could not make more than 23 knots. This was no more than a compromise speed, dictated by concern about fuel consumption. The demands of the day had been heavy, and if battle was resumed on the following morning then needs were unlikely to be any less onerous. Destroyers could not indulge in prolonged high-speed steaming, and the speed of 23 knots represented a compromise between the need for haste and the economical cruising speed of the escorts. Moreover, TG 58.4 was detached from the chase. Low on fuel, it was ordered to stay close to Saipan and to refuel and continue to keep the southern Marianas airfields in a state of disorder.

The other problems that confronted the American forces in their attempt to compel the enemy to undertake a battle of annihilation were linked. On the one hand, Spruance and Mitscher had no clear idea of the whereabouts of the enemy: on the other hand, they made very little attempt to redress this situation. Up to 19 June, the American command had only the occasional and fleeting indication of where the enemy might be, and on 19 June American aircraft from Saipan and Manus obtained only two contacts with the enemy, and of these only one report proved both accurate and timely. The fact of the matter was that the Japanese trail was cold even when TF 58 turned to the west, and Spruance's command hardly helped its own cause by nominal attempts to scout on its own behalf. During the pursuit phase at the Philippine Sea, Spruance's conduct of operations was very reminiscent of his handling of American forces at Midway on the day after his carriers had sunk the whole of the enemy's carrier task force. On that occasion he had failed to conduct his own reconnaissance until late afternoon with the result that a possible contact with enemy main forces had been missed.

Now, two years later, Spruance's carriers failed to carry out long-range searches on their own behalf both during the night of 19 to 20 June and on the morning of 20 June. At the very time when Spruance and Mitscher expected a contact with the enemy, their carriers were restricted to short-range reconnaissance and defensive patrolling. It was not until noon that TF 58 mounted a deep reconnaissance mission and then only on a very restricted search sector, and it was not before 1330 that it put together a reconnaissance both in-depth and in strength.

AMERICAN FORCES IN PURSUIT

An Avenger from the *Enterprise* from this scouting mission secured the all-important contact with Ozawa's forces at about 1540. The initial contact report was more confusing than enlightening, but this was remedied over the next 25 minutes with a number of accurate amplifying reports. These announced the presence of three enemy task groups steaming slowly west, apparently refueling. In fact they were not taking on oil from the tankers. Such had been the confusion in Japanese ranks on 20 June caused by Ozawa's being *incommunicado* in the *Haguro* that not one Japanese warship refueled during the day. The Japanese were steaming slowly into the wind in order to refuel the next day when they were found, and they in their turn were aware of their being compromised.

The American sighting reports were eavesdropped, and this combined with sighting reports of TF 58 by Japanese scouts served to convince Ozawa that his only hope lay in flight. The Japanese ships turned towards the northwest and Okinawa and began to work up speed, but their chance to escape had gone. The *Enterprise*'s scout had located the nearest Japanese task group at a range of 275 miles from TF 58. This represented extreme range for American strike aircraft, but what made American decision-making difficult was the fact that the lateness of the hour when the Japanese were found and their distance from TF 58 ensured that any American attack could not be made much before dusk. This in its turn meant that any attack had to involve a night recovery. Such were the hazards involved in these operations that no commander lightly considered such an option. However, Spruance and Mitscher had little choice but to undertake a dusk attack: it was inconceivable that TF 58 should pass up the chance of striking the Japanese when the opportunity finally presented itself. Thus the hazards of a night recovery were accepted, and a total of 216 aircraft were flown off by 11 of the carriers in just 15 minutes. Of these 85 were fighters, 77 were dive-bombers and 54 were torpedo-bombers.

A two-hour flight brought the first of these aircraft to a contact with the scattering Japanese task groups at about 1840. The three carrier groups had separated and had left their oilers and escorts trailing in their wakes as they tried to put themselves beyond the range of the American bombers. Ozawa had lacked either the time or the inclination to gather his capital ships together and to deploy them – or even the Van Force – between the approaching enemy and his two main task groups. Had Ozawa tried such a ploy, then he might have placed his surviving fleet carriers beyond the range of the Hellcats and Avengers, but even without such a deployment to distract or force a detour on the incoming American aircraft not all of the fleeing Japanese carriers were engaged in the last light of 20 June.

In the course of a wildly confused action as the sun set, the American attack achieved mixed results. The Japanese combat air patrol was swept aside by sheer weight of numbers as American aircraft moved against the oiler and all three carrier groups. Certain American aircraft attacked the first target they encountered with the result that two of the six units of the oiler group were crippled. Subsequently the destroyer *Ukuki* was forced to scuttle the *Genyo Maru* and *Yukikaze* had to administer the *coup de grace* on the *Seiyo Maru*. With regard to the carriers, the *Zuikaku* found that her previous immunity to damage that had stood her in such good stead over the previous 30 months had disappeared with her sister ship.

She was hit hard in the course of this attack and suffered a serious fire in her upper hanger. At one time it seemed that the fire was unmanageable and the order to abandon ship was given, but the fire was brought under control and the *Zuikaku* was brought back to Kure Naval Yard under her own power. Within the Van Force only the *Chiyoda* was attacked. The *Chitose*, protected by the *Musashi*, *Atago*, and *Takao*, and the *Zuiho*, escorted by the *Yamato*, *Kumano*, *Suzuya*, *Tone* and *Chikuma*, both escaped being attacked, and the *Chiyoda*'s damage control parties proved more than equal to the tasks imposed upon them by the Helldivers. The carrier was hit heavily aft by a single bomb, but she had no aircraft in her hanger and had drained her fuel lines prior to being attacked. Her foam system survived the damage caused by the hit and she was able to smother her fires quickly and efficiently.

In Joshima's force all three of his carriers were attacked. The *Ryuho*, on her first operation of the war, was very slightly damaged by near misses. She returned to Kure under her own power with no difficulties, but she was never again able to put to sea for want of an air group. The *Junyo* similarly emerged from the American attack with very slight damage despite being hit by two bombs on her flight deck abaft the island, but her sister ship was not so fortunate. The *Hiyo* was to earn the dubious distinction of being the only fleet carrier ever to be sunk solely by aerial torpedo attack. As with the

Taiho and *Shokaku*, the *Hiyo* was lost as a result of a series of self-induced explosions set off by a single torpedo hit, in her case one that was delivered by an Avenger from the light carrier *Belleau Wood*.

Amongst the various escorts, the battleship *Haruna* and the heavy cruiser *Maya* were slightly damaged, but more serious were the further losses incurred by the already hopelessly depleted air groups. In the course of the American attack the Japanese lost a total of 80 carrier aircraft and seaplanes, thereby leaving the six surviving carriers with just 35 aircraft, all but ten of them Zeke fighters. On the other side of the coin, American losses were heavy. Seventeen aircraft were lost in the attacks on the Japanese, and in trying to get back to their carriers another 82 either came down in the sea or were written off in deck crashes. Of the 209 aircrew involved in the loss of these 20 fighters, 49 dive-bombers and 30 torpedo-bombers, all but 49 were saved.

The American strike on the evening of 20 June was not quite the end of the battle. On 21 and 22 June, TF 58 continued to try to renew contact with the enemy, but when the enemy's withdrawal beyond range was finally admitted, it had to content itself with a strike against Pagan on 23 June and Iwo Jima and Chichi Jima by TG 58.1 on 24 June. Just as the earlier raid on these islands must be considered an integral part of the overture to the battle of the Philippine Sea, so these raids should be considered the finale.

In the course of the raid of 24 June, the Americans destroyed a minimum of 60 of the 122 aircraft on Iwo Jimo. Thus perhaps a total of 200 Japanese land-based aircraft were destroyed in the Bonins, Volcanos and Marianas before and after the battle of the Philippine Sea in addition to a total of about 450 aircraft and seaplanes from Ozawa's task groups shot down or lost between 17 and 20 June. Even though the Japanese surface forces escaped, such losses reduced them to little more than an impotent irrelevance. If as has been suggested Spruance fought a poor battle at the Philippine Sea and Ozawa deserved better than the defeat he suffered, there was no escaping the fact that TF 58 owed its victory to its fighter pilots. Whatever errors were committed on the American side were more than made good by Hellcat pilots who were infinitely superior in technique, organization and numbers to their counterparts in the Imperial Navy.

Herein lay the real difference between the American and Japanese navies by mid-1944: the discrepancy between the two sides' aircrews served as a microcosm for the navies and their nations. After more than two and a half years of war, the Americans were beginning to move towards the peak of their strength and effectiveness both at sea and in the air in the Pacific. Earlier losses had been more than made good, and the massive resources of the United States were then producing both mass and quality at one and the same time. The Japanese, on the other hand, were weakening and there was no means whereby increasing enfeeblement could be averted. The quality of Japanese aircraft and aircrew – and the whole of the Imperial Navy – was in decline, hence the recourse to *kamikaze* tactics in meeting the subsequent American offensive in the Philippines.

SAIPAN AND RITUAL SUICIDE

The victory at sea did little to speed the American cause on Saipan. Naturally the Japanese inability to reinforce their beleaguered garrison could not be anything but a boon to III Amphibious Corps, but it was no part of Japanese military philosophy to allow anything so minor as the annihilation of the Imperial Navy to affect the determination to fight on.

For the Japanese on Saipan, there was powerful inducement to resist. Tokyo was aware that it would come within range of Superfortresses once they were established in the southern Marianas, and even the most hardheaded of the Japanese militarists could dimly perceive that Japan would be at the end of her tether in that case. On the island itself, the Japanese garrison and civilian population had been brought up on a propaganda diet that vividly portrayed the fate that would befall any Nipponese unfortunate enough to fall into the hands of the Americans. So the failure of the Imperial Navy to fight its way through to Saipan had no impact on the will of the Japanese on the island to continue the battle, even though it obviously had an effect on their capacity to resist. Circumstances dictated that Japanese resistance and determination stiffened as a result of defeat, but few Americans were prepared for the horrific events on the island.

By nightfall on 22 June, III Amphibious Corps had cleared the whole of southern Saipan with the exception of the Nafutan headland. Thereafter Holland Smith determined on an advance up the length of the island, and it was this attempt that led to perhaps the most famous American inter-service dispute of World War 2. This was the dismissal by Holland Smith – actually by Spruance on the advice of Holland Smith and Turner – of Ralph Smith from command of the 27th Infantry Division on 24 June. What prompted this decision was the 27th's poor showing at the entrance to Death Valley.

As with all such controversies, the events were exaggerated as time passed, and in the final analysis it is rather difficult to quarrel with the verdict of the Army's official history on the affair. This set out the view that while Holland Smith had cause for displeasure with the performance of the 27th Infantry Division, whether the cure was any improvement on the disease was quite another matter. Ralph Smith's removal seemingly had no effect in speeding up the break through Death Valley, and the fact of the matter was that III Amphibious Corps faced a very difficult task in breaking through the Japanese defenses in the central part of the island. On 27 June the 2nd Marine Division took Mount Tapotchau and the 4th Marine Division took Donnay, but it was not until the last day of the month that the 27th Infantry Division was able to straighten the front by breaking through in the center, thereby completing the capture of the Japanese main line of resistance on the island.

On 9 July Turner was able to declare that Saipan was secure, although mopping-up operations continued for some days afterwards with the offshore island of Maniagassa being taken by a full assault on 13 July. But the end of Japanese resistance could be foreseen once the Americans broke through in the area of Mount Tapotchau and Death Valley.

The American capture of Garapan on 2 July was recognized by both sides to herald the end of the campaign. That end, however, involved two events that were fast becoming rituals of the Pacific war. The first was the final despairing massed *banzai* charge, though on Saipan there were to be two such attacks – the first on 27 June against American positions on the airfield at Aslito by Japanese forces from the Natufan area, the second on 7 July in the Makunsha area. This latter attack fell on two battalions of the illstarred 27th Infantry Division, and these lost about 1,000 men killed and wounded as they and the marine gunners behind them were overwhelmed by the Japanese attack. But the attack itself could only have one result, and with the American forces concentrating their artillery to halt the Japanese perhaps 3-4,000 Japanese were killed in this single episode. Its end marked the start of the second ritual – the mass suicide characteristic of the final stages of the breakdown of Japanese resistance.

In fact, the first mass suicides had taken place amongst the wounded in the emergency field hospitals near Dormay when the 27th Infantry Division began to emerge from the head of Death Valley on 30 June, but as resistance collapsed in northern Saipan the process of self-immolation amongst Japanese fighting men gathered pace. In one notable instance, incredulous Americans watched helplessly as in the distance enemy troops lined up to await decapitation by their officer. The garrison of nearly 32,000 soldiers died almost to the last man. In this Saipan was no different from all the earlier campaigns, but this time there was one very real change.

On Saipan the garrison had been matched by an equal number of Japanese civilians, and over 22,000 of these chose to join their service compatriots in death rather than allow themselves to be taken prisoner by the Americans. These suicides involved whole families, children being killed by their parents before the latter killed themselves. Scenes of unparalleled horror were played out in various caves or squalid buildings but mostly at two bluffs: the 1,000-ft Suicide Cliff over which hundreds threw themselves onto the jagged rocks below, and the 80-ft drop into the ocean at Banzai Cliff near Marpi Point. There the dead and dying were so thick that they fouled the propellers of destroyers trying to rescue the would-be suicides. American ships and boats moved over a carpet of drowned and injured, but plucked hundreds to safety.

SHOCK WAVES REACH JAPAN

In the month of June and the first days of July perhaps 70,000 men, women and children were killed or wounded in this series of actions on and around Saipan that formed a watershed in the Pacific war. After Saipan and the battle of the Philippine Sea, the Japanese had no chance whatsoever of avoiding defeat, and the Japanese leadership was not slow to read the meaning of events. Just as the battle of the Philippine Sea and the conquest of Saipan formed the basis of Roosevelt's nomination for an unprecedented fourth term (the invitation from Robert E Hannegan, chairman of the Democratic National Committee was penned on 10 July) so these defeats, plus those incurred in Burma, were the signal for the start of a short, intense but successful campaign within the Japanese establishment to drive General Hideki Tojo from his many posts.

At the time Tojo was minister of education, of munitions and of the army. Since February, he had also been Chief of the Army General Staff, but the post from which he had to be removed was, of course, the premiership. Tojo was regarded both by the Japanese themselves and their enemies as the embodiment of national determination, hardline nationalism and militarism. He had been the prime minister who had taken the country into war in December 1941, and the emerging peace faction within the country's ruling hierarchy saw his removal from power as the first essential step in bringing the war to an end. The battle of the Philippine Sea and the loss of Saipan ended illusions – or at least some of them – within the high command. The war was lost, and the Japanese had to find a way of ending it.

The problem for Tojo's opponents, however, was twofold. On the one hand, they did not realize the difficulties that they faced in trying to end the war. Japan had to deal with enemies willing to treat only on the basis of her unconditional surrender, and over the following year the Japanese leadership was left to ponder the truth of the dictum that wars are more easily begun than ended. On the other hand, and more immediately to the point, Tojo was not the embodiment of some form of Japanese fascism or militarism in the style of Mussolini or Hitler. The removal of Tojo from power would not decapitate the nationalist and militarist strands in society in the same manner as Mussolini's dismissal one year before had effectively spelt an end to Italian fascism. Tojo was an embodiment of *mainstream opinion* within the nation, the armed services and particularly the army. Tojo had powerful support, and by Japanese standards he was not extreme. Any move to oust him had to be made in such a way as to be acceptable to the armed forces.

THE *JUSHIN* ENGINEERS TOJO'S FALL

Tojo's opponents amongst the country's elder statesmen thus had to engage in a delicate balancing act, but on the first matter, the removal of Tojo, their course of action was relatively clear cut. Successive defeats had weakened the prestige and authority of the government and had enabled the committee formed by ex-premiers to emerge from the shadows with immense power and influence. After a series of meetings and attempts to get Tojo to resign, the *jushin* recommended to the Emperor their view that Tojo should not be allowed to stay as premier. The *jushin* advised against any partial reorganization of the cabinet. In effect, the ex-premiers advised the clearing out of the Tojo cabinet in one fell swoop.

Until this time, Tojo had argued that the situation facing Japan was so serious that she could not afford the luxury of political upheaval. He had even sought a sign of Imperial favor as the means of absolving him personally from recent defeats. Such approval had been denied him. Recognizing the strength of his opponents, he tried to bargain with the suggestion that he should reconstitute his cabinet, the very measure that the *jushin* damned as inadequate. Tojo had taken on too many posts for recent defeats to be paid for by sacrificing his colleagues. This was made very clear to Tojo who submitted his own and his cabinet's resignation on 18 July.

The immediate problem facing the Throne and the *jushin* was who should be Tojo's replacement. The initial inclination of the ex-premiers was that one of their number, Admiral Mitsumasa Yonai, should take over. Yonai was a choice that would have found favor with the navy, with the state bureaucracy and diplomatic service, and with the hitherto cowed liberal and 'peace' factions. Yonai, however, was not prepared to serve as premier. While he disclaimed knowledge of and partiality for politics and claimed that the new premier should really be a civilian, Yonai was pressing for the appointment of a soldier as prime minister.

In Yonai's view, the only way in which a fanatical army could be kept under control was by the appointment of one of its own as premier: a general was the obvious choice for maintaining control of the army. The logic of this view was that such an appointee would be the prisoner rather than the ruler of the army, but such a nicety was lost in this desperate hour.

Yonai's own recommendation was that General Kuniaki Koiso should become the new premier. Koiso served in Yonai's pre-war cabinet as army minister, was generally liked and regarded as moderate, and was in Korea and hence untainted by defeat. Yonai's recommendation, in the face of his refusal to serve as premier himself, was taken up by his colleagues as the only possible course of action open to them. Koiso was recalled to Tokyo and to the imperial palace for an audience with the Emperor. Naturally he suspected that he would be asked to form a government, but he most certainly was not prepared for the bizarre set of events that surrounded his audience with Hirohito.

Koiso was unable to speak to Yonai or anyone else before he and Yonai were ushered into the imperial presence by the Privy Seal, Marquis Kuniaki Kido. Koiso and Yonai were instructed to cooperate in forming a cabinet and then dismissed, and Yonai asked Kido whether he or Koiso had been appointed premier. Kido told him that Koiso was the new prime minister, thereby ending the general's doubts on the matter. It was an inauspicious start to the new government and the final period of Japan's decline.

FUTURE IMPLICATIONS

In the preceding chapters we have examined certain aspects of the campaigns that combine to give June 1944 its special significance in the history of World War II. Months of preliminary operations, planning and preparation came together at this time with a series of operations that spelt an end to any lingering Axis hopes of avoiding defeat.

In the European theater of operations the successful Anglo-American landings in northwest France, the fall of Rome, and the Soviet victories in the Belorussian and Viborg-Petrozavodsk offensives collectively marked the beginning of the end for Germany and her allies. They witnessed their enemies move in strength that could not be defeated into positions from which they would carry the war into the heart of Europe.

In the Far East, Japan – despite her success in southern China – found herself engulfed in general defeat, her divisions shattered in Burma and her navy broken in a battle that resulted in the control of the western Pacific passing finally and irrevocably into American hands. Certain military events have not been touched upon, the most notable being the upsurge of resistance activity throughout occupied western Europe that greeted the Normandy invasion. June 1944 probably saw the peak of resistance success even in such small states as Denmark which were hopelessly ill placed to mount any sustained resistance activity. But the significance of June 1944 lies not in resistance activity, however important that was in terms of redemption of national pride for the various occupied countries, but in the fact that the extinction of Axis hopes of avoiding defeat went hand-in-hand with the emergence to positions of dominance of two nations traditionally on the edges rather than at the center of power.

Even if it were possible to ignore the military aspects of this month, the pattern of the war could still be deduced by any observer willing to look at such matters as the scientific research and domestic legislative programs of the combatants. Germany and Japan for example, were so committed to the waging of war that this, in effect, became an end in itself that precluded consideration of postwar reconstruction. Such was the intensity of their war effort as the prospect of defeat hardened into certainty that while government in Germany and Japan continued to function and achieved unprecedented levels of production, administration could not plan or develop policies for the future.

This is not to suggest that there were no scientific or social developments in Axis countries, or that there were none of any value. June 1944 saw the Germans commission the first of their new-generation Type XXIII submarines and fire their first V-1 flying bombs. Within a matter of days after the end of the month the *Luftwaffe* brought its first jet fighters into service. Such developments were a formidable achievement for the hard-pressed German economy, but while many critics have noted that the massive investment in high technology needed to produce such weapons was a luxury that Germany could not afford at this time, little attention seems to have been paid to a more obvious point. Axis scientific development was very narrowly based, concentrating solely on military research and achieved at the expense of the economy as a whole. This was in sharp contrast to the various scientific and medical developments in the west in 1944. The Germans had no equivalent to the first successful heart operation on a blue baby by Bialock and Taussig, the synthesis of the antimalarial drug quinine, the first use (and then development) of DDT, the large-scale production of penicillin, and the completion of a cyclotron at Washington and the building of the second atomic pile at Clinton, Tennessee. The industrial, financial, scientific strength in depth of the Allied powers, particularly the United States, that made such developments possible could never be matched by nations too beset by immediate concerns to be capable of broadening research beyond the limits of immediate military applicability.

Moreover, none of the Axis powers could contend with the various political developments afoot in various countries, none more so than in Britain. In June 1944 the British government, goaded by the only major parliamentary revolt of the war, applied the final touches to a white paper on post-war employment policy. Largely prompted by William Beveridge's report *Social Insurance and Allied Services*, this policy document was to provoke Beveridge into parliament in October and print in November. His paper *Full Employment in a Full Society* provided much of the inspiration behind more than three decades of social welfare legislation.

Based on the belief that 'private enterprise of the means of production is not one of the essential British liberties', Beveridge expounded the belief that government policies to ensure full employment were not only possible but essential if the scourges of idleness, ignorance, disease, squalor and want were to be vanquished by a caring society that maintained individual freedom.

Few countries enjoyed Britain's fortunate position in developing ideas of social justice that arose partly in response to the successful management by government of a wartime economy, but even governments of still-occupied countries were well aware of the pressure and need for change. January 1944 had seen de Gaulle pledge a liberated France to a redefinition of her relationship with her colonies, and September saw the Netherlands, Belgium and

Luxembourg finalize negotiations with their joint declaration to form a post-war customs union. On 17 June, Iceland declared herself an independent republic and formally severed her links with Denmark, the Danish monarch wishing the new country well and expressing the hope that both countries would soon be free of foreign occupation. The Irish Free State in June 1944 saw something that was extremely rare in Europe between 1939 and 1945: a general election. This resulted in the minority Fianna Fail government of Eamonn de Valera being returned with an absolute majority.

In Italy, 1944 saw domestic political problems shelved rather than tackled, which was inevitable given the fact that the country was divided and occupied. On 5 June, however, King Vittorio Emanuele III appointed the crown prince *Luogotenente* (regent of the realm) and effectively withdrew from public life. This was a tacit recognition of his personal unacceptability to the Allies and indeed to many of his own people. The appointment of Prince Umberto, plus the formation of a new government under Ivanoe Bonomi's Committee of National Liberation on 22-25 June, in effect put 'the constitutional question' – the future of the monarchy – into abeyance for two years. But the failure of the Allies to clear northern Italy in the autumn and their refusal to deal with Bonomi's government on any basis of equality, plus the inability of the CNL to exercise real authority – to protect the population from the brutality of the occupying forces, and to deal with the problems of corruption, inflation and chronic shortages – ensured that the stock of the Bonomi administration rapidly fell amongst the fickle population. CNL rapidly came to stand for *come loro noi* (we are just like the others) and a rising tide of discontent with the occupation and Italian authorities culminated with a little known profascist uprising in Calabria in the second half of 1944.

Italy was one instance where liberation, or partial liberation, did not see radical and far-reaching changes implemented or even foreshadowed, but even here the position was very different from the situation that prevailed in those areas of Europe still under German occupation. There the Germans could make no overtures to conquered populations because Nazism could offer them only the stark alternatives of slavery or death. What had made the *Wehrmacht* so formidable in the offensive in the early years of the war, an elan borne of the certainties of racist ideology, precluded its being able to reconcile its enemies to their defeats because it had nothing to offer them except exploitation. Years of mistreatment of conquered nations ensured that by 1944 the only power remaining to Germany in occupied Europe was that of destruction.

But if in June 1944 Germany and Japan suffered defeats that ensured their final destruction, the fact remained that the war in

Europe still had almost a year to run and the war in the Far East slightly longer. Much bitter fighting lay ahead both in Europe and the Far East as the Axis armed forces roused themselves for a last desperate defense of their homelands; and 75 per cent of all bombs dropped on Germany and almost every bomb dropped on Japan were dropped after June 1944. Yet even as the Allied powers carried the war into central Europe the signs of divisions between the future victors appeared.

Throughout 1944 the Polish issue was never far from the surface, and especially in July when Soviet forces, complete with a stooge administration, arrived on territory that was undeniably Polish. In June negotiations between the exiled Greek authorities and the communist resistance broke down. This event foreshadowed an increasingly difficult situation in Greece that was only resolved by civil war. In China, too, all the indications of a resumption of conflict as the only means of deciding the nature of society were present. Thus, while in certain more advanced parts of the world ideas of democracy and social justice were advanced as a by-product of the war, in other areas war helped to foster the twin forces of nationalism and communism that were to play so important a role in shaping the future.

In a world that was to be dominated by the realities of American and Soviet military power, the development of regional identities, anti-imperialist nationalism, and revolutionary social ideas had the effect of bringing into focus the contradiction that lay at the heart of the post-war world. Just as Beveridge's ideas tended to deal with pre-war problems of poverty and mass unemployment that were in any event being eliminated in Britain, so the United Nations sought to deal with the old pre-war problem of collective security against war and aggression when the real issue was whether it had the means of preserving or changing the status quo. This contradiction between the creation of a new international order based on existing power, particularly American power, and the challenge to it presented by forces generally regarded as those of national liberation, was neatly summarized by two almost simultaneous developments. In an effort to prevent a return to the financial chaos that had proved such a destabilizing influence in the inter-war world, an international monetary and financial conference opened at Bretton Woods, New Hampshire on 1 July. On 30 June the Democratic Party of Vietnam was formed. This juxtaposition of these two forces, revolution and American power, somehow seems very appropriate.

GLOSSARY

Anvil
Planned Allied landings in southern France. Executed in August 1944 under the codename Dragoon.

Arcadia
Anglo-American conference Washington, December 1941-January 1942.

Bagration
Soviet offensive in Belorussia, June-August 1944.

Big Drum
Allied diversionary effort put into effect on 6 June 1944 in support of Neptune.

Brassard
French landings on Elba in June 1944.

CCS
The Anglo-American Combined Chiefs of Staff. This consisted of either both nations' chiefs of staff meeting in session or a permanent committee located in Washington that consisted of the American chiefs and British representatives.

COSSAC
The Chief of Staff to the Supreme Allied Commander. A position created in 1943 in order to formalize the planning for the invasion of Northwest France.

Diadem
Planned Allied offensive in central Italy. Put into effect in May 1944.

Epsom
British offensivc in Normandy, June 1944.

Eureka
Tripartite (British, American, Soviet) conference, Teheran, November-December 1943.

FEBA
Forward Edge of Battle Area.

FEC
French Expeditionary Corps.

Forager
Planned American landings in the southern Marianas. First part executed in June 1944, but the second part postponed because of the onset of the battle of the Philippine Sea.

Fortitude
Allied deception plan(s) put into effect in the spring of 1944.

Glimmer
As Big Drum.

JCS
American Joint Chiefs of Staff. Created in 1942.

LST
Landing Ship Tank.

Neptune
The naval plan of campaign for Overlord and the subsequent support of the ground forces in Normandy.

Overlord
Planned Allied landings in Normandy. Executed 6 June 1944.

Quadrant
Anglo-American conference, Quebec, August 1943.

Round-up
Name of various plans drawn up between 1941 and 1943 on the basis of earlier British plans for an Allied landing in northwest France in the final phases of war with Germany.

Sextant
Anglo-American and then Anglo-American-Chinese conference, Cairo. November and December 1943.

Shingle
Allied landings near Anzio, January 1944.

Sledgehammer
Plan for an Allied landing in France in 1942 as the means of either exploiting a German collapse or preventing one on the part of the Soviets.

Stavka
The Soviet high command.

Taxable
As Big Drum.

Trident
Anglo-American conference, Washington, May 1943.

APPENDIX I
WAR DEAD

Consideration of Soviet losses, real and admitted, prompts consideration of overall human losses in World War II. The table below gives an approximate total of military and civil losses on the part of twenty combatant nations:

	MILITARY	CIVIL	TOTAL	
BELGIUM	10,000	90	100,000	
BRITAIN	370,000	60,000	430,000	
BULGARIA	10,000	?	10,000	(+)
BURMA	?	1,000,000	1,000,000	(+)
CHINA	3,500,000	10,000,000	13,500,000	
CZECHOSLOVAKIA	20,000	330,000	350,000	
FINLAND	90,000	?	90,000	(+)
FRANCE	250,000	360,000	610,000	
GERMANY	3,480,000	3,890,000	7,370,000	
GREECE	20,000	140,000	160,000	
HUNGARY	120,000	280,000	400,000	
ITALY	330,000	90,000	420,000	
JAPAN	1,700,000	360,000	2,060,000	
NETHERLANDS	10,000	190,000	200,000	
NORWAY	10,000	?	10,000	(+)
POLAND	120,000	5,300,000	5,420,000	
ROMANIA	200,000	470,000	670,000	
SOVIET UNION	13,600,000	8,150,000	21,750,000	
UNITED STATES	220,000		220,000	
YUGOSLAVIA	300,000	1,360,000	1,660,000	
	24,360,000	32,070,000	56,430,000	

British totals refer to Britain only, and do not include imperial losses.
German totals refer to combined German and Austrian losses.
Soviet losses include those of Estonia, Latvia and Lithuania.

APPENDIX II – THE WESTERN ALLIES IN EUROPE 1944-45

American commitment intensifies

ORDER OF BATTLE 6 JUNE 1945

NATIONALITY AND TYPE OF DIVISION

ARMY GROUP	ARMY	NUMBER OF DIVISIONS	AMERICAN			mt	BRAZIL	BRITISH			CANADIAN		FRENCH		mt	INDIAN	NZ	POLISH		SA
15TH ARMY GROUP	5TH US	13	1	6					2											
	8TH BRITISH	12						1	2		1	1	3		1	3	1		2	1
		22																		
21ST ARMY GROUP	1ST US	8	2	6																
	2ND BRITISH	7						1	1	4		1								
		15																		
TOTAL NUMBER OF DIVISIONS IN ITALY		**25**	1	6	**7**			1	4	**5**	1	1 **2**	3	1	**4**	3	1		2	1
TOTAL NUMBER OF DIVISIONS IN NW EUROPE		**15**	2	6	**8**			1	1	4 **6**	1	**1**								
TOTAL DIVISIONS		**40**	2	1	12	**15**		1	2	8 **11**	1	2 **3**	3	1	**4**	3	1		2	1

ORDER OF BATTLE APRIL 1945

ARMY GROUP	ARMY	NUMBER OF DIVISIONS	AMERICAN	FRENCH		
6TH ARMY GROUP	RESERVE	3		1	1	1
	1ST FRENCH	7		2	4	1
	7TH US	12	9			
		22				

238

NATIONALITY AND TYPE OF DIVISION

ARMY GROUP	ARMY	NUMBER OF DIVISIONS	AMERICAN △	AMERICAN □	AMERICAN ⊠	AMERICAN mt	BRAZIL ⊠	BRITISH △	BRITISH □	BRITISH ⊠	CANADIAN □	CANADIAN ⊠	FRENCH □	FRENCH ⊠	FRENCH mt	INDIAN ⊠	NZ ⊠	POLISH □	POLISH ⊠	SA □
12TH ARMY GROUP	1ST US	17		5	12															
	3RD US	12		3	9															
	9TH US	13	1	3	9															
	15TH US	6	2	1	3															
		48																		
21ST ARMY GROUP	RESERVE	1								1										
	1ST CANADIAN	6						1			2	2							1	
	2ND BRITISH	10						1	3	6										
		17																		
1ST ALLIED AIRBORNE ARMY	BRITISH RESERVE	1	1																	
		1						1												
		2																		
15TH ARMY GROUP	5TH US	9	1	5	1		1			1										
	8TH BRITISH	8							1	2						2	1		2	
		17																		
IN GREECE		3			1											2				
TOTAL NO OF DIVISIONS IN S EUROPE		20	1	5	1		1	1	3				3	5	2	4	1		2	1
			7				**1**	**4**					**10**			**4**	**1**		**2**	**1**
TOTAL NO OF DIVISIONS IN NW EUROPE		89	4	15	42			2	4	7	2	2						1		
			61					**13**				**4**						**1**		
TOTAL DIVISIONS		**109**	4	16	47	1	1	2	5	10	2	2	3	5	2	4	1	1	2	1
						68	**1**			**17**		**4**			**10**	**4**	**1**		**3**	**1**

THE DISPARITY OF ANGLO-AMERICAN RESOURCES ENSURED THAT IN ANY DISAGREEMENT ABOUT ALLIED POLICY THE UNITED STATES WOULD HAVE THE FINAL WORD – WITH ALL THIS ENTAILED FOR THE POSTWAR LEADERSHIP OF WESTERN EUROPE.

APPENDIX III – SAIPAN AND THE PHILIPPINE SEA
AMERICAN AND JAPANESE ORDERS OF BATTLE

1. US GENERAL RESERVES

TG	TYPE	CVE	DD	DE	AH	AKA	AO	AP	APA	LCI	AUX
50.17	FUELLING	4	4	14	4		24				2
51.1	RESERVE	–	6	6		2		7	6	7	

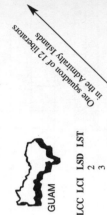

MARIANA ISLANDS

SAIPAN   TINIAN   AGUIJAN   ROTA   GUAM

Positions are not shown to scale

2. US AMPHIBIOUS TASK GROUPS

TG	TYPE	DD	SC	AK	AKA	AP	APA	APD	LCC	LCI	LSD	LST
52.3	TRANSPORT			2	3	2	10				2	
52.4	TRANSPORT				3	4	9				3	
52.5	TRACTOR											49
52.6	COMMAND		14					3	7	25		
52.8	TRANSPORT							6				
52.12	SCREEN	15	4					1				
		15	**18**	**2**	**6**	**6**	**19**	**10**	**7**	**25**	**5**	**49**

3. US SUPPORT GROUPS

TG	TYPE	BB	CVE	CA	CL	DD	DMS	AM	APD	AVD	AUX	AC
52.7	SERVICE										16	5
52.10	FIRE	3		4	2	9	2		2	1		
52.11	CARRIER		3			6				1		
52.13	MINESWEEPING						8	6			13	100
52.14	CARRIER		4	2	3	6						
52.17	FIRE	4				17						
		7	**7**	**6**	**5**	**38**	**10**	**6**	**2**	**2**	**29**	**105+**

One squadron of 12 liberators in the Admiralty Islands

Allied light forces in New Guinea

Diversionary American attack in Kurile Islands 13 June

4. US TASK FORCE 58:
THE FAST CARRIER TASK FORCE

AC	TASK GROUP	BB	CV	CVL	CA	CL	CLAA	DD
267	58.1		2	2	3		1	14
244	58.2		2	2		3	1	12
228	58.3		2	2	1	3	1	13
163	58.4		2	1		3	1	14
–	58.7	7			4			14
902		**7**	**8**	**7**	**8**	**9**	**4**	**97**

IMPERIAL JAPANESE NAVY
18 SUBMARINES

5. IMPERIAL JAPANESE NAVY 1st MOBILE FLEET

AC	FORCE	CV	CVL	BB	CA	CL	DD	AO
90	C		3	4	8	1	8	
135	B	2	1		1		10	
225	A	3		1	2	1	9	
–	OILER						6	6
450		**5**	**4**	**5**	**11**	**2**	**33**	**6**

US TASK FORCE 42
9 SUBMARINES

US TASK FORCE 17
19 SUBMARINES

Actual dispositions not shown to scale

PHILIPPINE SEA

SAIPAN

GUAM

MARIANA ISLANDS

PHILIPPINE ISLANDS

Glossary

AC	Aircraft		AVD	Seaplane tender
AH	Hospital ship		BB	Battleship
AK	Cargo ship		CA	Heavy cruiser
AKA	Attack cargo ship		CL	Light cruiser
AM	Minesweeper		CLAA	Anti-aircraft cruiser
AO	Fleet oiler		CV	Fleet carrier
AP	Transport		CVE	Escort carrier
APA	Attack transport		CVL	Light Fleet carrier
APD	Destroyer transport		DD	Destroyer
Aux	Auxiliary		DE	Destroyer escort
			DMS	Fast minesweeper
			LCC	Landing craft control
			LCI	Landing craft infantry
			LSD	Landing ship dock
			LST	Landing ship tank
			SC	Submarine chaser

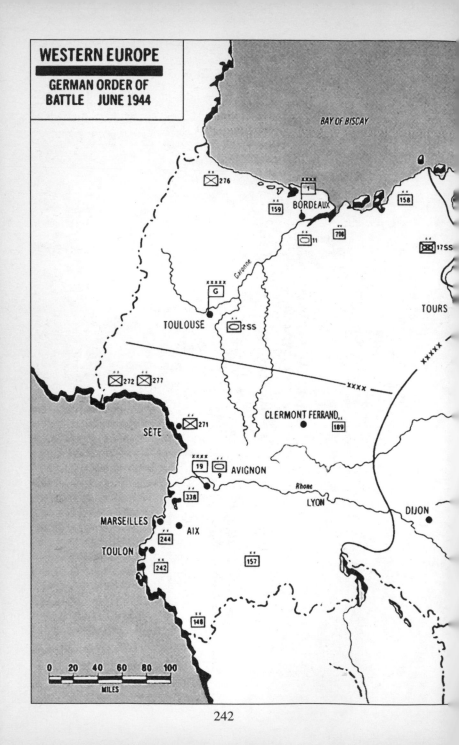

WESTERN EUROPE

GERMAN ORDER OF
BATTLE   JUNE 1944

BAY OF BISCAY

276

1

159   BORDEAUX   158

11   708

G   17SS

TOULOUSE   2SS   TOURS

272   277

271   CLERMONT FERRAND
SÈTE   189

19   9
AVIGNON
338   Rhone
LYON
MARSEILLES   DIJON
244   AIX
TOULON   157
242

148

0   20   40   60   80   100
MILES

BREST

343

3   353

265

266

275

77

319

NTES

5

243

ANGERS

91   CHERBOURG

709

35

7

21

CAEN   716

LE MANS

711   346

12SS   LE HAVRE

LEHR

84

17 LW

OB   ROUEN   245

WEST

B   116   DIEPPE

ORLEANS   BOULOGNE

BEAUVAIS   348

PARIS   344   49   47

CALAIS

2   58

182

COULOMMIERS   331   18 LW

326   15

COMPIEGNE   48

TOURCOING

712   165

19 LW

RHEIMS

BRUSSELS

ANTWERP   ROTTERDAM

155   719

347

LIÈGE   16 LW   AMSTERDAM

NANCY

METZ

AACHEN

COLOGNE

DUSSELDORF

COBLENZ   DORTMUND

FRANKFURT

BIRMINGHAM

MANCHESTER

SHEFFIELD

LONDON

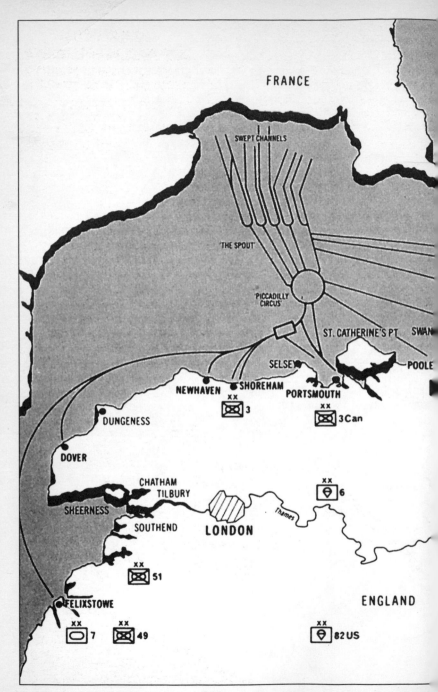

FRANCE

SWEPT CHANNELS

'THE SPOUT

PICCADILLY
CIRCUS

ST. CATHERINE'S PT   SWAN

SELSEY   POOLE

NEWHAVEN   SHOREHAM   PORTSMOUTH

xx
3

xx
3 Can

DUNGENESS

DOVER

CHATHAM
TILBURY

xx
6

SHEERNESS

SOUTHEND   LONDON

Thames

xx
51

ENGLAND

FELIXSTOWE

xx
7

xx
49

xx
82 US

OVERLORD

ALLIED DEPLOYMENT IN BRITAIN
AND PLANNED INVASION ROUTE

0   10   20   30   40   50
MILES

FALMOUTH

SALCOMBE

BRIXHAM   DARTMOUTH   FOWEY

PORTLAND   TORQUAY   4US   PLYMOUTH   29US

MOUTH   1US

9US

101 US

BRISTOL

CARDIFF   90US

SWANSEA   2US

245

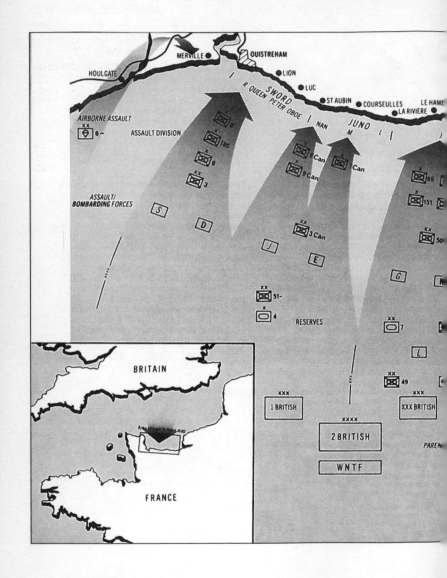

MERVILLE ● OUISTREHAM

HOULGATE

● LION

SWORD

● LUC

R QUEEN PETER OBOE

● ST AUBIN

● COURSEULLES

LE HAME

NAN

JUNO

● LA RIVIÈRE

AIRBORNE ASSAULT

6–

ASSAULT DIVISION

185

9

3

8

ASSAULT/
BOMBARDING FORCES

S

D

J

E

9 Can

8 Can

9 Can

3 Can

3 Can

69

151

50

G

51–

4

RESERVES

7

L

49

BRITAIN

1 BRITISH

XXX BRITISH

2 BRITISH

PAREN

WNTF

FRANCE

246

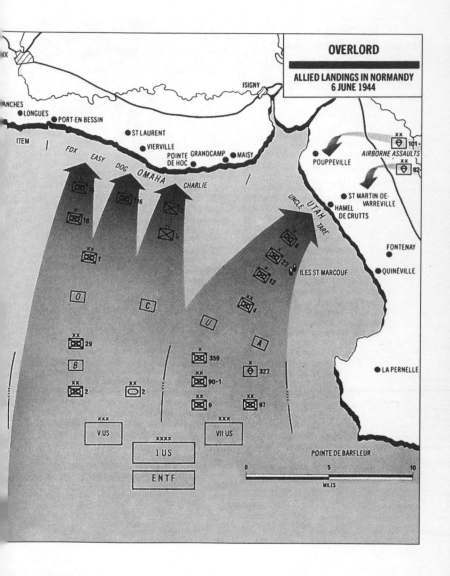

OVERLORD

ALLIED LANDINGS IN NORMANDY
6 JUNE 1944

ISIGNY

ANCHES

LONGUES ● PORT-EN-BESSIN

ITEM

ST LAURENT

VIERVILLE

POINTE GRANDCAMP MAISY
DE HOC

FOX EASY DOG OMAHA CHARLIE

AIRBORNE ASSAULTS

POUPPEVILLE

ST MARTIN-DE-
VARREVILLE

HAMEL
DE CRUTTS

UNCLE UTAH TARE

ILES ST MARCOUF

FONTENAY

QUINÉVILLE

O

C

U

A

LA PERNELLE

V US

VII US

1 US

POINTE DE BARFLEUR

ENTF

0   5   10
MILES

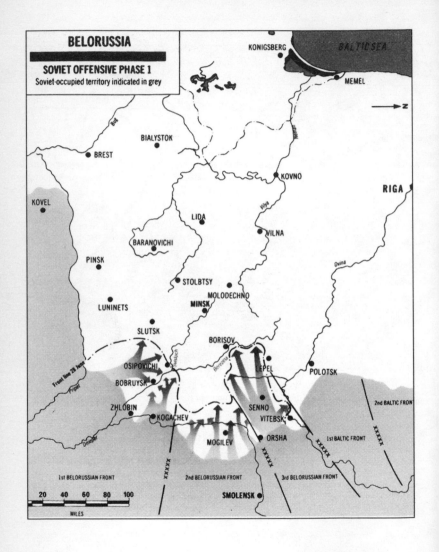

BELORUSSIA

SOVIET OFFENSIVE PHASE 1
Soviet-occupied territory indicated in grey

BALTIC SEA

KONIGSBERG

MEMEL

N

BUG

BIALYSTOK

BREST

KOVNO

RIGA

KOVEL

LIDA

VILNA

Vilya

BARANOVICHI

Dvina

PINSK

STOLBTSY

MOLODECHNO

LUNINETS

MINSK

SLUTSK

BORISOV

Front line 28 June

OSIPOVICHI

EPEL

POLOTSK

Pripet

BOBRUYSK

Berezina

2nd BALTIC FRONT

ZHLOBIN

SENNO

VITEBSK

KOGACHEV

ORSHA

1st BALTIC FRONT

Dnieper

MOGILEV

XXXXX

1st BELORUSSIAN FRONT

XXXXX

2nd BELORUSSIAN FRONT

XXXXX

3rd BELORUSSIAN FRONT

XXXXX

20 40 60 80 100

MILES

SMOLENSK

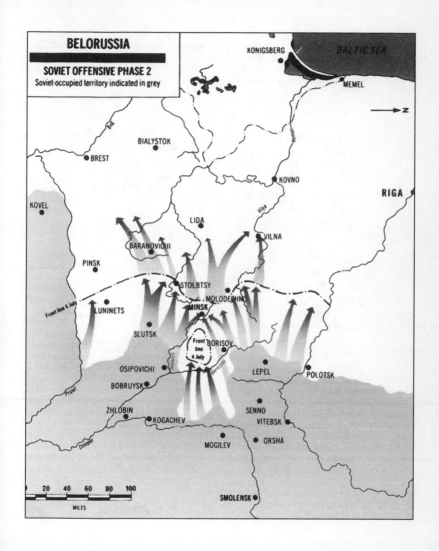

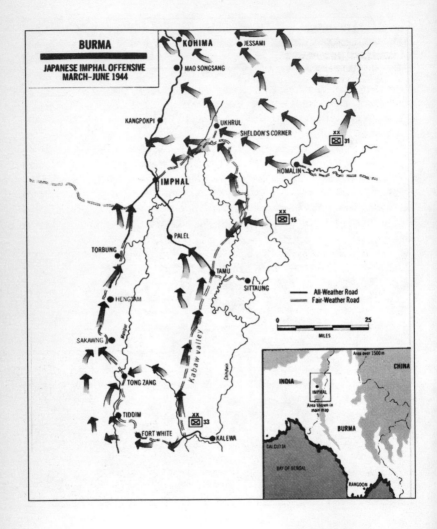

BURMA

JAPANESE IMPHAL OFFENSIVE
MARCH–JUNE 1944

KOHIMA
JESSAMI
MAO SONGSANG
KANGPOKPI
UKHRUL
SHELDON'S CORNER
XX 31
HOMALIN
IMPHAL
XX 15
PALEL
TORBUNG
TAMU
SITTAUNG
HENGTAM

All-Weather Road
Fair-Weather Road

0   25
MILES

SAKAWNG

Kabaw valley

TONG ZANG
TIDDIM
XX 33
FORT WHITE
KALEWA

Area over 1500 m
CHINA
INDIA
IMPHAL
Area shown in main map
BURMA
CALCUTTA
BAY OF BENGAL
RANGOON

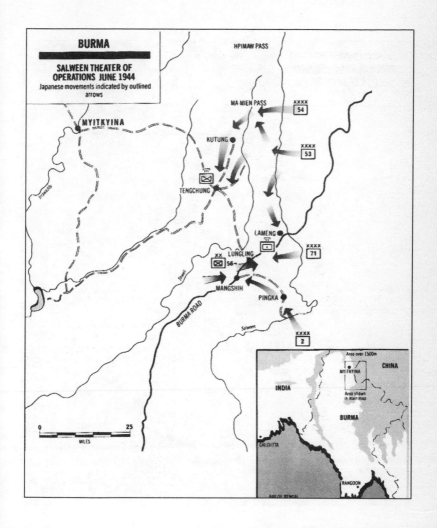

BURMA

SALWEEN THEATER OF
OPERATIONS JUNE 1944
Japanese movements indicated by outlined
arrows

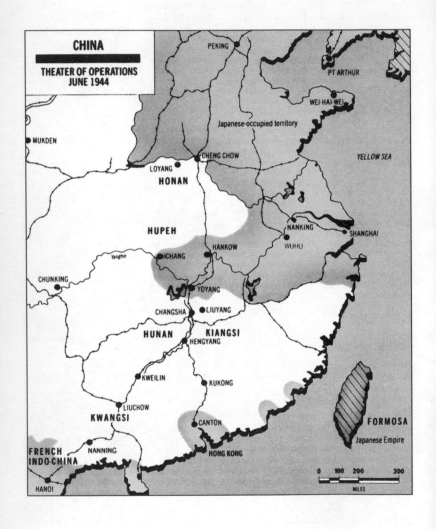

CHINA

THEATER OF OPERATIONS
JUNE 1944

PEKING

PT ARTHUR

WEI-HAI-WEI

Japanese-occupied territory

YELLOW SEA

MUKDEN

CHENG CHOW

LOYANG

HONAN

HUPEH

NANKING

SHANGHAI

WUHU

ICHANG

HANKOW

Yangtse

CHUNKING

YOYANG

CHANGSHA

LIUYANG

HUNAN

KIANGSI

HENGYANG

KWEILIN

KUKONG

FORMOSA

LIUCHOW

Japanese Empire

KWANGSI

CANTON

FRENCH
INDO-CHINA

NANNING

HONG KONG

HANOI

0   100   200   300

MILES

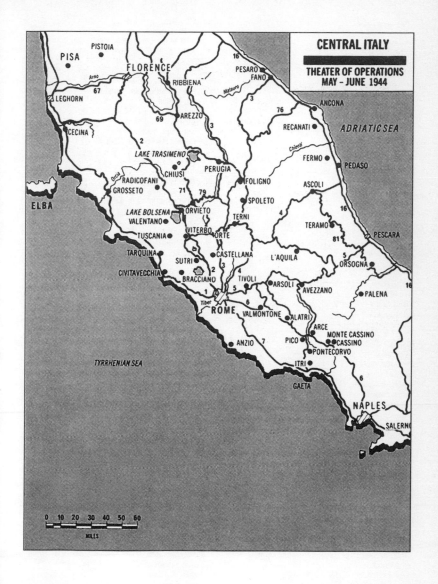

CENTRAL ITALY

**THEATER OF OPERATIONS
MAY – JUNE 1944**

PISTOIA

PISA

FLORENCE

Arno

RIBBIENA

PESARO

FANO

16

Matauro

3

ANCONA

76

ADRIATIC SEA

LEGHORN

67

CECINA

69

AREZZO

3

RECANATI

2

Chienti

LAKE TRASIMENO

CHIUSI

PERUGIA

FOLIGNO

FERMO

PEDASO

Orcia

RADICOFANI

GROSSETO

71

79

SPOLETO

ASCOLI

ELBA

LAKE BOLSENA

VALENTANO

ORVIETO

VITERBO

ORTE

TERNI

4

16

TERAMO

81

PESCARA

TUSCANIA

TARQUINA

SUTRI

CASTELLANA

2

3

4

L'AQUILA

5

ORSOGNA

CIVITAVECCHIA

BRACCIANO

1

Tiber

TIVOLI

5

ARSOLI

AVEZZANO

6

PALENA

16

ROME

VALMONTONE

ALATRI

ARCE

ANZIO

7

PICO

MONTE CASSINO

CASSINO

PONTECORVO

TYRRHENIAN SEA

ITRI

GAETA

6

NAPLES

SALERNO

```
0  10  20  30  40  50  60
|___|___|___|___|___|___|
        MILES
```

INDEX

255

Guadalcanal, 149, 183, 186-7, 203
Guam, 184, 202-3, 205, 207, 210, 213, 218, 220
Guderian, Gen H, 66, 75, 145-6

Ha-Go, Operation, 162, 164
Halmahera Island, 191, 193-6
Harding, Lt Gen J, 42-6
Harris, ACM A, 74
Le Havre, 22, 68, 70, 88-9
Hengyang, 173, 175
Hitler, A, 9, 11, 14, 25-6, 28-31, 40, 46, 50, 56,
    64, 75-7, 97-8, 100-1, 103-4, 111-12, 120-6,
    139, 142, 144, 228
Hollandia, 184, 190, 193-5
Honan province, 172-3, 219
Hukawng valley, 151, 161-2, 169
Hungary, 28-9, 117, 120, 145-6

Ichi-Go, Operation, 161, 172-3, 175, 177-8, 181-2
Imphal, 161, 163-5, 167-9, 172, 181-2
India, 15, 153, 155, 161-2, 168, 181-2
Indian Ocean, 23, 26, 151, 161
Indo-China (French), 153, 173, 182
Irrawaddy, River, 161, 169
Isigny, 38, 97
Italy, 14, 19-26, 28-37, 40-50, 57, 60-1, 104,
    113, 120, 134, 232
Iwo Jima, 190, 202, 223

Japan, 9, 22-3, 149-53, 155-7, 159-65, 167-9,
    171-2, 175, 177-96, 198-207, 210-13, 216-23,
    225, 227-9, 231-2
Japanese armed forces:
  Imperial Army, 161-2, 181-2, 229
    Armies:
      Burma Area, 162, 169
      Fifteenth, 162-3, 165, 168-9
      Thirty-Third, 162, 164
    Divisions:
      15th, 163, 165, 167
      18th, 162, 169, 172
      31st, 163, 167, 169
      32nd, 191, 193-4
      33rd, 163, 165, 167, 169
      35th, 191, 193-4
      55th, 162, 164
      56th, 162, 170-2
  Imperial Navy, 156-7, 183-5, 191, 193-6, 198,
    202, 206, 211, 225
  Formations:
    1st Mobile, 191, 202
    29th Air Flotilla, 196, 198
    Combined Fleet, 156, 184-7, 191-2, 197-200
    Van Force, 213, 216, 218-19, 223
  Ships:
    Chikuma, 216, 223
    Chitose, 185, 195, 213, 223
    Chiyoda, 185, 195, 213, 223
    Haguro, 217, 221-2
    Haruna, 216, 223
    Hiyo, 216, 223
    Junyo, 216, 223
    Musashi, 184, 200, 216, 223
    Ryuho, 216, 223
    Shokaku, 185, 192-3, 219
    Taiho, 185, 192-3, 219-20, 223

Tone, 216, 223
Yamato, 200, 216, 223
Zuiho, 185, 213, 219, 223
Zuikaku, 185, 216, 220-1, 223
JCS, 35-8, 40, 43, 48, 159-60, 186-7, 190-1, 203
Jessami, 163, 167
Jodl, Gen A, 91, 105, 113
Jordan, Lt Gen H, 141-2
Joshima, 216, 223
Juin, Gen A, 46, 56
Juno beach, 37, 82-4, 96-7

Kabaw, 161-3
Kamang, 169-70
Karelia, 14, 117, 120, 127-30, 133-4
Kesselring, Field Marshal A, 26, 30-3, 35-6, 38-
    40, 44-7, 49, 52, 56, 113
Kharkov, 124, 145-6
King, Adm E J, 157, 185-7, 190, 203-5
Koga, Adm M, 191-5, 204, 211
Ko-go, Operation, 173, 177
Kohima, 161, 163-4, 167-9, 172, 181-2
Kon, Operation, 198, 213
Konigsberg, 123, 135
Kovel-Sarny, 121-3, 126
Kuomintang, 172-3, 177-82
Kurita, V Adm T, 216, 218-19
Kwajalein atoll, 157, 183, 188, 203

Lagoda, Lake, 127, 129, 134
Lameng, 171-2
Lashio, 151, 170
Lee, V Adm W A, 202, 207, 218
Leigh-Mallory, ACM T, 37, 74
Leningrad, 117, 128
Leyte Gulf, Battle of, 216-17
Liri, River and valley, 30-1, 34, 38, 44-7, 60-1
Lisieux, 78, 88
Ljubljana, 48-9, 56
Loire, River, 68, 75, 87
Lublin, 121, 126, 142
Luxembourg, 11, 68, 232
Luzon, 181-2, 190
Lvov, 121, 126, 142

MacArthur, Gen D, 157, 159-60, 186-7, 190,
    193-4
Majuro atoll, 15, 183-4, 188
Malaya, 155, 159-60, 163, 181-2
Manchuria, 175, 177, 180-2
Mandalay, 151, 155
Manipur, 162-4, 168, 181
Manokwari, 190, 194
Le Mans, 68, 95
Mao Songsang, 167, 169
Marcus Island, 183, 196
Margival conference, 103-4
Mariana Islands, 11, 15, 156-7, 159-61, 184-92,
    197, 202-5, 207, 211-12, 216-23
Marshall, Gen G C, 22, 42
Marshall Islands, 157, 159, 183-4, 190-1, 196
Mediterranean Sea, 13, 15, 19-26, 32-3, 35-6,
    38-40, 42-3, 47, 68, 108, 168
Medvezh'yegorsk, 127, 132, 134
Merderet, River, 80, 101-3
Merville, 78-80

256